HOME OFFICE

A STUDY OF THE 1
COMPLAINTS SYS[

by M. Maguire and C. Corbett

LONDON: HMSO

ISBN 0 11 341007 7

For Ross

Mike Maguire is a Lecturer in Criminology at the Department of Social and Administrative Studies, University of Wales, College of Cardiff. Claire Corbett is a Research Fellow at the Department of Law, Brunel University. The study, commissioned jointly by the Home Office and the Police Complaints Authority, was carried out at the Centre for Criminological Research, University of Oxford.

Contents

Acknowledgments

The two studies which form the basis of this report were carried out at the Oxford University Centre for Criminological Research. While both authors are now employed elsewhere, they are extremely grateful to the director of the Centre, Dr. Roger Hood, and to their former colleagues and secretarial staff, for support and assistance throughout the period of the research. Valuable part-time research assistance, including some interviewing, was provided by Mrs Sally Simon.

The projects were both funded by the Home Office Research and Planning Unit, where Mr Mike Hough, Ms Julie Vennard and Mr David Brown acted at different times as intermediaries with police forces and the PCA. Their assistance, together with that of members of the 'customer division' in the Home Office (particularly Mr Brian Gange, Mr Eric Soden, Mrs Gloria Moody and Miss Irene Cole), proved invaluable in smoothing our passage.

We received very generous cooperation from the Chief Constables of the three forces in which fieldwork was carried out, as well as from numerous officers in their Complaints and Discipline Departments. As we have decided not to identify the forces, these individuals must remain anonymous. Similarly, all members of the Police Complaints Authority, especially the former Chairman, Sir Cecil Clothier, afforded us excellent hospitality at their offices and granted us full access to their files. Here, too, we would particularly like to thank Miss Kathy Hudson, a civil servant seconded to the PCA, who saved us a great deal of work by patiently extracting details from nearly 400 files.

Finally, we are most grateful to Linda Rose, Lesley Noaks, Jay Kynch and Gordon Shumack for comments and assistance in producing this published version.

Foreword

The research on police complaints procedures, which is contained in this book, was funded by the Home Office, either directly or by way of a grant to the Police Complaints Authority, in 1987.

Prior to 1987 little information was available as to the working of police complaints procedures and their impact on complainants. In the middle of that year, the Home Office published as Home Office Research Study 93 a survey of complainants' views. The research covered complaints made in 1982 and 1983, before the introduction of new procedures under the Police and Criminal Evidence Act 1984, but it gave the first clear picture of the attitudes of complainants as they were at the time and provides a useful comparison against which the current research can be assessed.

It was in fact in 1984, while this earlier research was in progress and the Police and Criminal Evidence Act still in its parliamentary stages, that plans were first made for a more ambitious piece of research into complaints and complainants. In the event, it was thought desirable to allow time for the new procedures under the Police and Criminal Evidence Act to settle in, and the research was not commissioned until early 1987.

During the process of designing the research, it became apparent that the most efficient way in which more serious complaints could be identified and studied would be by the use of records held by the Police Complaints Authority. Because of legal constraints on the disclosure of information the researchers were required to become servants of the Authority in order to examine these records. For this reason, the research was divided into two halves and although both were funded by the Home Office, one was commissioned by the Police Complaints Authority. The results of the latter part of the research, as well as being included in this publication, are also covered in a separate document which has been laid before Parliament.

The conclusions which the researchers draw in the present report do not necessarily reflect the views of the Home Office, the police or the Police Complaints Authority. However, the research has provided a number of useful insights into the handling of complaints about the police and the way in which complainants view the procedures, and those responsible for making and implementing policy in this area have already responded to these in a variety of ways.

The Home Office, for example, is considering in consultation with the police staff associations how police complaints procedures can best be adjusted to meet the needs of the public more closely, while the Police Complaints Authority has made changes to a number of its procedures. In addition, many police forces have acted individually to improve the way in which they respond to complainants.

In conclusion, the Home Office would like to put on record its appreciation of the hard work and professionalism which Mike Maguire and Claire Corbett have brought to bear on this interesting and difficult area of study.

Roger Tarling
Head of the Research
and Planning Unit
Home Office

List of Figures and Tables

Preface and Overview

In 1989, the police service was hit by a burst of bad publicity, including the case of the 'Guildford Four' and a major inquiry into the West Midlands Police Force. The next year, findings from the 1988 British Crime Survey (Skogan 1990) revealed that public satisfaction with the police had decreased since the 1984 survey (which itself had shown a fall since 1982). Other publications, such as the Wolff-Olins report on the Metropolitan Police (Wolff-Olins 1988) and the internally generated Operational Policing Review (Police Staff Associations 1990), have also drawn attention to continuing problems, both in the quality of face-to-face contact between the police and the public and in mismatches between police and public assumptions about policing priorities.

To the police's credit, they have set in motion a number of major initiatives—for example the 'Plus Programme' in the Metropolitan Police Force and the recent Strategic Policy Document (ACPO 1990) issued by the Association of Chief Police Officers—to try to recover the situation. These initiatives have focused upon the concept of 'quality of service', with particular attention to improving the attitude and manner of officers in their day-to-day dealings with the public. HM Inspectors of Constabulary, too, are now placing special emphasis upon this aspect of policing. One indicator they use in assessing performance is the level of complaints against the police, and many forces are now trying to reduce complaints by encouraging officers to adopt a more courteous and 'professional' manner.

However effective these preventive measures turn out to be, the police are still likely to be faced for the foreseeable future with the problem of responding to tens of thousands of complaints every year (in 1989, the total for England and Wales stood at 29,312, and there are no signs of a decrease at present). A vital part of any effort to increase public confidence in the police is to ensure that these complaints are dealt with fairly and effectively and that, as far as possible, both those who make them and the wider public audience believe this to be the case. The study described in this report was aimed at describing and elucidating the workings of the present system, which has in the past been shrouded in too much secrecy, and at eliciting the views and experiences of the parties directly involved—complainants, police officers subject of complaint, investigating officers, and members of the independent Police Complaints Authority (PCA). We were also allowed space in the 1988 British Crime Survey for some relevant questions to the general public. We were given almost unrestricted access to police and PCA complaints files, and spent a lot of time informally with PCA members and police investigators in their work settings.

While it was not our brief to make recommendations for change, we shall at least draw attention to what seemed from our research findings to constitute both the most encouraging features and the main shortcomings of the system. On the one hand, we found it difficult to fault the personal commitment or professionalism of those involved in the process full-time. We also found much to commend the new system of informal resolution. Against these positive features have to be weighed the very low levels of satisfaction among complainants; a sense of alienation—felt by complainants and police offers alike—from a complex, long-winded and secretive investigation process; failures in communication of the reasons for, and implications of, decisions; little external understanding of the role and input of the PCA; the difficulty for PCA members, given their present location and resources, in undertaking active and direct supervision of more than a few investigations; and, despite the undoubted improvements made by the Police and Criminal Evidence Act 1984, a continuing belief in many quarters that a system in which the police 'investigate themselves' is both wrong in principle and biased in practice. Some of these problems may be overcome by reforms within the present system. Others may demand a radical rethink of its aims and structure.

M. Maguire
C. Corbett
(February 1991)

PART ONE

THE COMPLAINTS SYSTEM AND PATTERNS OF COMPLAINT

CHAPTER 1

Background to the Study

1. Scope of the Report

The 1984 Police and Criminal Evidence Act ('PACE') introduced several changes to the system for dealing with complaints against the police in England and Wales, notably the establishment of the independent Police Complaints Authority (PCA) and the institution of a new procedure of 'informal resolution' for less serious complaints. In 1987, the authors were invited to carry out two studies of the system post-PACE. The first, commissioned and funded by the Home Office, entailed an analysis of patterns of complaints, an examination of how they were dealt with in three police forces, and an exploration of the views of complainants, police officers complained against and investigating officers. The second, also funded by the Home Office, but commissioned by the PCA, focused upon the work of PCA members, in particular their supervisory role in the investigation of serious complaints. At the same time, a postal survey was carried out to ascertain the reactions of complainants in such cases to the part played by the PCA.

The resulting reports were submitted to the commissioning bodies in late 1988 and early 1989. This publication is essentially an amalgamated version of the two reports, together with a brief review of the arguments which have surrounded the subject of police complaints for the past thirty or so years. It is not intended as a comprehensive 'audit' of the system, nor as a definitive statement of the researchers' own views on what changes should or should not be made. The main purpose here is simply the presentation of empirical findings emerging from the study, leaving proper consideration of the complex historical, sociological and political questions involved to later publications.

It is also important to stress that, like many aspects of policing today, the handling of complaints is a topic of frequent internal discussion (there is, for example, an active sub-committee of the Association of Chief Police Officers, which meets regularly to review the situation) and research findings can rapidly become out of date. This problem afflicted the study by Brown (1987) which was based on research carried out pre-PACE, but not published until three years later. We freely concede that there have been changes, for example in the use of informal resolution (Chapter 7) and in the work of the PCA

3

(Chapters 8 and 9), which already render some of our findings out of date. (Indeed, we flatter ourselves that findings presented in our initial reports have entered the policy-making process and have played some part in stimulating such changes). As far as possible, we have taken account of new developments in the following pages. But, even where the findings have been overtaken by events, we would argue that this is largely a matter of detail and that the general picture is still a valid one. It should be remembered, too, that there are 43 police forces in England and Wales and that the pace of progress varies considerably between them.

The shape of the report is as follows. Part One provides a general background to the research. In the remainder of this chapter, we briefly recount the recent history of the police complaints system, including the background to the creation of the PCA. We also outline the purposes which complaints systems generally are designed to fulfil, arguing that the possession by the police of unique coercive powers, together with shortcomings in other mechanisms of accountability, places a particularly heavy burden on whatever procedures are adopted in their case. Finally, we describe the research methods used in our study and the questions they were designed to answer.

In Chapter 2, we provide a more detailed account of current complaints procedures, both within police forces and at the PCA offices in London. We describe the basic rules and practices of recording and investigation, informal resolution, referral of cases to the PCA, supervision of investigations, discontinuance of cases, disciplinary decisions, and the role of the Director of Public Prosecutions.

In Chapter 3, we present some basic statistics on the substance and frequency of complaints, including recent trends and variations between forces. We identify three kinds of complaint—'arrest-related assault', 'traffic-related incivility'and 'inadequate responses to service requests'– which recur fairly frequently, examining the circumstances in which they arise and the characteristics of complainants and officers involved. We also note that cases dealt with by the PCA are untypical of the totality of complaints.

Part Two, consisting of Chapters 4-7, presents our main findings from the local study carried out in three police force areas. Chapter 4 looks at the system from the viewpoint of complainants, giving their accounts of initial police responses to their complaint (including perceived attempts to dissuade them from pursuing the matter), exploring their aims and motives in complaining and assessing their level of satisfaction, both with the outcome and with the system as a whole.

4

In Chapter 5 we turn to police perspectives. We first explore the views of officers who have experienced the complaints system, beginning with their images of situations which carry a high risk of complaint and of the kinds of people who complain. We also ask to what extent the prospect of receiving a complaint causes officers to alter their behaviour. We then examine their opinions of the fairness of the system and the extent to which they are prepared to co-operate with it. Finally, we view the system from the perspective of investigating officers, including their suggestions for change.

Chapter 6 is concerned with the new 'informal resolution' procedure. We describe the circumstances in which it is used and how it is 'sold' to complainants; the opinions of senior officers about its value; and some surprisingly common misconceptions and suspicions about the process which we discovered among the lower ranks. We also look at informal resolution in practice, noting that it is rare for meetings to be arranged between complainants and the officers they have complained against; and that, in many cases, the result is that both parties 'agree to differ' rather than a positive resolution being reached. However, we also show that complainants are much more likely to express satisfaction with informal resolution than with other means of handling complaints.

Chapter 7 covers withdrawn complaints. It is asked to what extent complainants experience 'pressure' to withdraw and what forms such pressure may take. We also outline their stated reasons for withdrawing and assess levels of satisfaction with this outcome.

In Part Three, we focus upon the role of the Police Complaints Authority. In Chapter 8, we describe the kinds of cases dealt with by the PCA, especially those supervised by members of 'I' (Investigation) Division. A number of examples are given of cases supervised mandatorily and of those selected for supervision by members. Finally, we look at 'Section 88' cases, which do not necessarily involve complaints, but are usually 'high profile' in terms of public attention.

Chapter 9 is concerned with the supervision of investigations—the decision to supervise, the nature of supervision, and whether it can be said to be effective. We distinguish between 'directive', 'active' and 'passive' styles of supervision, and look at the kinds of cases in which each tends to be used. We argue that it is unsafe to assess the effectiveness of supervision purely in terms of outcomes, and consider evidence which suggests that supervision may keep investigating officers 'on their toes', speed up the investigation of complaints, and/or reduce the likelihood of withdrawal.

In Chapter 10, we present the results of our questionnaire to samples of complainants whose cases had been considered or supervised by the PCA. We assess their level of satisfaction with the handling of their case, outline their views about the Authority and the complaints system in general, and record their comments on, for example, the style of letters they received from the PCA and the attitudes of investigating officers.

Finally, in Chapter 11 we attempt to pull the threads together and draw out some of the implications and questions raised by the findings.

2. Recent History of the Complaints System

The basic shape of the current complaints system retains a considerable amount in common with that first instituted by the Metropolitan Police in the 1830s and extended over the next one hundred years into a set of principles and procedures gradually adopted by other forces (see, for example, Select Committee 1834; Royal Commissions 1908, 1929). Official complaints can be made only against misconduct by individual officers, not against the force, force policy or operational decisions; complaints are closely tied to the internal police disciplinary system, being recorded and investigated as alleged breaches of a specified section of the disciplinary code; investigations are carried out by senior police officers, and in most cases a Superintendent or Chief Inspector from the same force; another senior officer (nominally, in provincial forces, the Deputy Chief Constable)[1] scrutinizes their reports to determine whether there is sufficient evidence to substantiate a disciplinary charge and, if so, whether to recommend a formal hearing or to deal with the matter by a warning; in the case of a hearing, he or she also frames the charges; and guilt or innocence and the level of punishment are then determined in most cases by the Chief Constable of the force concerned. All these practices are long established, and the majority of complaints continue to be handled in a manner which would not be unfamiliar to generations of police officers.

On the other hand, over the past 25 years, there have been grafted on to this basic pattern a number of new elements, designed primarily to rationalize and standardize procedures and, in the light of intensifying debate about police accountability (e.g. Marshall 1979; Scarman 1981; Jefferson and Grimshaw 1984; Lustgarten 1986), to make the whole system more open to external scrutiny. These include more rigorous recording practices, more specialization and centralization of investigators, independent monitoring and supervision of investigations, and the transfer of some decision-making powers (particularly decisions to prosecute or bring disciplinary charges) to outsiders. Over this period, complaints handling has developed from

6

a fairly marginal area of police activity to a publicly prominent specialism, accorded considerable priority—and greatly increased resources –within every force.

Official recognition of the importance of complaints to the wider topic of accountability can be traced back to the 1962 Royal Commission on the Police and the resulting Police Act 1964. Following a series of highly publicized complaints in which dissatisfaction with the outcomes was widely voted (LSPU 1987; Reiner 1985), the Royal Commission considered the idea of complaint investigations being conducted by a body external to the police, but in the end contented itself with measures to tighten up internal police procedures. Under the 1964 Act, chief officers were required to ensure that all complaints were recorded and investigated, to appoint investigators from outside forces for serious cases, and to refer all cases in which a criminal offence may have been committed to the Director of Public Prosecutions (DPP). All of these were practices already espoused in principle by most forces, although by no means regularly carried out. One obvious effect of the legislation was to bring about a dramatic change in recording practices. From an annual total of around 4,000 at the beginning of the 1960s, officially recorded complaints rose rapidly until stabilising towards the end of the 1970s at a figure approaching 30,000.

This growth in recorded cases, combined with the legal obligation to investigate every case and to notify the complainant of the outcome, soon resulted in a major increase in the time, money and manpower expended in dealing with complaints. Within a few years of the Police Act, concern was being expressed in police circles about excessive bureaucracy, long delays, and the waste of highly paid senior officers' time in the investigation of thousands of relatively minor grievances. One response, now fairly common practice, was to take investigations out of the hands of divisional Superintendents (who dealt with them largely in their 'spare time') and to set up specialist headquarters-based Complaints and Discipline Departments, seconding Superintendents, together with assistants from lower ranks, to work full-time on investigations. However, while perhaps enhancing the quality of investigations, this did little to meet the criticisms and, from the ordinary police officer's perspective, served only to make the whole system appear more remote and bureaucratic.

Meanwhile, the fundamental issue refused to go away. As further allegations of malpractice, particularly of corruption among detectives in the Metropolitan Police District, hit the headlines in the early 1970s, criticism became firmly focused upon the practice of the police 'investigating themselves'. Whatever the truth behind any individual

7

incident, and however fairly or thoroughly the investigation may have been carried out, the exoneration of officers almost inevitably led to suspicion of a 'cover up'. Despite a strong internal initiative against corruption in the MPD during which the new Commissioner, Robert Mark, required the resignation or early retirement of large numbers of detectives (Cox et al 1977; Reiner 1985; Hobbs 1988), pressure for the introduction of an independent element into the complaints system became irresistible. Strong opposition from the police lobby—a reaction experienced during attempts to introduce such reforms in many other countries (Brown 1983; Goldsmith 1991)—succeeded in blocking more radical change, but in 1976 the government set up a part-time lay body, the Police Complaints Board (PCB), to monitor retrospectively police decisions arising from investigations.

This compromise solution satisfied few people. The new watchdog was soon widely perceived as virtually toothless. Inundated with case papers, the PCB simply added more bureaucracy and delay to an already unwieldy system, rarely doing any more than 'rubber stamping' police reports. Between 1976 and 1985, members questioned chief officers' conclusions in only 210 cases among more than 50,000 examined, in most instances eventually accepting the original police decision (LSPU 1987).

Within ten years, the PCB was dismantled, to be replaced by the present independent body, the PCA. The latter emerged out of a fierce debate about police powers, beginning in submissions to a new Royal Commission (on Criminal Procedure) set up in 1979 and fuelled by the urban riots and subsequent Scarman Report in 1981. Between 1980 and 1984, in addition to the Royal Commission, no fewer than eight official committees and working parties reconsidered the specific issue of complaints (LSPU 1984; Cohen 1985). Eventually, the 1984 Police and Criminal Evidence Act (PACE) settled upon the 'solution' of the PCA, a full-time body with a new 'supervisory' role in investigations.

3. PACE and the PCA

A central aim behind PACE was to define more clearly than ever before the powers possessed by individual police officers, both on the street and in the station. Powers were increased significantly in several areas, but attempts were made to balance this with more precise specifications of their limits and with new mechanisms (in particular, strict requirements for making written records) to make officers accountable for their use. Detailed Codes of Practice were subsequently drawn up to regulate behaviour in relation, for

8

example, to the conduct of interviews. Any breach of these Codes now renders an officer liable to disciplinary, though not criminal, action. (For discussion of the aims and effects of the Act, see, for example, Alves and Shapland 1985; Freeman 1985; Zander 1985; Maguire 1988; Irving and McKenzie 1988.)

The handling of complaints, covered in Sections 83–105 of PACE, was seen as an important part of this 'after the fact' accountability for actions taken. Arguably the most significant innovation was the involvement of the Police Complaints Authority at an early stage in inquiries into serious complaints. Under Section 87, a PCA member must 'supervise' the investigation, still as before conducted by a senior officer, of any complaint in which it is alleged that the actions of a police officer led to the death of, or serious injury to, a member of the public. Members may also choose to supervise other cases in defined categories if they consider it appropriate (see Chapter 2). Before an investigation is deemed to have been completed, a member must issue an 'Interim Statement', certifying that thorough inquiries have been carried out and a report compiled to his or her satisfaction.

PCA members also inherited from their predecessors the duty of examining the files of all completed complaints investigations. Here they have a clear opportunity for affecting the final outcome of complaints, as, although the police recommend what action should be taken, and in most cases set up and administer disciplinary proceedings themselves, in the last resort members have the power to direct the holding of a disciplinary tribunal. Moreover, when such a direction is made, the panel hearing the case consists of the Chief Constable and two members of the PCA (selected from those who have no previous knowledge of the case).

In addition to the new procedures for serious complaints, the architects of PACE attempted to ease the problem of excessive formality in the handling of minor cases. The new system of 'informal resolution' is designed to dispense with such cases quickly, cheaply and, ideally, to all parties' satisfaction. The key feature of informal resolution is that police officers face no risk of disciplinary action: they can admit misconduct and/or apologise to the complainant without their statements being admissible as evidence against them and without any 'stain on their record'. This procedure effectively separates a proportion of complaints from the disciplinary system, with the aim of allowing more attention to be given to satisfying the complainant rather than to the demands of the system.

4. The Objectives of Complaints Systems
Most large organizations, particularly those which frequently deal

face-to-face with members of the public, have at least a rudimentary set of procedures for dealing with complaints. These can serve a number of different purposes, the relative importance of which varies with the kind of organization concerned. In commercial companies, the main object is often simply to keep customers happy, at the same time warding off potential adverse publicity about standards of service: emphasis is therefore likely to be placed upon apologising and, where appropriate, offering some form of compensation. They may, at the same time, use complaints as a tool for monitoring the company's standards of service, keeping records of the subject-matter and responding to increases in a particular kind of complaint by instigating new training initiatives or changing standard practices. Public bodies such as hospitals, schools, the Post Office, social work agencies and other central and local government institutions, may have similar aims in mind, but as they are using taxpayers' money to provide a service, they have in addition a duty to demonstrate publicly that they are doing so competently, efficiently and fairly. (This applies both to the formulation and implementation of policy and to the actions of individual employees.) An effective complaints system can make an important contribution in this respect, and hence emphasis is likely to be placed upon convincing outsiders of its thoroughness and impartiality.

Public accountability is also a central issue in complaints against members of recognized professions, whether publicly or privately employed. There is always a tension between the insistence of groups such as doctors and lawyers that their possession of specialist knowledge should preclude the fettering of their 'professional discretion' by outsiders, and the fact that their actions and judgements (and, sometimes, misconduct and misjudgements) can have a profound effect upon people's lives, indicating the need to question their actions when something goes wrong. The traditional response of such groups to calls for greater accountability has been to set up stronger internal regulatory mechanisms, including disciplinary codes and complaints systems, which, they claim, provide sufficiently tight controls over the behaviour of their members to obviate the need for external (and particularly governmental) 'interference' in their affairs.

All of the above considerations apply to the police: they are very conscious of their 'public image', they are providing a range of services paid for by the public, and they regard themselves as 'professionals' with particular forms of expertise which render it inappropriate for uninformed outsiders to judge many of their operational decisions. However, there is also a vital extra element in police work which distinguishes it from that of nearly all other public

10

services or professions: the right, in certain circumstances, to use force to carry out their duties. As Bittner (1974:35) put it in an often-quoted passage, "The policeman [sic], and the policeman alone, is equipped, entitled and required to deal with every exigency in which force may have to be used." There is a special onus on the police to reassure the public that such coercive powers are not being used excessively or repressively and to demonstrate that any specific allegations of their abuse are thoroughly and impartially investigated. This is the crux of the argument for singling out complaints against the police (perhaps along with those against one or two other occupational groups such as prison officers) as necessitating an exceptionally rigorous and independent system of investigation, whereby justice is clearly 'not only done, but seen to be done.'

Whether or not the above conclusion is justified, it is self-evident that, even during periods when policing issues attract relatively little public attention, the investigation of complaints is an intrinsically important responsibility. However, when, as over much of the past two decades, the credibility, and even the legitimacy (Reiner 1985), of the police is being called frequently into question, the effectiveness of the complaints system is likely to emerge as a vital issue. Indeed, one might add that over this period it has had to carry an extra heavy burden—perhaps an unfair one—by virtue of the failure of other mechanisms of accountability to help restore public confidence to its former level. The 'tripartite' system set up by the Police Act 1964, under which control of the police is theoretically shared between Chief Constables, the Home Secretary and local Police Authorities, has resulted in practice in a major loss of influence by the local elected bodies (Jefferson and Grimshaw 1984; Loveday 1984; Reiner 1985; Lustgarten 1986) and the capacity of outsiders to affect police policy or policing styles is regarded by many critics as unacceptably limited. A degree of local dialogue with Chief Constables has been achieved by the creation under PACE of Consultative Committees, but few would argue that these have had a great impact (Kemp and Morgan 1989). In the perceived absence of effective 'democratic' channels for seriously questioning or influencing major aspects of policing, the complaints system has come inevitably more into the limelight. Prominent cases have increasingly tended to spark off wider arguments about police practice, while for many critics the complaints system itself has become a symbol of the unresponsive and unaccountable organization which they perceive the police to be.

However, the important point is sometimes missed that the complaints system has never been designed as a forum for the airing of general grievances or dissatisfaction with policing methods. It is

11

concerned explicitly with individual officers and individual incidents: the primary task of the investigator is to determine whether or not there is sufficient evidence to substantiate specific allegations about that officer's behaviour at that time; if there is, the principal issue becomes one of individual punishment. In short, the complaints system embodies the 'bad apple' approach to concerns about misconduct. It does not encourage or seek to answer questions about the state of the barrel which contains the apples.

This, at least, has been the traditional approach—justified on the grounds that other mechanisms exist to deal with the broader questions. However, with the exposure of the limitations of these other mechanisms and the consequent greater demands being made of the complaints system, there are now some signs of change in this rigid interpretation of the latter's functions. Four particular developments may be briefly mentioned.

First, s.88 of PACE allows the PCA to supervise the investigation of incidents (not necessarily related to specific complaints) which the police choose to refer to the Authority by virtue of their gravity or exceptional circumstances. The PCA then has discretion whether or not to supervise: so far it has done so in 70–80 per cent of cases. A key feature of these 'Section 88' cases is that the terms of reference for the police investigation can be made much wider than in straightforward complaints cases. In practice, this means that the investigating officer is able to consider matters not directly related to possible offences committed by officers. For example, in cases arising out of the policing of demonstrations or picketing, the terms of reference can go beyond the determination of whether Officer A struck Complainant B, to include questions about the deployment and supervision of officers, and even the operational tactics, employed by senior officers.

Secondly, the introduction, under s.85 of PACE, of 'informal resolution' as an option removes a proportion of complaints from their traditional close relationship with the disciplinary system. The aim of the investigation in these cases is no longer the determination of whether or not a provable breach of the disciplinary rules has occurred, but the provision of an opportunity for complainant and officer to 'bury the hatchet' through explanations of the actions which took place and, if appropriate, apologies and admissions of mistakes. Ideally, both parties should be satisfied with the outcome, and lessons should be learned by erring officers without the risk of formal punishment or threat to promotion prospects (informally resolved complaints are not recorded on officers' personal files). While still essentially concerned with individual rather than general police behaviour, informal resolution at least offers the possibility of less inhibited dialogue with the public, getting away from the formalised

12

and inherently adversarial relationship engendered by the standard complaints system.

Thirdly, we found evidence of police forces beginning to look at patterns of complaints, in order to identify possible continuing problems in particular areas and to take remedial action at a wider level than simply individual punishment or advice. For example, an abnormal number of complaints about operational support groups which patrolled town centres in transit vans led one force to limit their deployment, while the overall level of complaints of incivility contributed to the same force's decision to initiate a major training initiative to improve the quality of routine contacts with the public.

Finally, the Police Complaints Authority, to a much greater extent than its predecessor, the PCB, has regularly commented in its annual reports upon matters of general concern arising from individual complaints it has dealt with. For example, it has made recommendations, some resulting in concrete changes, concerning the supervision of armed operations, the use of police computers, the identifiability of police vehicles, the care of drunken detainees, and the techniques used to make forcible entry (PCA 1987, 1988, 1990).

These developments may presage a considerably expanded role for the complaints system in the future, and consequently a rethinking of the criteria by which its effectiveness might be judged. Be that as it may, we would argue that, even now, there are at least four main objectives to the achievement of which it is reasonable to expect the current system to make some contribution. These are:

(a) The maintenance (through punishment or general deterrence) of 'discipline in the ranks.'
(b) The satisfaction of complainants.
(c) The maintenance of public confidence in the police.
(d) The provision of 'feedback from consumers' to police managers.

In the course of this report we shall summarise evidence from our own and other research about the extent to which each of these aims is being served. Particular attention will be paid to any contribution made by the creation of the PCA or the way it carries out its functions.

5. Outline of the Research

(a) *Three police forces*
As mentioned earlier, the research involved two separate, but linked, studies. The first, commissioned by the Home Office, entailed fieldwork in three police force areas, which we have called 'County', 'City', and 'City II'. As the names partly imply, the first was a large

county force which included several important towns but also extensive rural areas; the second was a force covering a major conurbation; and the third was a force dominated by one large city, but which also contained an extensive surrounding area of mixed urban and rural character. In each of these areas we carried out the following research tasks:

(i) *Local casefile analysis*

The files relating to fifty recently completed cases, randomly selected and including investigated, withdrawn and informally resolved complaints, were examined in each of the three force headquarters. From these 150 files, detailed information was extracted concerning the nature of each incident, the characteristics of those involved, and the path which the investigation took. This part of the research will be referred to as our 'local casefile analysis'.

(ii) *Interviews with samples of complainants*

These samples were drawn from consecutive cases in batches of recently completed complaints files (not the same cases as those used in the local casefile analysis). Appendix 1 gives a full account of the samples taken and the response rates achieved. Exactly 100 complainants were interviewed out of a total sample of 168: 40 whose cases had been formally investigated, 30 whose cases had been withdrawn, and 30 whose cases had been informally resolved. As explained in the Appendix, possible doubts exist about the representatives of those interviewed, particularly because the majority came from the County Force area and because there was a slightly lower response rate among those who had withdrawn their complaint (59 per cent) than among those who had proceeded with it or had accepted informal resolution (71 and 67 per cent, respectively). Non-respondents were also more likely than respondents to be young, unemployed and to have previous convictions, which suggests that if there is a general bias in the findings, it is in the direction of showing more satisfaction with the system and more 'pro-police' attitudes than actually exist.

In these interviews, as in interviews with other participants in the system, we used semi-structured questionnaires and recorded responses in note form. One of us also used shorthand, which was useful for recording longer comments made by interviewees: some of these are quoted in the report.

(iii) *Interviews with samples of officers complained against*

These, again, were drawn from consecutive cases in batches of recently completed files in the three police force areas studied. Some cases were the same as those used for constructing the complainant samples, but no systematic attempt was made to link the two sets of responses: we did not wish to be perceived by either side as 'rehearing the case'. The samples of cases were not stratified, so they contain representative proportions of investigated, withdrawn and informally resolved complaints. However, in cases in which four or more officers were complained against, we limited ourselves to interviews with half of those named (up to maximum of four officers per case). A total of 63 officers were asked for interviews, and 50 (79 per cent) of these agreed. Again, for reasons explained in the Appendix, the majority of the sample (40 of the 63) was taken from the County force, but no major differences in their responses were apparent between areas.

(iv) *Interviews with investigating officers (IOs)*
We spent a considerable time in the headquarters of all three forces, and interviewed fourteen of the Superintendents and Chief Inspectors attached as full-time Investigating Officers (five each from two of the forces, four from the third). We also interviewed five Superintendents 'on division', who were occasionally instructed to investigate cases as part of their general duties (which often meant, in reality, cutting into their evening leisure time). However, the practice of allocating complaints investigations to divisional officers had virtually disappeared in two of the forces, and was becoming less common in the third. This appears to be a countrywide trend.

(v) *Conversations and formal interviews with other interested parties*
These included senior officers in Complaints and Discipline (C & D) departments, members of Police Authorities and officials of police unions. Our frequent presence in C & D departments also allowed us to get to know staff and investigators personally and to observe the daily routines in the offices.

In addition to the fieldwork in local areas, we obtained data indicating the national picture from a number of sources. Useful statistics were obtained, for example, from F2 Division in the Home Office and from the Police Complaints Authority. We were also permitted to include a number of questions in the 1988 British Crime Survey, aimed partly at exploring the 'dark figure' of potential complaints which fail to reach the official records, and partly at measuring attitudes to the system of investigation.

(b) *The Police Complaints Authority*
The second part of the research entailed a special study of the PCA, commissioned by the Authority under s.97 of PACE.[2] There was a

15

problem, in that s.98(1), which establishes the confidential status of information received by the Authority, seems to preclude outsiders from seeing PCA files. To overcome this obstacle, we were given a contract which put us temporarily in the position of employees of the Authority. This did not in practice affect our independence: we were given complete freedom in the design and execution of the research. The arrangement also allowed us virtually free access to files and guaranteed the co-operation of members. Over a period of more than six months, we made many visits to the Authority's offices in central London, where we spent time informally with members and their support staff, engaging in frequent discussion and observation of their work. At the same time, we carried out a number of more formal research procedures:

(i) *Interviews with members and staff*
We formally interviewed all members of 'I' Division (those concerned with the supervision of police investigations) as well as four 'D' Division members (those concerned with disciplinary matters). We also interviewed eight of the seconded civil service staff who provided administrative support to both divisions, and the two police advisors then attached to the PCA.

(ii) *PCA casefile sample*
We took a stratified sample of 100 supervised cases, about which we extracted detailed information from PCA files. These were cases which had been completed by the Authority in 1986 or 1987, and were selected at random within each of three categories. They consisted of:

—40 cases supervised mandatorily under S.87(1)(a)(i) of the Police and Criminal Evidence Act 1984.
—40 cases referred under S.87(1)(a)(ii), (1)(b) or (2) and subsequently selected for supervision.
—20 cases selected for supervision after referral under S.88.

The first category comprised cases which the PCA had been obliged to supervise, as the complaints amounted to allegations that the conduct of police officers had led to the death of, or serious injury to, members of the public. The second category consisted of complaints investigations chosen for supervision by the PCA, after either mandatory or voluntary referral by the police.[3] The final category comprised cases referred under s.88, which concern matters, not necessarily related to a complaint, which the police wish to investigate under PCA supervision. (For relevant Statutes and Regulations, see Appendix 2).

Our samples thus cover the full range of cases supervised by the PCA, although, as they are separate stratified samples, they cannot, strictly speaking, be amalgamated into one 100-case group to represent all PCA cases, without an adjustment through 'weighting' to allow for the slight underrepresentation of mandatorily supervised cases. (During the period in question, about 55 per cent of all cases taken on by 'I' Division were supervised under the mandatory system, compared with the 40 per cent in our sample.)

(iii) Questionnaire sample

In order to obtain the views of complainants in supervised cases, we also extracted from PCA files a separate stratified sample of 382 cases—156 supervised mandatorily, 76 supervised at members' discretion, and 150 initially referred to the PCA but not selected for supervision. In February 1988, questionnaires were sent to one complainant from each of these cases, asking them about their impressions of the investigation and of the PCA and its work. (The questionnaire is reproduced in Appendix 5). 186 replies were received and a further 35 questionnaires were returned marked 'gone away'—a response rate among those who received our letter of at least 54 per cent. This is well above average for postal questionnaires. As we had no systematic information about the social characteristics of the complainants in these cases, we cannot be certain that there is no response bias affecting the results. The only such bias we could detect was that replies were received from a higher proportion of complainants whose cases had been supervised than unsupervised: there were no significant differences between respondents and non-respondents where the formal outcomes of cases were concerned.

As the above 'questionnaire sample' contained a higher number of cases than our 'PCA casefile sample', it was useful for checking the validity of some of the findings from the latter, as well as allowing a certain amount of comparison between supervised and unsupervised cases. More general statistics on the PCA caseload, and on its relation to the total sum of recorded complaints, were extracted from a variety of sources, including PCA reports and internal documents, and annual returns by the police to the Home Office.

Finally, an important general comment to make about the data we gathered is that, in order to cover the several different ways in which complaints against the police are handled—investigated, withdrawn, informally resolved, supervised by the PCA and so on—and in order to interview participants on all sides of the system, we were unable to create samples as large as we would have liked in every instance. We are well aware that, for example, to interview only 30 complainants whose cases have been informally resolved, leaves some doubt about the representativeness of their views. Nevertheless, we would emphasise that the total numbers of cases in the stratified samples of casefiles and of complainants are quite large: with appropriate weighting, their strata can be analysed together to form the equivalent of representative samples—e.g. of 'complainants of all kinds'—of sufficient size to allow a reasonable degree of confidence in the results. The overall picture which emerges from the sum of its smaller parts we believe, is relatively clear, coherent and consistent. (For further discussion of sampling issues, see Appendix 1).

NOTES
1. This, like many other responsibilities in the system, is often delegated in less serious cases to a lower ranking officer. Throughout the text, in order to avoid unnecessary complication, we shall refer to officers responsible for particular tasks according to the situation obtaining in forces other than the Metropolitan Police District, where the rank structure is somewhat different.
2. Section 97 of the Police and Criminal Evidence Act 1984 states that the Authority has a duty 'to report on such matters relating generally to their functions as the Secretary of State may specify, and may for that purpose carry out research into any such matters.'
3. Under s.87(1)(a)(ii), the police must refer to the PCA certain types of complaint—as laid out in Regulation 4(1) of the Police Complaints (Mandatory Referrals etc.) Regulations 1985. These include allegations of assault occasioning actual bodily harm, corruption and other serious arrestable offences. The police may also refer complaints voluntarily under s.87(1)(b), and the PCA may 'call in' any other complaint it wishes under s.87(2).

CHAPTER 2

An Outline of Complaints Procedures

The complaints system in England and Wales is subject to a confusing array of legal requirements, regulations, instructions to chief officers, and local force orders. It is further complicated by local traditions, which produce considerable variations in practice and in ways of interpreting the regulations. Similarly, recording practices are subject to local variation, so caution must always be exercised in comparing forces solely on the basis of their statistical returns. The object of this chapter is to provide a simplified picture of the main recording rules and practices, systems for the classification and allocation of cases, and basic investigative and disciplinary procedures.

1. Recording, Classification and Allocation

Complaints against the police in England and Wales do not become 'official' until they are recorded by the police. The independent Police Complaints Authority receive and note a number of communications from potential complainants who telephone, write to, or occasionally visit, their offices. Callers are generally advised to contact their local police station to initiate the formal procedures—though the Authority also send letters on to forces where appropriate. This requirement to address complaints in the first instance to the police is common to many countries, although it has been criticised as a barrier which dissuades or deters some people from using the system. A few jurisdictions in the USA and Canada, for example, now allow complaints to be made direct to an independent body (Loveday 1989; Goldsmith 1991).

The majority of complaints are recorded following a visit by a member of the public to a local police station, where, provided there is a clear intention to complain, staff on the front desk will normally call the shift Inspector to deal with the matter. However, our research indicated that people are sometimes incorrectly advised by desk staff to return home and write a letter (see Chapter 4). Others write in the first instance to the Chief Constable or to police headquarters, and a smaller proportion telephone: the latter, again, may be advised to come to the station or to put their complaint in writing.

An unknown number of potential complainants are deflected from their initial intention during these early stages. As will be discussed in Chapter 4, this can be brought about by their receiving, for example from a desk Sergeant, an informal apology, a reasonable explanation of the 'offending' officer's actions, or a promise to 'have a word with him'; by charm or 'soft soap'; by being deliberately or unintentionally confused about technical points; by becoming persuaded that it is 'not worth the effort' to invoke the formal machinery; or by real or perceived threats of reprisals for complaining.[1]

However, assuming that any such initial hurdles have been overcome, the key stage in the recording process is usually a face-to-face interview with an Inspector or, less frequently, Chief Inspector. This may take place on the spot, or later by appointment, in the police station or the complainant's home. (Even when people write in directly to the force headquarters, Complaints and Discipline (C & D) staff will normally ask a local Inspector to see them first to clarify the nature and details of their complaint.) At this interview, the complainant is asked what happened and, after discussion, whether he or she wishes to pursue the matter further.

If the complainant is happy with an explanation, an informal apology, or a promise that the matter will be looked into—or if he or she simply decides, on reflection, that it is not worth persisting with the complaint—it is open to the Inspector to take no further action. A record of the conversation is usually kept locally and the officer may make a note of it in his or her pocket book:but the matter is not recorded as a complaint and does not therefore feature in statistical records. In police jargon, the Inspector is said to have 'allayed the sense of grievance'.

Alternatively—particularly if the headquarters C & D department is already aware of the matter—the Inspector may suggest that it be dealt with by means of the 'informal resolution' process (i.e. under s.85 of PACE). This can only be used if (a) the complainant (but not necessarily the officer complained against) agrees, and (b) 'the chief officer is satisfied that the conduct complained of, even if proved, would not justify a criminal or disciplinary charge' (s.85(10)(b)).

In its simplest form—known in some forces as a *'desk top'* resolution—informal resolution is little different from the totally informal allaying of grievance described above, except that an official complaint form is filled out and the case will eventually enter the force's statistical records. The Inspector will speak to the officer(s) involved—occasionally in the presence of the complainant—and may, if he/she feels it appropriate to do so, convey an apology on the officer's or the force's behalf; equally, the complainant and the police may 'agree to differ' and let the matter rest. Normally, the whole process will be concluded within a few hours, all that remains being to prepare a brief report for headquarters records.

If, despite the willingness of the complainant to engage in informal resolution, the Inspector prefers not to deal with the matter personally at that time, he or she may decide instead to record a complaint and pass it on to C & D with a recommendation that it be informally resolved. If they agree with this recommendation, Headquarters will then nominate an 'Appointed Officer' (AO) to carry out the procedure. (It should also be noted that, provided the complaint is of a sufficiently minor nature, C & D departments may, even without any indication or recommendation from the referring Inspector, decide to appoint an AO—as opposed to an investigating officer (see below)— in the hope that the complainant can be persuaded to accept informal resolution.) This may be one of their own staff, another middle-ranking officer in the relevant police station or from a neighbouring area, or even—increasingly—the very Inspector who recorded the complaint. A similar process then ensues: the officers involved are interviewed informally and the complainant is informed of their responses. Again, an apology may be offered by the officer concerned, or one may be made on behalf of the force if this appears appropriate.

After an AO has made efforts to achieve an informal resolution, it is still open to the complainant to express dissatisfaction with the outcome and to insist instead upon a formal investigation. In this case, the whole process must begin again, as interviews conducted under the informal resolution rules cannot be used as evidence to charge an officer with a disciplinary or criminal offence. However, it is rare for complainants to take this option: as will be shown in Chapter 4, even if officers totally deny the allegations, complainants are usually persuaded to 'agree to differ' and, indeed, are by no means always made aware of their right to pursue the issue further (Corbett 1991).

A quite different situation arises if a complainant is unwilling from the outset to agree to informal resolution, or if the police consider the complaint too serious to be dealt with in this way: as noted earlier, PACE precludes the use of the informal system unless 'the chief officer is satisfied that the conduct complained of, even if proved, would not justify a criminal or disciplinary charge'. In these circumstances, formal investigative procedures are set in motion. If the complaint has been made in the first instance to a local Inspector, the latter will play little further part in the process, beyond recording brief details of the allegations and telexing them to the headquarters Complaints and Discipline Department. He or she has, however, one other important duty—that of preserving any ephemeral evidence which may be relevant to subsequent investigations (see below).

21

Normally, the abovementioned telex includes a provisional classification of the complaint or complaints being made—a translation of the complainant's (sometimes long and rambling) account into one or more official categories, such as 'incivility', 'assault', 'oppressive conduct', or 'neglect of duty'.[2] This is by no means always a straightforward process, particularly if the allegations relate to a series of incidents involving several officers, several complainants and a variety of locations (e.g. a fracas starting with arrests at a public house, and continuing in police vehicles and cells at the local police station). The original classifications are quite often changed, added to or reduced in number by headquarters staff, in the light of subsequent examination. The wide discretion allowed here has important consequences for statistical returns, as most published figures refer to totals of individual *complaints*, rather than totals of *cases*:[3] a change in interpretation can artificially inflate or depress a force's complaints figures, when in fact there has been little movement in the total of incidents leading to complaint (see Chapter 3 below and Maguire and Corbett 1989).

On receiving a complaint, senior officers at C & D take a number of important preliminary actions and decisions. Such departments are usually under the overall control of the Deputy Chief Constable (DCC) of the force, and it is he or she who is ultimately responsible for ensuring that the duties of the 'chief officer', as laid down in many sections of PACE, are properly carried out. In very serious cases the DCC may well be called in to take immediate charge. Otherwise, depending upon the sensitivity or importance of the case, decisions will be made either by the senior manager in charge of the department (normally a Chief Superintendent) or by an administrator of lower rank.

Under PACE (s.84(1)), the first duty of the 'chief officer' is to ensure that evidence is preserved. This is an urgent matter in many complaints of assault in particular, not necessarily because unscrupulous officers might seek to destroy it, but because it can deteriorate quickly. For example, there may be truncheons to check for signs of impact, or injuries to photograph. (Not only C & D departments have this duty: if criminal allegations are involved, the officer—usually an Inspector—to whom they were first made also has a duty, as with any other crime report, to seize evidence as soon as practicable).

Another early consideration for senior officers is whether the case must or should be referred to the PCA, for a decision on whether the investigation is to be independently supervised by one of their members. The rules on referral and supervision are reproduced in Appendix 2, but they may be briefly summarized as follows:

22

(i) The police *must* refer—and the PCA *must* supervise—the investigation of cases in which it is alleged that an officer's actions led to the death of, or serious injury to, a member of the public (s.87(1)(a)(i)).

(ii) The police *must* refer—and the PCA *may* supervise—cases in which there are allegations of misconduct amounting to assault occasioning actual bodily harm, corruption, or any other serious arrestable offence (s.87(1)(a)(ii)).

(iii) The police *may* refer—and the PCA *may* supervise—any other complaint which the chief officer 'deems it proper' to refer (s.87(1)(b)), as well as any other matter, not necessarily related to a complaint, which it appears advisable to refer 'by reason of its gravity or other exceptional circumstances' (s.88).

(iv) The PCA may 'call in' and supervise the investigation of any other complaint of which they are made aware (s.87(2)).

Complaints falling under the mandatory referral rules (i) and (ii) above must be notified to the PCA without delay, by telex or fax. If the allegations are extremely serious, or, for example, a fatal shooting by police officers has occurred, the DCC may even telephone the relevant PCA member[4] at his or her home in the middle of the night, suggesting immediate attendance at the scene. However, in most cases, the member will receive a copy of the initial complaint form in his or her 'in tray' within 24 hours of its reception by the local Complaints & Discipline department, and will contact the investigating officer (see below) by telephone as soon as is convenient. In Chapter 9, an account will be given of the decision-making process at the PCA in relation to discretionary supervision.

Again in exceptionally serious cases, officers may be suspended immediately from duty pending the outcome of the investigation—a decision taken by the Deputy Chief Constable, sometimes in consultation with the PCA. Officers complained against may also be transferred temporarily to other duties.

The other main decision to be taken at an early stage concerns the appointment of an 'Investigating Officer' ('IO'). If the complaint does not fall within a category which necessitates its referral to the Police Complaints Authority for possible supervision, or if the PCA decides not to supervise, the appointment of the IO is left to the C & D department—the choice usually being delegated to the Superintendent or Chief Inspector in charge of administration. However, if a PCA member does decide to supervise, he or she may reject the recommended IO and insist upon a new appointment. (In our experience, this happened rarely.)

Where necessary, the IO will be of Superintendent rank, but in practice most investigations are performed by Chief Inspectors or

23

Inspectors acting on a Superintendent's behalf. Until relatively recently, in most forces, any Superintendent at all might be called upon to act as an IO, with the proviso that he or she came from a different division than that of the officer(s) complained against. However, it is becoming common practice for IOs to be appointed, as far as possible, from among officers seconded full-time to Complaints and Discipline departments. This is generally considered both a more efficient use of resources and more likely to produce competent investigations and reports: standards vary considerably, and officers without much experience of complaints investigations (and/or without CID experience), trying to fit the work in between their other duties, may do a less satisfactory job.

Finally, in the most serious cases, the PCA, usually with the police's ready agreement, may appoint an investigator from another force. Indeed, if the complaint is against a senior officer,[5] or concerns allegations of widespread serious misconduct, an outside officer of Chief Constable, Deputy Chief Constable or Assistant Chief Constable rank may be appointed.

2. Investigative Procedures

We now turn to the investigation itself. In theory, the procedure followed should not differ substantially from that of any other police investigation, be it into a reported crime, a road accident or a sudden death. This, indeed, is a central plank in the argument of those who resist the notion that there should be a fully independent system for investigating complaints: senior police officers, especially those with CID experience, possess a rare expertise and familiarity with a set of proven techniques. Assuming (and of course, depending upon the state of the police force concerned at any one time, this could be an assumption open to serious question) they can overcome any inherent bias or reluctance to convict a fellow officer, the argument runs, complaints investigation is 'no different' and such officers are the people best equipped to carry it out.

By the same argument, of course, one would not expect the shape of an investigation to be any different if supervised by an outside body like the PCA. However, we leave discussion of the quality of investigations and the related question of whether PCA supervision has any effect, to later chapters. For the moment, we will look at the main elements of the investigative task as a set of formal procedures.

As in any investigation, the main prescribed task of the IO is to establish the truth and, ideally, to gather evidence sufficient to prove or disprove that a criminal or disciplinary offence has been committed by particular individuals. As mentioned earlier, the first priority is to obtain and secure any physical evidence which exists. It is also standard practice, as early as possible, to conduct a full interview with the complainant and to obtain a signed statement outlining his or her version of what happened. At this meeting, the IO usually explains what will be done and may outline the possible consequences for the officer(s) concerned. Complainants are also likely to be asked, for the last time, whether they still wish to proceed, or whether, on reflection, they might agree to withdraw their complaint. About 40 per cent of all recorded complaints are officially withdrawn, the majority of withdrawals occurring at this first interview with the IO (Chapter 7).

Assuming the complainant wishes to continue, a full investigation will then take place, although there is an important factor which delays further action in quite a high proportion of cases. If there are criminal charges outstanding against the complainant, the matter may be considered *sub judice*. As will be shown in Chapter 3, a considerable proportion of complaints arise from situations in which somebody has been arrested and allegations and counter-allegations of violent behaviour are made by both parties. Particularly if the suspect faces charges of assaulting the police or resisting arrest, the investigation of his or her complaints against the arresting officers is likely to be suspended until the conclusion of the court case.[6] (The allegations of police misconduct may be brought up in court as a defence, although solicitors sometimes advise their clients not to raise them, on the grounds that, if the court fails to believe them, their chances of acquittal may be jeopardised or a longer sentence may be imposed.) Investigating officers quite often attend the court case, and immediately afterwards approach the complainant to ascertain whether he or she still wishes to pursue the matter.

Quite a few complaints are officially withdrawn in these circumstances, sometimes because those making them are persuaded that the court's reluctance to believe their story makes it unlikely that their complaint will succeed (see Chapter 6) and sometimes, no doubt—the explanation usually put forward by the police—because the allegations were made originally as ploys to confuse the case against them and avoid conviction: once the court case is over, they have served their purpose and the complainant has no interest in pursuing them. A counter-claim made by some complainants and some commentators (cf. Russell 1986) is that the sequence is often the reverse: people who complain of assault by the police upon arrest are likely to find themselves subsequently charged with assaulting the police, this being a ploy by officers to protect themselves against the allegations.[7] Further comment on this issue will be made in Chapter 3.

Once any *sub judice* obstacles have been removed—a process which can take months or even years—the full investigation can proceed.

Fairly standard procedures include the examination of evidence in the form of, for example, computer records, notes on message pads, custody records, tape recordings, or officers' pocket books; the seeking and interviewing of witnesses, both police and members of the public; and—usually at a later stage—interviews with the officer(s) subject of complaint. All interviews are transcribed and each page signed by the person concerned.

If the complaint includes an allegation that an officer has committed a criminal offence, he or she has the same rights accorded to any citizen interviewed as a possible suspect. There is no obligation to answer questions and a legal advisor may be present if requested.

If there is no question of a criminal offence, or, alternatively, once a criminal offence-related interview has been terminated, the officer(s) complained against may be asked to answer allegations relating to possible breaches of discipline. This second kind of interview is conducted under different conditions. Officers must be issued with a 'Regulation 7' form (see Appendix 3), informing them of the nature of the allegations against them and warning them that anything they say may be used in any subsequent disciplinary proceedings.[8]

There has been some debate over the timing of the issuing of 'Reg. 7s', as some investigators prefer to wait until the last minute before alerting officers to the existence of the complaint, in order to 'catch them on the hop' and to give less opportunity for the concoction of stories. However, cases against officers have been dismissed on the grounds of unfair delay in warning them of the allegations against them,[9] and it is now standard practice to issue notices at an early stage. When formally interviewed about a potential disciplinary matter, officers under investigation are allowed to bring with them an advisor, usually an official of the Police Federation, but not a solicitor. They are under no formal obligation to answer questions, but it was said by many we interviewed that the senior rank of the IO makes it difficult to refuse, as he or she may in the future become their commanding officer or may have a say in their posting or promotion: stubborn maintenance of silence may be seen as a 'black mark' against them.

During the investigation, all statements, photographic and documentary evidence, transcripts of interviews and any medical or scientific reports are marshalled into a (usually fairly bulky) file, to which the IO finally adds his or her report. The latter consists of a detailed summary of the allegations and the evidence, together with the IO's own conclusions and recommendations. Before being deemed complete, the file will be checked by a manager in the Complaints & Discipline department for any flaws or omissions: on occasion, IOs are instructed to re-interview witnesses or to explore new avenues. If the case has been supervised by the PCA, a complete copy of the file is also considered by the supervising member, who finally signs an 'Interim Statement' to certify that the investigation has been carried out to the Authority's satisfaction. The IO's involvement then ceases and the process enters the decision-making phase.

3. Criminal and Disciplinary Procedures

(a) *The chief officer and the PCA*
The key police officer in the post-investigation procedure is, in most forces, the Deputy Chief Constable, in the role of 'chief officer' under PACE, who initially decides whether or not the case merits (a) referral to the Director of Public Prosecutions (DPP) for a decision on criminal prosecution, and/or (b) the holding of a disciplinary hearing before the Chief Constable. The Deputy Chief Constable (DCC) is also responsible for sending copies of all completed investigation files to the disciplinary division of the Police Complaints Authority and for negotiating with its members about any outcomes with which they disagree.

The chief officer (the DCC) must first consider any evidence of criminal behaviour in the investigative report. If coming to the conclusion that this indicates that 'a criminal offence may have been committed by a member of the police force for his area' and that 'the offence indicated is such that the officer ought to be charged with it' (s.90(3)), a copy of the file must be sent to the DPP. Normally in such instances, copies are sent to the DPP and PCA simultaneously, the latter awaiting the DPP's decision before proceeding to consider disciplinary questions. If the chief officer decides that there is no evidence of crime, the file is sent to the PCA alone. However, if the PCA are not satisfied with this decision, and feel that an officer *should* be charged, they can—indeed, have a statutory duty to—overrule the chief officer and direct him or her to send the file to the DPP (s.92). The final decision on prosecution rests entirely with the Director and his staff in the Crown Prosecution Service, who determine whether there is sufficient evidence—and, if so, whether it is in the public interest—to bring any officer before a criminal court.

If the DPP decides to prosecute, the truth or otherwise of the relevant allegations will be settled in court, and court alone: no officer can undergo the 'double jeopardy' of facing a disciplinary charge which is 'in substance the same as the offence of which he has been acquitted or convicted' (s.104(1)). Officers surviving a prosecution can, however, later face disciplinary charges on related or subsidiary matters—for example, be disciplined for making racialist remarks to

27

a prisoner although acquitted in court of assaulting him. Convicted officers may also face dismissal on the disciplinary charge of 'having been found guilty of a criminal offence' (s.104(2)).

Any criminal proceedings having been completed, the only other barrier which may delay the final stages of the complaints process (i.e. the decisions about discipline) is the initiation by a complainant of civil proceedings against the police. There has been a growing trend in recent years for people claiming to have suffered material loss or damage as a result of police misconduct to initiate such an action at the same time as (or in lieu of) making a formal complaint. The reasons for this include the belief that, as the standard of proof is lower in civil courts than in the complaints system (see below), they are more likely to 'win their case'; another reason is that a successful outcome may include financial recompense, rather than simply an acknowledge-ment by the police that misconduct has taken place (Clayton and Tomlinson 1987).[10]

If there is no prosecution, or once any court case is settled, it must be decided whether there are grounds for any disciplinary action to be taken against individual officers. This decision, again, is made in the first instance by the DCC, who conveys his or her conclusions to the PCA in a memorandum. A member of 'D' Division in the PCA (see Chapter 8) reviews the evidence and reaches his or her own con-clusion. If this differs from that of the DCC, discussions will take place by telephone or letter. In the great majority of cases, one or other party is persuaded to change their mind and agreement is reached. However, as will be outlined below, in the few instances where no compromise can be found, the PCA may use its statutory power to direct the holding of a disciplinary tribunal (s.93(3)).

As far as police records are concerned, every individual complaint which has passed through the full investigation process is deemed eventually to have been either 'substantiated' or 'not substantiated'.[11] Substantiation does not necessarily mean that an officer will face formal disciplinary proceedings. On the contrary, the most common outcome is for 'advice' to be given. This entails an instruction to a senior officer (often a Superintendent) in the offending officer's station to deliver a formal homily to the latter in private, making it clear that a breach of discipline has occurred and that it should not happen again. To receive such 'advice' is certainly not considered a trivial matter in the police service: it is recorded in the officer's personal file, and can prove a hindrance to promotion. More serious, from an officer's point of view, is a formal 'admonishment'. Advice or admonishment can also be ordered when no complaint has been substantiated but other irregularities have come to light during the investigation—for instance, failure to make proper records in a pocket book, irregularities in overtime claims, or neglect of standard procedures after arrest.

In more serious cases, if the DCC considers—or is persuaded by the PCA—that there is *prima facie* evidence of a breach of discipline, he or she will frame a set of charges to be heard by the Chief Constable at a full disciplinary hearing. Such hearings are quasi-judicial in nature. The case is presented by a senior officer and the officer facing charges can be defended by a 'friend' from the police service (often an official of the Police Federation). Furthermore, if the officer faces charges serious enough to result in dismissal, requirement to resign, or reduction in rank, he or she may be represented by counsel or a solicitor. Witnesses, including the complainant, can be called and cross-examined by both sides. The complainant is entitled to be present to hear the evidence, but must leave before the verdict is announced and is not always informed of the outcome or any punishment awarded (see PCA 1990:14). The Chief Constable decides whether the case has been proved, using a standard of evidence—'beyond reasonable doubt'—identical to that employed in the criminal courts. A wide range of punishments can be imposed, from a reprimand to dismissal from the force. Officers have a right to appeal to the Secretary of State against conviction and awards.

Somewhat different rules apply on the rare occasions (averaging about six cases per year) when a DCC fails to be persuaded by the PCA that a hearing should be held and is then directed to set up a disciplinary *tribunal*. In this case, the PCA not only can frame the charges, but is required to nominate two of its own members—ones who have had no previous involvement in the case—to sit as members of the tribunal. These members have full voting rights in determining guilt or innocence, so can between them overrule the Chief Constable. However, they play no part in deciding upon the punishment to be awarded.

It should be noted that the PCA is unhappy about the tribunal system, and would prefer not to take part in the proceedings. In the Authority's Triennial Review 1985–88, it was noted:

"The Authority have been somewhat uneasy about their dual role. On the one hand they are effectively instigating the prosecution; on the other as members of a tribunal they are required to make an impartial judgement based on the evidence presented."

Finally, perhaps the most frequent criticism made of the disciplinary system concerns the standard of evidence required, not only to convict at a hearing or tribunal, but to substantiate even a minor case of incivility. Whereas those concerned with discipline in most other professions have to show only on the 'balance of probabilities' that a breach of a code has occurred, the much more rigorous test applied by the police makes it inevitable that only a small minority of complaints will result in substantiation. This problem was highlighted by the PCA in its 1987 Annual Report, and also underlay some controversial comments it made in the 1986 report concerning the difficulties of removing unsuitable officers from the force.[12] The problem is that, even when senior officers are convinced, for example, that a particular officer is persistently 'roughing up' arrested persons or dealing rudely with the public, it can be very difficult to produce sufficient evidence to take decisive action.

(b) *The Director of Public Prosecutions*

Although our interest is principally in complaints and discipline, rather than in criminal procedures, it is appropriate to add a few comments about the role of the Director of Public Prosecutions. This is the part of the system in which decision-making power by outsiders is the clearest and the longest established. It was first recommended by the Royal Commission of 1909 that decisions to lay criminal charges should be the prerogative of the DPP, whose office had been formally established a year earlier. Most forces soon co-operated fully with the DPP, although it was not until 1964 that the referral of papers was put on a statutory footing.

Criticism of prosecution decisions has focused upon the apparent 'caution' or 'conservatism' of the DPP: the proportion of cases received by his office which are rejected for prosecution is considerably higher than average when police officers are the subject. In responding to allegations of pro-police bias, the DPP has pointed out first of all that many police cases, unlike ordinary cases, are referred to his office without even meeting the standard of *prima facie* evidence (because Deputy Chief Constables are obliged to forward papers when they consider an offence *may* have been committed).

The DPP has also spelled out the implications of the primary test which he has decided to apply to all cases submitted to his office, whoever is involved. Before bringing any prosecution, he wishes to be satisfied that there is a 'reasonable prospect' of conviction.[13] 'Reasonable prospect' is a much more stringent test than that of evidence amounting to a *prima facie* case, in that the question asked is not simply whether a jury *could* convict, or even whether a jury *should* convict on the available evidence, but *whether it is more likely than not that it will convict* (Peay and Mansfield 1988:12). This element of prediction has particular significance for police cases, the DPP claims, because juries are traditionally more reluctant to convict police officers than other members of society. Thus he rejects many cases which, although apparently containing sufficient evidence, have in practice a poor chance of persuading a jury to bring in a guilty verdict. Indeed, he has taken the argument a step further, asserting that the high acquittal rate in police cases indicates that his office, far from favouring the police, may be prosecuting in *too many* such cases. These arguments have brought vigorous responses from Williams (1985) and Lustgarten (1986), among others, who assert that the whole approach is untenable in principle. Lustgarten, indeed, describes it as 'a flagrant violation of the rule of law'.

NOTES

1. It is interesting to speculate whether the trend to civilianisation on front desks will affect the 'attrition rate' of potential complaints.
2. The complaint categories used in statistical tables are incivility, assault, irregularity in procedure, traffic irregularity, neglect of duty, corrupt practice, mishandling of property, irregularity in relation to evidence/perjury, oppressive conduct or harassment, irregular arrest, irregular stop/search and irregular search of premises (PCA 1990:42). However, there are some variations in the classifications used by different forces. The full Discipline Code is provided in Appendix 6.
3. Generally speaking, the term 'case' refers to one incident, or set of related incidents, where one Investigating Officer is appointed and the evidence is collected in one file. It can involve any number of individual complainants, complaints or officers complained against. In exceptional circumstances, such as the investigation into the policing of the Wapping dispute, hundreds of all three categories can be involved (see also Chapter 3).
4. 'I' Division members were each allocated a number of police forces, and in normal circumstances any supervision required was carried out by the member in whose area the complaint was registered. However, the Deputy Chairman selected some cases from all areas for his own supervision and, if workloads were unbalanced, might allocate some to other members (including 'D' Division members).
5. Complaints against a Chief Constable or other officer above the rank of Chief Superintendent are officially (under PACE s.84) the province of local Police Authorities, rather than the PCA, although the former can ask the PCA to supervise on their behalf.
6. There are also practical difficulties which cause complaint investigations to be deferred until after a court hearing. In practice, defence solicitors are rarely prepared to permit their clients to be interviewed by the police to establish the facts of the complaint in advance of the court hearing, lest their clients inadvertently prejudice their own case. Conversely, the duty imposed on the police to conform to the Code of Practice on interviewing persons charged with an offence may present difficulties for them too.
7. In either event, Home Office officials point out, the existence of a complaint is not, and is not designed to be, a substitute for the assembly of evidence to provide a defence to charges against either party.
8. Although quite commonly referred to as 'Reg 7s', these forms vary between forces and are known locally by different form numbers.

9. This was one factor in the dismissal of summonses against officers arising out of the Wapping disorder on 24th January 1987 (see PCA 1990: para 5.5).

10. For these reasons, together with a general lack of faith in the complaints system, some solicitors regularly advise their clients to initiate a civil action without registering a complaint. Of course, this may result in a court decision (eg an award of damages) which satisfies them; but as any such action must be initiated against the force (or Chief Constable) rather than against the officer alleged to have caused the harm, the latter is likely to escape disciplinary sanctions even if the police lose the case. Moreover, the PCA (1988a: para 2.25) has noted the problem of complaint investigations being delayed for years by the refusal of complainants, on legal advice, to co-operate with them until civil proceedings have been completed.

11. The term 'substantiation' is not used by the PCA, who record outcomes in their annual reports in terms of criminal and disciplinary charges brought, advice or admonishment, and 'no action'.

12. PCA Annual Report 1986 (PCA 1987:11). The point was made that in, for example, the civil service and the armed forces, staff performing unsatisfactorily could receive a series of warnings and finally be dismissed, without having to be found guilty of serious misconduct at a hearing using the standards of a courtroom.

13. He must also be satisfied that prosecution is 'in the public interest'.

CHAPTER 3

The Nature and Frequency of Complaints

The classification and counting of complaints against the police is a complex business, as a single incident may result, directly or indirectly, in one or more complaints, made by one or more people, against one or more officers. Related incidents (such as an alleged assault in the street and subsequent alleged unlawful detention in a police station) are normally investigated together as a single case, however many different complaints, complainants or officers are involved. If Home Office guidance is followed correctly, the number of separate complaints recorded for any one case depends not on the number of officers or complainants, but on how many different kinds of police misconduct are being alleged against how many different 'victims' (Home Office 1985: s.3.14). Thus, for example, complaints by three different people about a series of related assaults on one person by three officers (say, in the street and later in a police van) should be recorded as only one complaint of assault. On the other hand, if all three complained that they had been assaulted, and one that he had later been denied access to a solicitor, four complaints should be recorded (three assaults and one 'irregular procedure').

The national statistics provided by F2 Division of the Home Office indicate that, on average, each case involves about 1.7 complaints, 1.1 complainants, and two officers complained against. On reading complaints files, however, we found many cases where the complexity of the incident or lack of clarity in the complainant's statement made precise classification difficult and, unsurprisingly, the recording rules were not always followed religiously. Overall, there is probably some underrecording of individual complaints within cases. For these reasons, the total of *cases* is probably the most meaningful figure and the most reliable indicator of trends. Unfortunately, most official statistics are based upon numbers of *complaints*, so, although we shall refer mainly to cases when describing our own research, we are forced when assessing national patterns and trends to use complaint-based figures more than we would wish.

1. National Patterns

(a) *Recent Trends in Complaints*

Between 1979 and 1989, the annual total of completed cases—i.e. those resulting in complaints being officially substantiated or not substantiated, informally resolved, withdrawn or not proceeded with—in England and Wales varied only narrowly, between a minimum of 16,206 and a maximum of 18,780 (see Table 1). The totals of recorded complaints contained within these cases were a little more volatile, varying between 27,932 and 32,443: this may simply reflect variations in classification practices, as discussed in Chapter 2.

However, while the overall totals have remained fairly stable, they conceal a difference in trends between the majority of forces and the largest, the Metropolitan Police District (MPD). In most areas, case totals have been increasing gradually, but in the MPD they fell markedly between 1979 and 1987—from almost 5,500 in 1979 (when they made up nearly a third of all cases in England and Wales) to under 3,000 in 1987 (only 18 per cent of all cases). This could reflect (a) a change in police behaviour in London, (b) a decline in public confidence in the MPD's complaints system, or (c) greater efforts by MPD shift Inspectors to allay grievances on the spot and dissuade people from making a formal complaint. On the other hand, there may be a simpler explanation, evidenced in a sudden increase in MPD completions in 1988: this followed criticism by the PCA (PCA 1987) of delays and administrative problems in the MPD, of which the force took serious note.[1] Whatever the answer, the fluctuations provide a

---

Table 1: Annual totals of completed cases and completed complaints against the police: MPD and all other forces in England and Wales, 1979–89

	Numbers of Cases			Numbers of Complaints		
	MPD	Other	TOTAL	MPD	Other	TOTAL
1979	5,487	11,441	16,928	8,786	20,597	29,383
1980	5,136	12,236	17,372	8,607	22,402	31,009
1981	4,849	12,527	17,376	9,178	23,265	32,443
1982	4,387	12,975	17,362	8,617	23,469	32,086
1983	4,240	12,887	17,127	7,711	22,970	30,681
1984	3,459	12,973	16,432	6,594	24,580	31,174
1985	2,838	13,368	16,206	5,462	22,791	28,253
1986	2,915	13,747	16,662	5,093	24,085	29,178
1987	2,981	13,432	16,413	5,236	22,696	27,932
1988	4,863	13,917	18,780	6,934	21,825	28,759
1989	4,786	13,868	18,654	6,873	22,439	29,312

Table 2: Outcomes of all completed complaints, England and Wales, 1979–1989

	Total complaints	Substan-tiated (%)	Unsubstan-tiated (%)	Withdrawn/ not proc. (%)	Informally Resolved (%)
1979	29,383	1,338 (5)	13,326 (45)	14,719 (50)	—
1980	31,009	1,288 (4)	13,476 (43)	16,245 (52)	—
1981	32,443	1,542 (5)	14,660 (45)	16,241 (50)	—
1982	32,086	1,787 (6)	14,702 (46)	15,597 (49)	—
1983	30,681	1,448 (5)	13,570 (44)	15,663 (51)	—
1984	31,174	1,561 (5)	15,549 (50)	14,064 (45)	—
1985	28,253	1,155 (4)	11,650 (41)	13,286 (47)	2,162 (8)
1986	29,178	1,129 (4)	12,676 (43)	11,335 (39)	4,038 (14)
1987	27,932	924 (3)	10,432 (37)	11,491 (41)	5,085 (18)
1988	28,758	853 (3)	9,848 (34)	12,144 (42)	5,913 (21)
1989	29,312	765 (3)	8,464 (29)	12,958 (44)	7,125 (24)

Source: F2 Division, Home Office

useful illustration of the confusing and misleading nature of police complaints statistics in general.

Complaints are distributed somewhat unequally between police forces, not only in terms of absolute numbers, but in relation to the numbers of officers employed. The highest annual rates seem to be of the order of 30 cases per 100 officers, and the lowest around ten per 100.[2] Again, it is impossible to say without further investigation whether these differences tell us more about variations in styles of policing or simply in recording practices.

Table 2 shows the outcomes of complaints over the same eleven-year period. It can be seen that a declining minority result in a formal decision as to whether they are or are not justified: in 1989, 44 per cent were withdrawn or not proceeded with, while a further quarter were informally resolved. Overall, the proportion of complaints undergoing full investigation has fallen from 50 per cent in 1979 to 32 per cent in 1989. This seems to be largely a consequence of the growing popularity of Informal Resolution, which has accounted for an ever larger proportion of all complaints. It might have been expected that its introduction in 1985 would have led to an overall increase in recorded complaints, with local Inspectors beginning to use it where in the past they would have tried to send complainants away happy without a formal record being made ('allaying the grievance', in police parlance). However, Table 2 suggests that this has not happened: Informal Resolution has been used much more often as a substitute for investigation. This is encouraging at least for the designers of the new system, one of whose main intentions was to reduce the amount of time and money spent on detailed investigation of relatively minor complaints.

The other striking trend in Table 2 is the falling proportion of complaints which result in substantiation. The 1989 proportion was probably a 'record low' in this respect: only 2.6 per cent of all complaints were substantiated. Between 1979 and 1984, by contrast, the average substantiation rate was 4.8 per cent. This trend, again, is partly explained by the advent of Informal Resolution,[3] although it should be noted that the substantiation rate has fallen in recent years even when expressed as a proportion of all fully investigated complaints: it averaged 9.5 per cent over the years 1979–84 and 8.3 per cent in 1985–89.

(b) *Types of complaint and their outcomes*
Table 3(A) shows a breakdown of complaints completed in 1989, in all English and Welsh forces except the MPD, according to the official

---

Table 3: Completed complaints against the police in 1989: types and outcomes

A. *Proportions recorded in each category: all forces except MPD*

COMPLAINT CATEGORY	%	%
Aggressive behaviour/rudeness		
Assault	28	
Incivility	21	58
Oppressive conduct/harassment	9	
Irregularities/neglect		
Irregular procedure	10	
Unlawful arrest/detention	6	
Neglect of duty	9	29
Traffic irregularity	2	
Impropriety in search	3	
Dishonesty		
Perjury/irregular evidence	3	
Mishandling property	2	6
Corrupt practice	0	
Other		
Racial discrimination	1	
Other disciplinary	4	6
Other criminal	2	
TOTAL	100	(N = 22,439)

Source: Home Office, F2 Division.

Table 3 (continued)

B. Outcomes, by complaint category: all other forces, with MPD appended

COMPLAINT CATEGORY	Substantiated N (%)	Not substantiated N (%)	Withdrawn/ not proc'd with N (%)	Informally resolved N (%)	All N (%)
Aggressive behaviour/rudeness					
Assault	90 (1)	2001 (32)	3762 (60)	463 (7)	6316 (100)
Incivility	70 (2)	917 (20)	1184 (25)	2479 (53)	4650 (100)
Oppressive conduct/harassment	36 (2)	483 (23)	770 (37)	796 (38)	2085 (100)
SUBTOTAL	196 (2)	3401 (26)	5716 (44)	3738 (29)	13051 (100)
Irregularities/neglect					
Irregular procedure	105 (5)	687 (32)	840 (39)	509 (24)	2141 (100)
Unlawful arrest/detention	57 (4)	484 (36)	619 (46)	199 (15)	1359 (100)
Neglect of duty	163 (9)	521 (27)	573 (30)	660 (34)	1917 (100)
Traffic irregularity	16 (4)	106 (29)	130 (35)	119 (32)	371 (100)
Improper search	17 (3)	213 (31)	251 (36)	209 (30)	690 (100)
SUBTOTAL	358 (6)	2011 (31)	2413 (37)	1696 (26)	6478 (100)

Continued overleaf

Table 3—*Continued from previous page*

B. Outcomes, by complaint category: all other forces, with MPD appended

COMPLAINT CATEGORY	Substantiated N (%)	Not substantiated N (%)	Withdrawn/ not proc'd with N (%)	Informally resolved N (%)	All N (%)
Dishonesty					
Perjury/irreg. evidence	16 (2)	354 (54)	220 (34)	66 (10)	656 (100)
Mishandling property	25 (5)	162 (30)	290 (54)	63 (12)	540 (100)
Corrupt practice	12 (14)	34 (40)	34 (40)	4 (5)	84 (100)
SUBTOTAL	53 (4)	550 (43)	544 (43)	133 (10)	1280 (100)
Other					
Racial discrimination	3 (2)	53 (32)	70 (42)	41 (25)	167 (100)
Other disciplinary	42 (4)	348 (37)	302 (32)	257 (27)	949 (100)
Other criminal	10 (2)	195 (38)	256 (50)	53 (10)	514 (100)
SUBTOTAL	55 (4)	596 (37)	628 (39)	351 (22)	1630 (100)
TOTAL ALL FORCES EXCEPT MPD	662 (3)	6558 (29)	9301 (41)	5918 (26)	22439 (100)
TOTAL MPD	103 (1)	1906 (28)	3657 (53)	1207 (18)	6873 (100)
ALL FORCES	765 (3)	8464 (29)	12958 (44)	7125 (24)	29312 (100)

category in which they were finally classified.[4] The central message from this Table is that well over half of all complaints allege some form of aggressive or incivil behaviour, verbal or physical. Most of the remainder contain allegations of irregular or negligent conduct. In fact, as we shall show later, if one looks at *cases* rather than complaints, the proportion containing at least one allegation of assault emerges as considerably higher than the 28 per cent indicated by the Table. This is because several of the other types of complaint (particularly incivility, neglect of duty and irregular procedure) tend to be secondary complaints in assault cases.

It is also interesting to note how different categories of complaint tend to be dealt with in different ways. This is shown in Table 3(B), where it is particularly striking to find that 60 per cent of all complaints of assault were withdrawn and that 53 per cent of complaints of incivility were informally resolved (the corresponding figures for all complaints were 44 per cent and 24 per cent, respectively). Comment on both these points will be made later in the report.

In investigated cases, too, there are clear differences apparent between the categories in terms of results. For example, nearly a quarter of the 'neglect of duty' complaints which went to investigation were substantiated, compared with only four per cent of investigated 'assault' complaints and five per cent of 'racial discrimination' complaints: indeed, only three of the latter, out of a total of 167 registered, were eventually substantiated. Possible reasons for the low substantiation rate in complaints of assault—only 90 out of 6,316 recorded—will be discussed in some detail below.

2. A Profile of 'Complaint Incidents', Complainants and Officers Complained Against

None of the above figures, of course, tell us anything about the *context* in which complaints most commonly arise, let alone offer any details of the behaviour complained about. No relevant official statistics are kept, so we have used file analysis, complemented with information from interviews with complainants and police officers, to build up a picture of the most common elements of incidents which resulted in a complaint being made. The following analysis is based upon random samples of cases from each of the three force areas in which we conducted fieldwork. These include withdrawn as well as investigated and informally resolved complaints.

Our base figure for the incident analysis is 264 cases, made up of the 50 casefiles selected in each of the three research areas, together with another 114 cases from the County force area which formed the basis of our interview sample there. (See Chapter 1 and Appendix 1. All these samples consisted of consecutive cases in batches of recently completed complaints files.)[5] Where there were any significant differences between the areas, we shall show findings separately for the 164 cases in the County force and the 100 cases in the two City areas.

The 264 cases involved a total of 347 complainants (1.3 per case) and 685 officers complained against (2.6 per case). However, as the quality and completeness of the information about the officers varied considerably, we are not able to use the full sample to describe them. Also, where complainants are concerned, we have analysed the characteristics of the 'principal' complainant.[6] Here, again, where appropriate, we show any major differences between 'County' and 'City' complainants. In the remainder of this chapter, we present a brief statistical overview of the salient characteristics of the incidents, the officers complained against and the complainants. We then illustrate and discuss three of the more common kinds of complaint— arrest-related assault, driving-related incivility, and failure to provide a requested service.

(a) *The incidents*

—Overall, 87 (33 per cent) of the 264 cases included at least one allegation of an assault by a police officer. This proportion was lower (30 per cent) in the County force than in the City forces (37 per cent). Among the remainder, 70 cases (27 per cent of the total) contained one or more complaints of incivility.[7]

—133 (50 per cent) of the 264 incidents occurred during the night shift (10 p.m. to 6 a.m.), with a concentration between the hours of 10 p.m. and 2 a.m. Among all incidents for which a definite time could be established, 42 per cent occurred during this four-hour period. Furthermore, more than half of the latter took place on Friday and Saturday nights: in other words, more than 20 per cent of all complaints were generated within these two key periods each week-end. The second most common period for complaints to arise was in the afternoon. There were only small differences between areas where these variables were concerned.

—Nearly half (46 per cent) occurred in the street or on the road, with about two-thirds of the complainants on foot and one-third in a vehicle. Other common locations were in or around the complainant's home (24 per cent of cases) and in a police station (18 per cent).

—Alcohol was involved rather less than one might infer from the above time patterns and from our police interviewees' accounts of 'typical complaints' (see Chapter 5), but one or more of the complainants had been drinking prior to the incident in at least one third of all cases. And 71 (27 per cent) of the 264 were described by police or other witnesses as 'drunk'.

—In just under three-quarters of the cases, there were two or more police officers present at the time of the alleged misconduct. And in roughly half, there were uninvolved members of the public who witnessed at least part of the incident.

(b) *The officers complained against*

—Unsurprisingly, Constables—who represent the bulk of police manpower—were complained against much more frequently than any other rank. However, there is some evidence that both Inspectors and Sergeants are equally—if not more—likely to be complained against when account is taken of their numbers.[8]

—Constables in their 'early middle' years of service were more likely to attract complaints than those at the beginning or end of their careers. The average age of PCs complained against in the County force was 29, and the average length of service was nine years. In the City force, where there was a computer record of the details of all cases, we were able to look at the position in more detail.[9] Here, as Table 4 shows, both the highest total of complaints and the highest ratio, taking into account the service-length structure of the force, were made against officers who had served 7–8 years. The chances of attracting a complaint more than doubled after a Constable had completed two years' service, decreasing rapidly after about 16 years' service. Such a pattern is similar to that found in a small study in the Thames Valley area (Emment 1984). How much it is explained by changes in attitudes over time (e.g. as the closely supervised probationary period ends and the effects of training 'wear off', before a more 'mellow' approach is adopted in the last few years of service) and how much to increasing and then declining exposure to 'sharp end' policing, is an interesting subject for further study.

—Where postings were concerned, by far the highest number of complaints in all three forces were against ordinary uniform patrol officers (Table 4). But when relative numbers of officers were taken into account, there was generally little difference between the proportions complained against in different departments. For example, among a sample of 200 officers from the City force, Detective Constables were slightly less likely than PCs to attract complaints, but more senior CID officers received a higher than average proportion. The most striking finding, however, was an overrepresentation of complaints in both forces among members of Operational Support Units. These officers frequently travel in groups in transit vans or similar vehicles, and are used as 'trouble-shooters' anywhere in the force area. They appear to attract considerable numbers of

41

Table 4: Characteristics of officers complained against: City force, 1987.

Years service (Police Constables only)

Years service	% of total PCs in force[1]	% of all PCs complained against[2]	Number complained against per 100 PCs in force
0–2	15	8	12
3–4	8	11	28
5–6	14	16	26
7–8	13	22	36
9–10	10	14	31
11–12	8	10	28
13–14	6	6	22
15–16	5	5	23
17–18	4	3	16
19–20	5	2	10
21 +	12	4	8
All	100	100	22

Posting[3]	Constables %	Other ranks %	All %
Uniform patrol	60	63	60
Operational support unit	14	0	7
Permanent beat officer	7	10	8
CID	8	20	11
Traffic	4	2	4
Other	7	0	3
N/K	12	5	7
Total	100 (N = 159)	100 (N = 41)	100 (N = 200)

Notes
1. The force strength and the proportions of PCs in each service-length group change somewhat throughout a full year, so the figures are inevitably approximations. Those used are based the distribution of Constables at a point early in 1988, adjusted backwards with estimations of retirements, etc. The total PC strength was approximately 4,400.
2. Based on all cases completed in 1987.
3. Based on a sample of 200 officers complained against in 1987.

complaints of assault in particular. (These findings are in accord both with the impressions of our police interviewees, and Emment's study.)

(c) *The complainants*

The 264 principal complainants in our samples were predominantly (75 per cent) male. Their other main characteristics, which are summarised later in the last column of Table 5(B), were as follows:

—Overall, nearly 60 per cent were in employment, and just under half of these were in non-manual jobs. Twelve per cent of the whole sample held professional or executive jobs. However, there were differences here between areas: those in the City areas were twice as likely to be unemployed as in the County area (32 per cent, compared with 16 per cent) and much less likely to be in non-manual jobs (16 per cent, compared with 36 per cent).

—49 per cent of the full sample were under the age of thirty, those in the City areas being slightly younger as a group (54 per cent under 30, compared with 46 per cent in the County area).

—45 per cent were known to have one or more previous criminal convictions. Complainants in the City forces were marginally more likely to have previous convictions.

—The great majority of those we interviewed stated that this was the first time they had complained against the police (again, see Emment 1984, where 82 per cent were first time complainants).

As will be described in Chapter 4, conversations with police officers revealed a widely-held image of the 'typical complainant'. This was of a young, aggressive, anti-police male, engaged in some form of criminal activity and likely to be intoxicated during the incident he complains about. The above figures suggest that such a picture is false where the majority of complaints is concerned. However, it is important to note that the characteristics of complainants varied significantly according to the type of complaint lodged. As we shall now illustrate, those complaining of assaults by the police were more likely to fit the 'stereotype'—i.e. to be young and working class, to have previous convictions, and to have been drinking prior to the incident in question. Those complaining of incivility or neglect of duty, by contrast, spanned a wide range of ages and social backgrounds.

3. Recurring Types of 'Complaint Incident'

(a) *Arrest-related assault*

Most complaints of assaults by police officers are arrest-related: 87

(33 per cent) of the 264 cases included a complaint of assault, and in 79 of these the alleged police violence either followed or preceded an arrest. Indeed, at least four of the other eight (which included incidents at a 'stop search' and in court cells) indirectly involved a suspected offence. The victims of the alleged assaults were predominantly males under the age of 30, and three-quarters had at least one previous conviction (see Table 5).

Nearly all the complainants asserted that they had been assaulted at the scene of the arrest—predominantly in the street. As Table 5 shows, allegations of assaults in vehicles or in police stations were less common, and most of these were said to involve a continuation of the initial violence.

The circumstances of the arrests were of three fairly distinct types: those planned in advance (as when a warrant was effected), those where the complainant was suspected of a recent offence (thought to be driving a stolen car, leaving the scene of a burglary, etc.) and 'immediate' arrests for offences (usually assaults or public order offences) either witnessed by the police or arising out of a confrontation between police and public. The majority of complaints of assault followed arrests of the last two kinds, in which the decision to arrest was often taken in difficult or confused circumstances. This may partly explain the fact that only about 60 per cent of those arrested were later charged with an offence.

A fairly typical example of a complaint arising from an 'immediate' arrest occurred when the police, called to an incident in a pub, had arrested the complainant's friend and were allegedly mistreating him. The complainant's story was that he asked the arresting officer not to be so rough and tried to restrain him, whereupon another officer turned to him and said 'We'll have you and all', assaulting him in the process of arrest. The complainant was later bound over to keep the peace. Another case of this type illustrates how the complainant's and police officers' versions of the same incident tend to differ greatly. The complainant, who had been out drinking, saw a group of policemen, including a Special Constable whom he recognised as someone he had previously known socially. According to the complainant, he greeted his friend jovially: 'Hello, X. What are you doing with that jacket on?' Met by silence, he then asked 'What's up, mate?' At this point he was bundled into a police vehicle and assaulted by officers in the back. The officers all claimed that the complainant had been drunk and abusive and refused to move on. He was therefore arrested and conveyed, struggling, to the vehicle. The conversation, too, was reported differently, with the complainant's opening gambit recorded as 'Fuck me, if it isn't X the fucking Special,' followed by 'Am I fucking seeing things? Is this cunt for real?' Cases of this

Table 5: Three common types of complaint: a profile.

1. *Elements of the incident*

Arrest-related assault (N = 79)		No.	%
Arrest for:	instant offence	32	41
	suspected recent offence	28	35
	pre-planned arrest	15	19
	other/not clear	4	5
Assault alleged in:	street	42	53
	home	18	23
	police vehicle	17	22
	police station	18	23
Time:	hours of darkness	55	70
	10 p.m.–2 a.m.	44	56
Alcohol:	some consumed	44	56
	'drunk'	29	37

Traffic-related incivility (N = 36)		
Stopped for driving behaviour/vehicle fault	21	58
Parking ticket being issued	8	22
Accident	3	8
Road check	2	6
Asked police for information	2	6
(Reported for traffic or parking offence:	22	61)

Inadequate response to service request (N = 26)		
Failure in investigation of offence	21	81
Failure to attend call	2	8
Failure to inform re recovered property	3	12

2. *Characteristics of complainants*

	Arrest–related assault (N = 79)*	Traffic–related incivility (N = 36)*	Failure in service (N = 26)*	All cases City and City II	All cases County	All (N = 264)*
Characteristics of complainants	%	%	%	%	%	%
Male:	85	75	58	73	76	75
Aged under 30:	82	19	31	54	46	49
non-manual	6	72	35	16	36	28
manual	48	17	42	26	33	30
rtd/hsewife/stdnt	16	8	23	26	15	19
unemployed	29	3	0	32	16	22
Known previous convictions:	75	17	6	51	42	45

*Percentages are based on totals excluding cases with missing data.[10]

45

general kind contain many of the ingredients (late evening, rowdiness in the street, alcohol, young males, complainants with previous convictions, etc.) of situations seen by our police interviewees as having a particularly high risk of generating complaints. However, although they form quite a large proportion of all complaints of assault (see Table 5), they constitute only about one in eight of all cases. As we now illustrate, large numbers arise from very different sets of circumstances.

(b) *Driving-related incivility*

Ninety-one (34 per cent) of the 264 cases included a complaint of incivility. In 21 of these, the incivility was simply a secondary complaint to an assault, and there was little to distinguish the incident from the kinds described in the previous section. Otherwise, the cases covered a wide range of people and circumstances, including alleged rudeness at the front desks of police stations, at arrests (in several cases to friends of those arrested), during searches, and even during a talk to a school group. Here, however, we concentrate upon the largest identifiable group: in 36 of the 70 incivility cases which did not include a complaint of assault, the complainant alleged rudeness by an officer in the course of contact relating to driving behaviour. Most of these incidents were initiated by the police stopping the complainant for a minor driving offence or faulty vehicle (Table 5). Indeed, most of the complainants conceded that they had committed an infraction, but had clearly been upset or annoyed by the officers' manner in dealing with it. For example, a doctor who inadvertently turned the wrong way into a one-way street in a strange city, claimed that a police officer adopted an officious approach and took over half an hour to 'book' him. And another motorist, trying to ascertain his whereabouts on the hard shoulder of a motorway, complained about the unhelpful attitude of the traffic constables who stopped to issue him with a fixed penalty notice, but left him none the wiser about where he was.

As a group, the complainants in these situations had very different social characteristics from those complaining of assault. The majority were middle-aged people in middle-class occupations, and only six had any known previous convictions—indeed, most of those we interviewed held (or used to hold) the police in reasonably high regard.

The 'genesis' of many of these complaints makes fascinating reading, and might repay study by those interested in reducing the incidence of complaints. Quite often, there was a clear 'escalation' of ill-natured discussion between the police officer and the complainant, a process which might have been stopped at some point by more thoughtful or more professional behaviour on the officer's part before it reached the stage of 'triggering' a complaint. Several times, too, the rudeness seemed to arise from misunderstandings or misinterpretations of the complainant's words or behaviour. The following case provides a good example. There was some dispute over the true sequence of events and the tones of voice used, but this is unimportant for our purposes here. It is clear from both sides' accounts that the incident started off in a routine manner, but soon escalated into an aggressive exchange of words.

A schoolteacher, who stopped to let a friend out at a roundabout, was approached by traffic police, who first told her that it was an unsuitable place to stop, then examined her car and pointed out a bald tyre. They asked her to stand by the kerb while they issued a ticket, whereupon she tripped over it. She was then asked (rudely, she claimed) if she had been drinking and was requested to take a breathalyzer test, being told ('aggressively') to 'do it properly' or else she would be arrested. When she asked what the test indicated the reply was, 'It tells me that you've been drinking'. When she repeated the question ('hysterically', according to the officer), one of the officers replied ('loudly', according to her), 'It tells me that I'm not going to arrest you'. She then told him to stop shouting at her, and when he responded ('in a booming voice'), 'I'm not shouting', she burst into tears.

(c) *Inadequate responses to service requests*
One or more 'neglect of duty' complaints appeared in 37 of the 264 cases. Quite a few of these were subsidiary to other complaints and concerned technical breaches of procedure, of only marginal interest to the complainant. However, one type was of primary concern to complainants: an inadequate response to a request for service. This was the essence of the complaint in 26 cases, in most of which crime victims claimed that the police had failed to carry out proper investigations.

A few of these complaint-producing incidents reflected a disjunction between police and public perceptions of the proper response to reports of minor offences (or—the police might argue—lack of appreciation by the public of the pressures upon their time). For example, one person complained that police officers had failed in their duty by not arresting two drunks who had banged on his door and acted aggressively. A comparable complaint arose when an officer seemed disinterested in investigating an 'assault' by a passenger on a mini-coach driver. The officer apparently believed the driver's injuries too minor to record a criminal offence. Similarly, two complaints arose from the police's 'graded response' approach to reports of minor offences, in which the victims considered officers—who had followed force instructions on priorities correctly—to have been neglectful in their duty by not dispatching a patrol car.

However, the majority of crime victims' complaints concerned failures to follow up 'leads' in investigations or to inform them about recovered property. For example, one victim told the police she had found an eye witness to her burglary, but the responding officers were apparently 'too busy' to take a statement. In another case, a victim of a serious assault complained that the police had failed to arrange an identity parade as promised. And one irate victim learned that his stolen car had been located, but that the police had failed to inform him of this, the result being that it was stolen again.

4. The untypical nature of cases dealt with by the PCA

A final point to note about the nature of complaints is that there is a considerable difference between those routinely dealt with at force level and those which come to the attention of the independent Police Complaints Authority. As one would expect, investigations supervised by the PCA, which amount to a few hundred each year, generally involve very serious allegations—most frequently, of assault. Similarly, the 5,000 or so cases sent to the PCA at an early stage for a decision on whether or not to supervise arise predominantly from allegations of assault on arrest. When one also takes into account that the PCA see none of the files of informally resolved cases, it can be seen that by far the greater part of members' time is spent dealing with 'complaint incidents' and complainants quite untypical of the overall picture: in short, the bulk of their work derives from people in conflict with the law. Whether this gives members a distorted picture of disputes between the police and the public—or in any way affects their attitudes towards officers and complainants—is an interesting question, to which we return in Part Three.

NOTES

1. There is some support for the explanation that shift Inspectors have been allaying more grievances informally, in that, between 1985 and 1987, despite the decreasing totals, the number of *serious* complaints did not appear to decline in the MPD. Indeed, it may even have increased: certainly, over this period, there was an increase in the MPD 'share' of cases referred to the Police Complaints Authority as serious enough for either mandatory or discretionary supervision. In April to December 1985, 469 (19 per cent) of 2,521 such cases came from the MPD; in 1987, 1,224 (29.5 per cent) of 4,148 came from the MPD.

   A general reluctance among Inspectors in London to record minor cases may also be indicated by the fact that relatively little use was made in the MPD of the

Informal Resolution option—which, despite its informality, does result in a recorded complaint. In 1987, 686 Informal Resolutions were carried out in the MPD—13 per cent of all those concluded in England and Wales. This compared with an MPD share of 20 per cent of all investigated cases.

On the other hand, the sudden increase in 1988 seems to be largely explained by a response to PCA criticism, as outlined in the text. Whereas completed cases rose from 2,981 in 1987 to 4,863 in 1988, new cases opened fell from 5,748 to 5,294 over the same two years.

2. That is, with the exception of the small City of London force, which, owing to the unusual area it covers, receives a tiny number of complaints. The rates referred to are based upon totals of cases completed or pending, in relation to force strength.

3. If Informal Resolutions are excluded from the complaints total, 3.4 per cent were substantiated in 1989.

4. Initial classifications (usually made by a local Inspector who has spoken to the complainant at an early stage) are quite often changed during the course of investigations as it emerges from complainants' statements or from other sources what precisely the complaint involves.

MPD figures are not included in the Table, as F2 Division of the Home Office, who supplied the detailed breakdown of complaints, is not responsible for collecting statistics from this force.

5. These extra 114 County cases were selected randomly, not stratified to overrepresent withdrawn or informally resolved cases. The City and City II interview samples, however, were stratified in this way and cannot, therefore, be included in this analysis.

6. Where more than one exists, we have defined the 'principal complainant' as follows: a 'victim' takes precedence over someone complaining on his or her behalf, and a more serious allegation takes precedence over a less serious one. Where doubt still exists, we have taken the first named.

7. In addition, 21 contained a complaint of incivility secondary to one of assault.

8. For example, in a small study in the Thames Valley area (Emment 1984), Inspectors were found to be involved in 12 cases per 100 of those holding that rank, Sergeants in nine cases and Constables in eight. In many cases, the supervising officer is alleged to have been neglectful in his or her supervision of junior officers.

9. Information about age and length of service was not always available in the complaints files and had to be extracted from other sources. Owing to shortage of time these other sources were not used in the City II force.

10. There were eleven cases in which there was no information retrievable concerning previous convictions, nine in which it was not stated (or could not reasonably be inferred) whether the complainant was under 30, and nine in which there were no details or clues as to the person's occupation.

PART TWO

THE COMPLAINTS SYSTEM AND PARTICIPANTS'
VIEWS IN THREE POLICE FORCE AREAS

The next four chapters are based on our research in three police force areas, in which we looked at samples of complaints of all kinds, whether dealt with by investigation or informal resolution, or not investigated owing either to withdrawal by the complainant or to an official decision not to proceed. Cases supervised by the Police Complaints Authority will be discussed in Part Three.

In discussing the local situation, we shall look at the system from the point of view, in turn, of each of the three main parties concerned: the complainant, the officer complained against and the investigating officer. We shall identify points of agreement, as well as points of contention, among these groups, in relation to the standards of fairness and effectiveness which the present system delivers. We shall also focus attention upon withdrawal and informal resolution, which together account for the majority of outcomes of complaints against the police.

CHAPTER 4

The Complainants' Perspective

1. The 'Dark Figure': From Dissatisfaction to an Official Complaint

Officially recorded complaints represent only the tip of the iceberg of public dissatisfaction or annoyance with the behaviour of police officers. As pointed out in Chapter 3, the published statistics are the end product of a 'filtering' process, in which, at each of a series of decision-making stages, some incidents which might have generated an entry in official records disappear from view. The decision at each stage on whether to continue may be made independently by the potential complainant (depending upon the depth of grievance felt), or influenced by police officers or by a third party such as a solicitor. Although there is a fair amount of evidence available from previous work (Russell 1976, 1986; Brown 1987) about decisions to withdraw, little is known about early decisions on whether and how to bring dissatisfaction to official notice. One of the few sources of data here is Tuck and Southgate (1981), who surveyed random samples of 568 'West Indians' and 255 'Whites' in an inner city area. They found that 111 people (comprising 16 per cent of the former, and 8 per cent of the latter) had at some time in their lives wanted to complain about the behaviour of a police officer. However, of these 111, only 11 (seven West Indians and four Whites) had taken any steps to complain, and in every case they had fallen short of activating formal investigative procedures. As this was pre-PACE, and hence pre-'Informal Resolution', one assumes that no complaints were officially recorded, either because the police did not construe what was said as a complaint, or because the respondents agreed to let the matter drop.

The responses to questions we were permitted to include in the 1988 British Crime Survey (BCS) may throw some new light on this complex matter of the 'dark figure' of potential complaints which do not reach the recording stage. Other evidence comes from our interviews with people whose complaints *were* recorded, looking back at the 'hurdles' they had to cross to achieve this. Finally, we have some relevant information from discussions with police officers, particularly Inspectors working on division.

We begin with the BCS data. Among respondents to the survey's special follow-up questionnaire on the police (a random sample of over 6,000 households), 20 per cent said that they had been 'really

53

annoyed' by the behaviour of a police officer during the past five years. Half of these (10 per cent of the whole sample) said that they had felt strongly enough about the matter to make a complaint, but only a fifth of the latter (i.e. 2 per cent of the whole sample) had taken any steps to do so: it is not known how many actually had one recorded. Among those who had wanted to complain but did not go ahead, 31 per cent gave the reasons that they thought a complaint would have no effect, not be taken seriously, or not be investigated properly (see also Skogan 1990).

We turn now to evidence from our interviews. First of all, only ten of 100 complainants in our interview sample from three forces said that they had had any clear idea of how to go about complaining or how the system worked. This suggests that a considerable number of potential complaints may 'fall by the wayside' because of a lack of knowledge about how to proceed. Secondly, among those interviewees whose first move in making their complaint had been to visit or telephone a local police station, almost 30 per cent had been 'put off' at that stage, and had had to take the initiative themselves to register it on a later occasion. For example, several who went to police stations had been told by officers or civilians on the desk to write to the Chief Constable or to the local Superintendent, and one had been told to write two letters to different stations. Another had been informed that she would have to visit headquarters (nearly 20 miles away) to register her complaint. Others, too, had been told to come back later when an Inspector was on duty. Those who had tried to complain by telephone, but whose complaint had not been recorded at that time, said they had received courteous replies aimed at convincing them that 'the officer was only trying to do his job', but had been given little information about complaints procedures and no efforts had been made to arrange a meeting to take the complaint.

Most of the above complaints would never have come to the attention of an Inspector or other senior officer if the complainant had not persevered—which suggests that there are many others which do not get any further. Moreover, even among potential complainants who do see an Inspector, there is evidence that at least half leave without an official complaint being recorded. In an exercise carried out on our behalf, a group of 18 Inspectors in the City force were asked to fill in forms (anonymously) with the number of complaints they could recall having been brought to their notice over the previous (a) four weeks and (b) twelve months. They were also asked to state how many of these they had recorded officially. Between them, they recalled having recorded four (19 per cent) of 21, and 52 (50 per cent) of 103, respectively.

54

None of this necessarily means that the police are constantly trying to deflect legitimate complaints which should be investigated. In many cases, the potential complainant is fully satisfied with an explanation and freely decides not to pursue the matter. However, it is also obvious from discussions we have had with Inspectors that many have considerable powers of persuasion and are able to nudge people in the direction they wish them to take. Thus, while there are always some complainants who will not be diverted from their purpose, the number of complaints recorded has considerable elasticity, dependent largely upon the responses of middle-ranking officers (influenced, of course, by force instructions and informal policies.)[1] Our best guess is that at least one in three people who make a definite attempt to complain are dissuaded (for good or bad reason) from so doing, but that the proportion varies widely both between forces and between individual police stations.

2. The Motivation of Complainants

(a) 'Genuineness' and perseverance
It is our firm impression that, among people who take the step of making a formal complaint and who persevere with it after being offered the option of withdrawing, the majority are genuine in the belief that they had been wronged, and do not take this course lightly. We say this for four main reasons. First, as will be shown in Chapter 6, a considerable proportion experience but resist strong 'pressure to withdraw' (see also Brown 1987). Secondly, both in our interviews and in the responses to our postal questionnaire to complainants in PCA cases, we were continually struck by the intensity of feelings expressed by complainants. Justifiably or not, many retained a lasting sense of grievance about what occurred. Thirdly, as stated in Chapter 3, the great majority are complaining for the first time in their lives. And finally, it is clear that, even without any pressure from police officers, many find it quite a daunting step to make a complaint against a powerful and generally respected body like the police. About one third of our 100 interviewees said that they had felt apprehensive about complaining, two fairly typical statements being:

"I felt very frightened and nervous, especially when waiting in the station foyer, since I was brought up not to question the police, and I felt guilty just even being there"

"It takes guts to complain, rather like walking up to a six foot man".

The apprehensions of those among them who had previous convictions—but also of several others—were focused particularly upon the possibility of police harassment as a consequence. Comments included 'They know my car now' and 'I expected a bit of aggro'. However, it should be noted that only seven of the full sample of 100 claimed that any harassment had actually materialised, and in most cases they provided only vague evidence of this.

The decision to complain was not always made immediately, and only about a third of first moves to complain were made within two hours of the incident. Incivility was the type of complaint most likely to be made soon after the event, many complainants feeling so incensed that they went out of their way—literally—to register their displeasure. Frequently the 'trigger' in such cases was something specific the officer had said—a 'punchline' or 'final straw' to an increasingly ill-natured dialogue. For instance, an elderly driver described to us how he stopped to ask about the duration of some roadworks. He claimed that the officer gradually became more impolite with each exchange, and finally, when the driver told him his age, the officer's retort—which triggered the complaint—was 'Well, you shouldn't be driving then'.

Those who delayed complaining gave a variety of reasons for this. Some had simply been too drunk to think about complaining. Others had been in detention and wanted their freedom first. Several said that they had needed time to calm down to see if they still felt upset or annoyed about the incident. And quite a large number, too, did not finally decide to complain until encouraged to do so by a third party: mainly a relative, solicitor, GP or another police officer. An interesting finding here was that, among those 43 interviewees who had not registered their complaint until between 24 hours and three weeks after the incident, eight had sought the advice of a police acquaintance. Most of those who had waited longer complained on a solicitor's advice. It seems that many people turn initially to someone who will 'know about these things', seeking advice on whether their subjective view that officers have overstepped the mark is correct and whether it is worth complaining. Unlike in these cases, some solicitors regularly advise clients against complaining, but to consider a civil action (Clayton and Tomlinson 1987; Christopher and Noaks 1989).

(b) *Aims and expectations*
Using the sample of 100 complainants we interviewed from three areas (40 of whose cases, it will be remembered, had been fully investigated, 30 withdrawn and 30 informally resolved), let us now look at what people wished and expected to achieve by complaining. First of all, it can be said unequivocally that only a minority felt especially vindictive towards the individual officers they had complained against. When asked 'Why did you complain? What did you

Table 6: Complainants' primary desired outcomes when making a complaint

DESIRED OUTCOME	Investi-gated No.	%	With-drawn No.	%	Inform-ally resolved No.	%	All (No. = %)	(W)*
Expression of anger/ 'justice'/prove truth/make a point	8	20	6	20	3	10	17	(17)
Formal discipline/ punishment	9	23	13	43	2	7	24	(28)
'Education'/stop repetition/'ticking off' for officer	7	18	5	17	15	50	27	(22)
Apology	8	20	2	7	10	33	20	(17)
Compensation	5	13	2	7	0	0	7	(8)
Stimulate police action/get charges dropped	3	8	2	7	0	0	5	(6)
Total	40	100	30	100	30	100	100	

TYPE OF CASE (header spanning Investigated, Withdrawn, Informally resolved, All)

*Weighted data (see note 2, this chapter).

hope would come out of it?' only about one quarter of the whole sample[2] expressed as their main goal a desire for the officer to be formally disciplined, and only five of these had actually wanted him or her dismissed. As Table 6 shows, the desire for punishment was most common in withdrawn cases. Perhaps surprisingly, however, it was not significantly higher in assault cases than in other (generally less serious) types of case. This is quite different to the finding from our postal questionnaire to complainants in cases supervised by the PCA, that about three-quarters of those complaining of assault wanted the officer punished. The reason may be that the injuries sustained in the PCA cases were generally much more serious than those in the local samples.

A fairly similar proportion (22 per cent overall, if the data are weighted to allow for the overrepresentation of informally resolved cases) had wanted their complaint, first and foremost, to serve some sort of educative function, either for the officer concerned—so that he or she would learn from the experience and not repeat the perceived misconduct—or for senior management. This included in many cases a 'ticking off' or 'carpeting' of the officer, but not any other punishment: in other words, what is known in the police service as 'advice'. Such answers were given by half the complainants who accepted informal resolution, and were especially common in incivility cases, however resolved. Some of these complainants were very 'pro-police' and were concerned that rudeness was bad for police-public relations. They hoped their complaint would bring the matter to the attention of senior officers who would take steps to put their house in order.

The other two primary goals most commonly mentioned were (a) to extract an apology, either from the police in general or from the officer concerned and (b) to 'make a point'—complainants wishing either simply to register their anger or to have it proved that they were telling the truth. Other less common aims were the payment of compensation for damage to property or emotional distress caused; and the stimulation of police action in their case (usually 'proper investigation'of a reported crime). Although it is virtually received wisdom among police officers that the majority of complaints are made by criminals in the hope of affecting the outcome of charges against them (see Chapter 5), this was not borne out by our evidence. Most of the 'criminal' complainants we interviewed doubted that complaints were effective in this way, and seemed anyway to have had other motives for complaining: like most other complainants, they believed they had been treated wrongly and wanted this recognised and 'put right'. Most of them, too, despite adversarial contact with the police in the past, were complaining for the first time in their lives.

Where their expectations were concerned, we found that most people had embarked upon their complaint in a reasonably optimistic frame of mind. About half had been 'very' or 'fairly' confident that their complaint would be taken seriously, and more than half had thought they would achieve at least some of their objectives. Overall, roughly equal numbers had expected a full investigation and an informal response, but there were variations according to the type of complaint. Thus, while most complainants of assault had expected a 'proper investigation', the most common expectation among complainants of incivility had been an apology to them and an informal reprimand for the officer concerned.

3. Levels of Satisfaction and Views about the System
Our interviews with people who had experienced the complaints system produced a clear majority of negative views. Over two-thirds of the full sample of 100 interviewees (and 74 per cent when the data were weighted) were dissatisfied with the outcome of their complaint,

Table 7: Levels of satisfaction by method used to handle case

	TYPE OF CASE						
	Investigated		Withdrawn		Informally resolved		All
	No.	%	No.	%	No.	%	(No. = %)
LEVEL OF SATISFACTION							
Very satisfied	0	0	3	10	9	30	12
Fairly satisfied	4	10	7	23	8	27	19
A bit dissatisfied	9	22	7	23	5	17	21
Very dissatisfied	27	68	13	43	8	27	48
Total	40	100	30	100	30	100	100

and most of these were 'very' dissatisfied. However, as Table 7 shows, there were considerable differences in levels of satisfaction between those whose cases were investigated, withdrawn and informally resolved. The most content were those who had experienced informal resolution, 57 per cent of whom declared themselves very or fairly satisfied. The attraction of this option for complainants was further emphasized by the fact that almost half of those whose cases had been formally investigated said that they would have preferred a less formal approach, involving either a meeting with the officer and his or her superiors, or some form of inquisitorial hearing, with themselves and the officer present.

Those who had withdrawn were less likely to be satisfied with the outcome (33 per cent very or fairly satisfied), but by far the greatest amount of dissatisfaction was to be found among complainants whose cases had been formally investigated. Among the 40 we interviewed, we found only four who described themselves as even 'fairly' satisfied with the process. The main reasons for the dissatisfaction were the length of time taken to deal with the case, the absence of any apology, and the inadequacy of, or lack of explanation for, the decision made. Only half said that they would complain again in similar circumstances (compared with 85 per cent in informally resolved cases).

Perhaps surprisingly, satisfaction did not appear to be related to the official outcome of the investigation. Five of the 40 had had at least one of their complaints substantiated (although in two cases these were 'secondary' complaints, not their main reason for complaining), but four of these five declared themselves dissatisfied. The following are some of the explanations they gave. (The letter to which each refers was that sent by a PCA member at the conclusion of the investigation.)

"*I read the letter twice. I was angry over it. I phoned the PCA to talk to the person who signed it. It was just a statement, a load of bumpf, a lot of made up pages. I wanted to talk specifically to X, but I was told I was not allowed to. I knew I was talking to a policeman. I asked him 'was he a policeman', and he said 'we are only civilian employees'. I'm sure he was a policeman though. He said I could talk to him and he pulled out my file. I told him that it hadn't been investigated right and I wasn't happy, but I just got fobbed off. I wanted to know who was interviewed, what was in their statements, what exactly happened to the officers, and why the police I complained about still hadn't done the investigation into the attack on me* [by a member of the public.] *They should have been found guilty of negligence.*"

"*The letter didn't say a lot, or who was responsible. They didn't investigate it properly. They sort of omitted to get at the truth. They should have found out who was the officer who kept misinforming us about their detention—saying they weren't there when they were—and I want to know what the 'appropriate method of dealing with the custody officer' is. There should be new rules that relatives should be informed when people are held in custody.*"

"*I got an official letter from an official department. Nobody felt sorry at all that it had been allowed to take place—and I've lost my livelihood over it. It just said that the officer had been caught and would be dealt with by his local Chief Superintendent. We have a right to know what action is taken against them—like a criminal in a court. Why hush it up—because if they do, that implies that perhaps nothing happened—he wasn't reprimanded. Perhaps he was patted on the back—there's no way of knowing if justice has been done. He's probably in the same position to do it again to somebody else.*"

The basic message from these comments is that 'winning the case' is not in itself sufficient to satisfy complainants, if they feel cheated of full information about the investigation and its outcome. The comments also illustrate the considerable degree of ignorance and confusion to be found among complainants about the procedures involved, and especially about the role and identity of the PCA (see also Chapter 9). Another area about which there was only hazy understanding was that of 'advice' to police officers found to have committed breaches of discipline. It was simply not appreciated that formal advice is regarded in police circles as a serious matter, with potentially adverse effects upon an officer's promotion prospects.[3] Moreover, five of ten complainants in whose cases some advice had been given to the officers were unaware of the fact, either because they had not been told or because it had not registered in their minds as important when reading the letter from the PCA.[4]

4. The Problem of Communication

The findings outlined in this chapter clearly suggest that failures in communication lie at the root of much of the dissatisfaction to be found among complainants, and hence constitute an area in which reforms might profitably be sought—most obviously in cases where complaints have been found to be justified. For example, although communication of the outcome of investigations is a PCA responsibility, there is a case for a senior officer (preferably the original IO) to contact the complainant at the conclusion of any case in which any fault has been found with police behaviour, in order to explain precisely what the decision meant and to answer any questions. Communication by post—despite the great deal of trouble taken by the PCA in composing letters to complainants (see Chapter 10)—appears to create too many misunderstandings and to leave too many questions unanswered.

The above suggestion is further supported by the finding that the one aspect of the system which did seem to satisfy complainants was the visit by the IO to take their statement. In just over half the 40 fully investigated cases we examined, IOs were reported to have been caring, interested and/or sympathetic. However, this initial good impression was gradually dissipated by the long wait for the result, and finally extinguished by what many complainants perceived as the impersonal communication of a result which they did not fully understand, by a body about which they knew very little. In particular, terms like 'advice' to officers, 'substantiated' and 'unsubstantiated', need to be explained much more carefully, as does the level of proof required. Consideration might also be given to introducing a new result of 'not proven' to indicate to complainants that they are not necessarily disbelieved—it is merely that there is insufficient evidence to prove the case.

Problems in understanding the outcome were only part of a general picture painted by complainants of a system lacking effective communication with those on the receiving end. (As we shall see in Chapter 5, this applied to officers complained against as well as to complainants and, in Chapter 6, to people involved in informally resolved as well as investigated cases.) Over 80 per cent of complainants in investigated cases felt that they had not been kept sufficiently well informed of the progress of their case, and several had taken the initiative themselves—by telephoning the IO—to find out what was happening.

Apart from frustration at not being told what stage the investigation had reached, many complainants also felt annoyance at what they saw as deliberate exclusion from the whole investigative system. Several complained that they were not told which witnesses had been interviewed, let alone what they had said. About 20 per cent were upset that people they themselves had put forward as witnesses had not been interviewed. And as mentioned above, few were told whether individual officers had been 'spoken to' by senior officers or whether steps had been taken to prevent a recurrence of the situation leading to their complaint. The situation seemed to be somewhat analogous to that of people reporting a crime to the police, where, as has often been pointed out, the machinery of the criminal justice system takes over and largely excludes the victim (Shapland *et al* 1985; Maguire and Pointing 1988); similarly, the mechanics of the disciplinary system take over the complainant's dispute with the police and his or her wishes or feelings become subordinate to the needs of that system.

While, naturally, the rights and feelings of police officers have to be respected, this should not preclude attention to the aims which are paramount in most other complaints systems—those of satisfying the complainant and rekindling his or her faith in the organization concerned. At present, it appears that these objectives are not being fulfilled by the police complaints system. As many as 28 (70 per cent) of the 40 interviewees whose cases had been investigated claimed that the investigation had changed their view of the police for the worse. It is important to stress that these complainants were not generally 'anti-police' at the outset: a minority (35 per cent) had previous convictions and just under two-thirds thought that the police generally behaved well. (This contrasts with complainants in serious assault cases, the majority of whom have previous convictions and most of whose injuries are sustained in struggles in the course of arrests—see Chapters 3 and 8).

Finally, in addition to their other criticisms, a majority of the 40 complainants declared themselves unimpressed with the thoroughness of the investigation. About 70 per cent felt that, despite his charm when interviewing them at the outset, the IO merely 'went through the motions' of investigation. Only four (ten per cent) thought that he had 'tried to get to the bottom of the matter'. These opinions were arrived at mainly by deduction, few having been told precisely what the investigation had entailed. A typical example was:

"*He said he couldn't find one* [a witness] *although I'd given him the address, another was back in the local prison so he could have easily have interviewed him, and the man who could testify that I had had no alcohol on my breath at the time I was arrested for being 'drunk' is in the same place every day. I think they just sent my statement to London and didn't interview anyone.*"

Those who had experienced investigation of their complaints by the police were also the most adamant of our interviewees that the system should be changed to one of investigation by outsiders. No fewer than 85 per cent supported this viewpoint, the remainder being content with the oversight by the PCA as at present. When asked (in a free response, not precoded, question) what kind of outsiders they had in mind, about a quarter referred to people with legal qualifications. Interestingly, a similar number seemed to think that 'ordinary people' could do the job; and despite the objection often raised that independent investigation is impractical because of the dearth of trained investigators outside the police force, hardly any of our interviewees saw this as a problem. They tended to perceive the handling of complaints as a fairly straightforward matter, in which, ideally, witnesses would be called to a hearing and an assessment would be made by an independent arbitrator. The police practice of meticulously marshalling documentary evidence into a thick file was not the image they held of an 'investigation'.

NOTES

1. In the County force, for example, it was widely felt among Inspectors that there was a risk of 'trouble from above' if it was suggested that they had failed to record a complaint. This went back to circulars sent out by a previous DCC who had been keen to see all complaints 'put on paper'. The complaints rate in the force was above average, a fact attributed by many officers to this 'tradition'. However, at the time of our research, the Complaints and Discipline department was encouraging Inspectors to take more responsibility themselves and to 'allay grievances' without recording a complaint if this seemed appropriate.

2. Strictly speaking, findings based upon the full sample should be weighted to allow for the oversampling of withdrawn and informally resolved cases in the two City forces (the distribution of cases in our final set of interviews was 40% investigated, 30% withdrawn and 30% informally resolved, while the overall distribution in the three forces together was of the order of 45%, 40% and 15%, respectively). If the figures are weighted, the proportion wanting punishment emerges as 28 per cent rather than 24 per cent.

3. This could be formal or informal advice, directly related to the complaint, or on matters coming to light during the investigation. In the latter case, the complainant was not always informed that this had happened, which may explain some of the lack of knowledge referred to.

4. This is usually explained in an accompanying note sent by the PCA, but complainants did not often seem to recall the document or to have absorbed its contents.

CHAPTER 5

Police Viewpoints

In this chapter, we discuss findings which bear upon police officers' reactions and attitudes towards the complaints system. We begin with officers subject of complaint, moving on to examine the views of senior officers involved in the investigation of complaints.

1. Officers Complained Against

Outside police circles, little attention tends to be paid to the feelings or opinions of officers complained against. But if the complaints system is to have any beneficial effects upon police behaviour, it is most important to understand how it is viewed by ordinary officers. We use the term 'ordinary officers' deliberately, because, although there are in every force a small proportion who tend to accumulate complaints (and whose names are mentally noted by senior officers in Complaints and Discipline departments), almost every police officer is complained against at least once in the course of his or her career.[1] Thus, although the experience is by no means commonplace, it is one with which most are acquainted, both directly and through the experiences of colleagues.

As stated in Chapter 1, we sent letters requesting interviews to random samples of officers from three force areas who had been the subject of a complaint upon which the file had recently been closed. (These included withdrawn and informally resolved, as well as investigated, complaints.) Out of 63 contacted, 50 agreed to be interviewed, a satisfactory response rate of 79 per cent. While some may have been reluctant to say anything 'self-incriminating' to us, despite our assurances of confidentiality and despite the fact that the investigation was over, we established good open relationships over an hour or more in many cases. Several officers were also very frank with us about other incidents in the past. We tended to believe the general tenor of their accounts—or, at least, that most were conveying honestly their perceptions of what had happened.

Over three-quarters of these officers said that they had in their minds a clear image of types of situation which held a high risk of generating a complaint. Such situations could quite often be recognised in advance, and some said that their approach was dictated partly by the desire to avoid a complaint—or at least to ensure that no allegation against them would be substantiated. This applied particularly to planned operations like raids on houses (which were seen as likely to produce complaints of assault and of damage to property) and the policing of demonstrations, but also to some more common types of incident in which there was less time for preparation. Those most frequently mentioned were arrests, interventions in fights, 'domestics', and attempts to control alcohol-inflamed disturbances on the streets in the late evening. Particularly in this last case, however, there was a general feeling that it was wrong to worry too much about complaints: the 'good policeman' always 'went in' when the situation demanded it, and anybody at the 'sharp end' of policing who did not occasionally attract complaints was likely to be 'avoiding responsibility'.

One set of features which their images of 'complaint situations' seemed to have in common was volatility, unpredictability and difficulty for the police in maintaining full control. Many officers pointed out that quick decisions had to be made, often in the face of possible violence against themselves, and argued that if 'the job' was to be done effectively, it was inevitable that people would sometimes be treated roughly or property would be damaged in the process.

Secondly, such incidents were regarded as likely to involve people ready to complain without valid cause—either maliciously because they are 'anti-police' or in the hope of charges against them being dropped. Ten per cent of our interviewees dismissed virtually all complaints as 'gross exaggerations' or 'complete fabrications', and described 'typical complainants' as 'toe-rags' or 'trouble-makers'. And while most conceded that some complainants may have been roughly treated, they claimed that this had almost always been justifiable, provoked by violence on the latter's part.

Finally, it was notable that, although they were asked about complaints in general, nearly all those interviewed spoke about the subject mainly in terms of alleged *assault*. Incivility—although making up a fair proportion of complaints—was rarely afforded much attention, and complaints of irregular procedure or neglect of duty were usually mentioned as unpleasant 'side effects' of another complaint (the results of a perceived tendency of investigating officers to go 'digging' in search of technical breaches of regulations).[2] This tendency to focus on assault—understandably of particular concern to police officers, as it is a criminal offence, conviction of which means almost certain dismissal from the force—was also evident in answers to our question as to whether they regarded any particular officers they knew as especially 'complaint prone'. Well over half agreed that they did, and the most common description produced was of policemen with 'short fuses' (or, more graphically, as one put it 'a bit punchy')—i.e. people who were good officers in every other way, but who tended to lose their temper when provoked. The point was also made that such officers could create trouble for their colleagues:

"Going around with one or two is like walking about with a stick of dynamite in your pocket."

Interestingly, although several interviewees had numerous unsubstantiated complaints on their records, hardly any of these put *themselves* in the 'complaint prone' category.

When asked about their own complaints, 60 per cent claimed that the most recent complaint against them had come as a surprise, or, in some cases, concerned an incident which they could not immediately recall. This is quite understandable, considering that the majority were not informed of its existence until at least three weeks afterwards.[3] Generally speaking, they did not consider the incident in question to have been highly unusual, although feelings may have been running high at the time. From their point of view, they were simply unlucky enough to have 'collected a complaint' from a difficult situation that was a normal part of policing—dealing with drunks, stopping a motorist, making an arrest, and so on. And although a small proportion (8 per cent) admitted to us in confidence that they had for example, 'lost their cool' for a moment, most insisted that the complainant had either misunderstood the situation or had been behaving aggressively or unreasonably.

As we have shown in Chapter 3, the main aims people gave for complaining were to stop recurrence of poor police behaviour by drawing it to the attention of senior officers, to see offending officers disciplined, to gain an apology, and to express their anger and 'make a point'. However, officers' perceptions of the public's reasons for complaining were quite different. When we asked them their understanding of why the person had complained against them, the two most common replies were 'to try to get off charges against them' and 'dislike of' or 'retaliation against' the police (about a third giving each of these responses).

We turn now to the important question of whether complaints affect officers' subsequent behaviour on duty. The majority (80 per cent) claimed that no complaint made against them had significantly influenced their future conduct—in most cases because they did not think they had done anything wrong. However, the other 20 per cent said that complaints had had an undesirable effect on their style of policing. As one put it:

"You start to back away from situations when you should be taking action . . . There are particular people known to make trouble with complaints and you tend to avoid them . . . And if there's an obvious risk

of a complaint you pass the buck. Why should I risk my mortgage by giving some little yobbo the chance to have a go at me?"

Of course, the line between 'backing away' wrongly when firm action is required and taking a more cool-headed approach to confused or potentially violent situations is fairly narrow. It could be argued that consciousness of the possibility of a complaint, which most said they had in certain kinds of situations, has a beneficial deterrent effect against hasty behaviour. Certainly, nearly all our interviewees recognised 'complaint-prone' situations—domestic disputes and planned raids on houses, for example—in which they sometimes made a conscious effort to avoid complaints (or, at least, complaints that might 'stick'). Most agreed that the existence of the complaints and discipline system tended always to be in the back of their minds, and with promotion seen as partly dependent upon the possession of a good disciplinary record, complaints were certainly something to be avoided if possible.

Apart from the matter of possible blots on their record (even unsubstantiated, withdrawn or informally resolved complaints being seen by most as such blots—few junior officers will believe assurances that these are not 'recorded against them'), most interviewees agreed that one of the most unpleasant aspects of receiving a complaint was 'coming under the spotlight' from an officer of superintendent or chief inspector rank. Even if they were certain that they had nothing to fear from the complaint—allegations of minor assaults on arrest, for example, causing them little worry, as they expected senior officers to support them in handling violent people firmly—investigation remained an uncomfortable experience, and there was always the possibility of some other misdemeanour coming to light in the course of inquiries. Errors in pocket book entries, breaches of PACE custody rules, and so on, could lead to incidental discipline while the complaint itself was completely dismissed. (This actually occurred in 5 of the 35 unsubstantiated cases in our sample.) Moreover, investigators from Complaints and Discipline departments—much more so than divisional senior officers, who were thought closer to 'real' police work—were regarded with some distaste and a little fear, and, contrary to the public image of complaints investigations as 'whitewash' exercises, IOs had a reputation of giving junior officers a rough ride in interviews. It should be mentioned that a number of officers—about one in five—took an outwardly cavalier or 'gung-ho' approach to complaints, claiming, for instance, that they used them to paper their walls, or that they were 'water off a duck's back'. Two put it thus:

"They're an occupational hazard. I usually stick them in my bin. Most PCs see them as quite amusing, a change to the day's routine."

"There's some camaraderie about having a complaint: a bit like being one of the boys. When I was in Traffic, I put them up on the wall."

However, most of these, when questioned further, admitted that they did not treat them quite as lightly as they pretended to colleagues. (Such attitudes were most prevalent among members of support units.)

This raises the issue of stress caused by being under investigation. For younger officers, in particular, the long period of waiting for the outcome of a complaint could be very unsettling, and in the case of serious complaints—particularly anything involving alleged dishonesty–even experienced officers were likely to experience considerable stress. Among those we interviewed, 47 per cent said that they or their family had experienced some form of stress as a result of their most recent complaint, and 70 per cent that they had experienced it at some time in the past. For example, two recalled their first complaints as probationers:

"During the first month, psychologically it was quite devastating just thinking about it. For so long I'd wanted to be a policeman and on the word of one person I could lose the whole thing, irrespective of my guilt or innocence. It sent me into fits of quietness and depression."

"I suffered untold anxieties until it was finished. It only took a few weeks, but it seemed like a lifetime at the time."

Other comments included:

"Any allegation will cause you pain, discomfort and disgust. You think you're only doing your job to the best of your ability and then you get a complaint."

"I was fairly confident about the outcome, but it didn't stop me worrying about it. I went home and said to my missus, 'Before I tell you this, there's nothing in it.' It came as a great shock to her and she was very worried."

Finally, although we interviewed only one officer who had experienced it, we were informed several times of the devastating effect that suspension from the force could have on a police officer. Anyone in this situation tends to be avoided by colleagues and, as one senior officer put it,

"They have feelings of being abandoned and deserted by their fellows. Their emotions range from anger and frustration to being let down and alone, bordering, in some circumstances, on suicide. How can anyone assess the psychological damage this does? I appreciate there are some bad

eggs in the job, but how do you compensate officers in the case of unfounded and malicious complaints?"

About two-thirds of our interviewees were critical of delays (a) in notifying them of the existence and full content of complaints and (b) in completing the investigation and telling them the outcome (in fact, the officer is usually the last person to be officially informed of the result). They also, like complainants, felt excluded and alienated from the process, receiving no information about the stage the investigation had reached, nor being told what precisely complainants or witnesses had alleged against them.

While IOs sometimes pointed out that it is more effective to 'hit'officers suddenly with the complaint after marshalling evidence quietly, this was regarded as unfair. Overall, both complainants and officers complained against tended to agree that the system was too impersonal and was steeped in excessive secrecy and excessive 'red tape'. Both sides were in favour of more openness and exchange of information.

Finally, what changes would those who had undergone investigation wish to see in the complaints system? Almost half our police interviewees made some positive comments about the idea of outside investigators replacing senior police officers—particularly where the complaint did not amount to a criminal investigation. Most of these argued that outsiders would have more credibility with complainants and the public, and therefore they could 'weed out' trivial or malicious complaints at an early stage without being suspected of doing so unfairly, while police investigators have to go through a full investigation unless they can get a dispensation not to proceed—possible only in the most clear-cut instances. Several also made the point that it would be to their own advantage to have the same rights in practice as a member of the public under investigation: with superintendents, there was no effective 'right of silence', as the latter used their rank to oblige officers to answer their questions. As one put it, 'I could say nothing, but a few months later I might find the same man as my governor'. Even so, just over half were in favour of police investigating their own, mainly because it was felt that outsiders would never understand the pressures of policing on the ground. Three comments illustrate these views quite well:

"You've got to know how things happen on the street . . . lay people will not look at the outside influences that affect the performance of a given officer. Lay people couldn't be trained to understand the pressures—you have to have done it to understand it."

"If you've never been in a situation of fear, you won't be able to understand why a police officer acted that way. A police investigation is

70

fairer from the officer's point of view because police understand each other."

"Outsiders wouldn't be aware of the slippery eels they are dealing with!"

Nevertheless, about 60 per cent admitted the existence of something like a 'code of silence' among junior officers, and told us that the knowledge police officers gain through dealing with suspects can be used to advantage when they themselves become subject to investigation. Whoever does the questioning, they told us, will almost always find themselves up against a skilled 'opponent' with allies among his colleagues. So long as a 'them and us' way of thinking persists, in relation both to senior officers and to members of the public, this is an inevitable consequence. Our interviewees generally agreed that, despite some serious efforts within the police to change such attitudes, they still remained deeply entrenched. It was also pointed out by one or two that, if one is going to have the benefits of high morale and a strong 'esprit de corps' among the 'troops' in difficult situations, it is difficult to erase the negative, self-protective aspects of such a spirit which emerge when something goes wrong.

2. Investigating Officers

A majority of the 19 investigating officers we interviewed also thought that the police should retain the task of investigating complaints. Once again, the importance of 'insider knowledge' was stressed, although from a different point of view to that of officers complained against: most IOs though that they were more effective than civilians in penetrating the 'wall of silence' which develops when officers are under investigation, and also that by knowing their way around police stations and police bureaucracy, were able to lay their hands on evidence much more effectively. For example:

"Outsiders would find it hard to move around as freely as us inside a police station. If I want charge sheets, logs or tapes, I just walk in and take them. Outsiders would have to have someone with them."

"If I'm inside I can talk informally to a lot of people. I can ask 'What's such and such like?'. I can tell him to get his act straight—to think about it. I can ask his Inspector what he's heard about the complaint. I've got an inside line, haven't I?"

Even so, about one-third favoured an independent system, partly because they recognised that the public would never have faith in the impartiality of internal investigation, and partly because they thought that the present system sometimes resulted in ill-feeling and divided loyalties. It was also frequently said that the cost of using highly

71

experienced senior officers to investigate 'rubbish'—minor or groundless complaints—was a misuse of resources. Several claimed that the proportion of these kinds of complaints in their caseload had risen recently because increased attention to complaints had resulted in Inspectors 'going by the book' and, instead of attempting to allay the member of the public's sense of grievance there and then, recording an official complaint. Moreover, rather than taking the initiative and carrying out an immediate ('desk top') informal resolution, Inspectors were said to find it, as one IO put it, both 'less work and less risky' to refer the case to headquarters for informal resolution by an Appointed Officer (AO) from the Complaints and Discipline Department. (This trend was beginning to be combatted in one headquarters by routinely appointing the referring Inspector as the AO.) At any rate, the vast majority of IOs we interviewed were in favour of informal resolution, and wished to see its use expanded.

More generally, IOs, like the managers of C & D departments, saw the complaints system as a useful management tool—or, at least, potentially so. While reluctant to take complaint statistics too seriously, they could be used to identify and take action over emerging problems. For example, it might be noticed that complaints were increasing in a particular subdivision or specialist group, and this could be used as a starting point for a closer look by senior officers. While it was doubted that complaints often threw up problems about which local supervisors did not already know, they could be used as a lever for dealing with particular officers or even for senior officers in C & D to give a slack local supervisor a 'kick in the pants'.

These comments illustrate the tendency of senior officers to regard the complaints system as an adjunct to the general disciplinary system of the force. As one IO put it, 'I'm a complaints *and discipline* officer'. They spoke less often about the objective of satisfying complainants, which, they seemed to assume, was an almost impossible task given the low substantiation rate. Their main effort in this regard was confined to their interview with the complainant early on in the investigation, when most took the trouble to be polite and to listen to his or her concerns, as well as trying to assure them that the investigation would be thorough. However, few re-contacted complainants after the conclusion of the case, leaving this to the PCA and/or DCC.

Their general attitude to investigations seemed to be a desire to do a 'good professional job' with a thorough report, although they said that the standard of proof was so high that they embarked upon most investigations with little expectation of substantiating the complaints. This applied particularly to complaints of assault, where it usually came down to 'one person's word against another' about how injuries had been caused. The complaints system was seen as more effective in what was done behind the scenes than in its official results. For example, if it was believed that an officer had behaved unprofessionally but this could not be proved, 'quiet words' could be had with the senior officer in his division and transfers or changes of duty might result. As one IO put it, 'He can be posted, counselled, told to mend his ways, or put with a stickler of an Inspector rather than a gung-ho Inspector'. Of course, the complainant would be unlikely to learn of such consequences.

In all, then, IOs tended to have a certain amount of faith in the system as a deterrent and as a tool for managers. Although most grumbled about what they perceived as a preponderance of trivial and groundless cases in their daily workload, not worth the attention of a highly paid senior officer (as was often pointed out, some rape and other serious crime investigations are led by more junior officers than those put in charge of investigations of minor complaints), they still felt that C & D work was important. The point was made that senior officers had to be closely involved, so that incisive action could be taken in the occasional case in which it turned out to be essential. Few actually enjoyed C & D work, although one or two found it a temporary holiday in comparison with previous posts and some recognised its value as a way of keeping in touch with 'the ground'.

The most frequent suggestion for change in the system—apart from those who wanted to hand it over to outsiders—was to find ways of reducing the amount of time wasted in investigating minor cases. (Informal resolution, it was felt, had had some beneficial effect in this direction, but had not solved the problem.) Their own suggestions included the idea that more complaints should be investigated by supervisors in the local division concerned, and that IOs should be given greater powers (or the PCA should use their existing powers more often) to dispense with cases at an early stage if there was early evidence that the allegations were groundless. Other suggestions for reforms included better induction or training for IOs (although some argued that this was unnecessary as most senior officers had ample investigative experience) and improved feedback to IOs, especially to those on division, about the quality of their reports as well as about any action taken as a result of them. It was widely recognised that some IOs were much better than others, but unless there were major omissions in a report, it was rare for either praise or constructive criticism to come back to an individual investigator.

NOTES

1. A random sample of 200 officers' records in the County force showed that 73 per cent had been complained against at least once in their careers, and only 14 per

cent of those with seven or more years' service had never been the subject of a complaint.

2. While this is a widely held belief among junior officers, we found that in the County force, at least, it was rare for technical breaches of discipline to be added formally to lists of complaints.

3. On the other hand, several said that they had been told informally by an inspector or sergeant to expect a 'Regulation 7' (the official notification and caution).

CHAPTER 6

The Informal Resolution Process

1. Introduction

Prior to the implementation of the Police and Criminal Evidence Act, the full weight of the police investigative machinery was required in order to process even the most minor complaint (unless withdrawn or not proceeded with). However, under S.85(1)(b) of PACE a chief officer may now appoint an officer to seek to resolve a complaint informally, provided he 'is satisfied that the conduct complained of, even if proved, would not justify a criminal or disciplinary charge'. The appointed officer's ('AO's') official task is 'to achieve a position in which the complainant is satisfied that his complaint has been dealt with in an appropriate manner' (Reg. 4(1) of the Police (Complaints) (Informal Resolution) Regulations 1985). Thus the formality and rigidity of a full investigation, along with the 'black or white' result demanded by the adversarial process, can be dispensed with. Instead, the views of both parties can be relayed informally to the other, the officer may admit fault without risking disciplinary action or even an entry on his or her personal record, and an apology may be tendered to the complainant if this is thought appropriate. The regulations further provide that a meeting can be arranged if it appears to the AO useful in seeking a resolution, and if both parties consent.

As an alternative to passing a complaint to HQ for a decision, Regulation 4(1) provides for an immediate (or 'desk top') resolution to be effected by a local supervisor. At first, this was interpreted narrowly in many forces, to mean that the process had to be completed either during the shift or within 24 hours. However, in two of the forces we studied the understanding was now that it should be completed within 72 hours—the objectives being both to encourage divisional supervisors to take more initiative in complaints and to save resources.

In spite of the advantages which informal resolution (IR) offers the police over formal investigation—particularly its speed and lower cost—the extent of its use has varied widely between forces. In 1989, for instance, one force resolved informally 48 per cent of its totals of recorded complaints, while, at the other end of the spectrum, another dealt informally with only 12 per cent. In the forces we looked at, there was also evidently considerable variation between divisions.

Such differences may be explained in part by variety in the mix of complaints—for instance rural areas tend to receive a higher proportion of complaints of incivility and urban areas more of assault, the latter generally unsuitable for IR. The Recording practice may also vary between forces, some of which actively encourage what has been called 'informal informal resolution' or 'allaying grievances' (i.e. Inspectors attempting to satisfy complainants without recording an official complaint) while others have a tradition whereby supervising officers tend to 'get a form out' at the first hint of a complaint.

The extent of the use of IR can also be affected by individual Inspectors' knowledge of the rules. For example, we came across several who did not know that it was unnecessary to obtain the officer's agreement in order to initiate IR, and therefore tended to pass complaints on for investigation if there was any doubt about their officers' willingness to co-operate. Equally important, Inspectors vary in their readiness to take responsibility. As senior officers in Complaints & Discipline departments pointed out, it was the 'easy path' simply to pass complaints on to headquarters, whereas to initiate a 'desk top' informal resolution not only gave them more work, but could mean an awkward interview with one of their officers. Some Inspectors, too, may be influenced by the fairly widespread reservations about the IR procedures to be found among PCs, many of whom object to it in principle as implying an 'admission of guilt' when the officer in fact denies the allegations. On the other hand, there is no doubt that police attitudes are changing quickly on this subject. Informal discussions we have had recently with senior officers suggest that there is a continuing trend towards acceptance of IR at all levels, and there is every likelihood that the proportion of complaints informally resolved will continue to increase. Between 1986 and 1989, the proportion nationally rose from 14 per cent to 24 per cent (see Chapter 3, Table 2). Eventually, too, we may see a reversal of the increase in withdrawn complaints, with informal resolution being seen as a better option in many cases (see also Chapter 7).

We begin with an account of what was, at least at the time of our research, the somewhat haphazard process by which complaints entered or failed to enter the IR system, looking at the influence of some common misconceptions and at how the option of IR was 'sold' to the complainants. We then outline some of the general views and personal experiences of IR described to us by complainants, officers subject of complaint, investigating officers and appointed officers.

2. Attempts to Initiate Informal Resolution
In the forces we studied, most informally resolved complaints

involved an AO or IO appointed by headquarters, with relatively few divisional Inspectors having taken the initiative to carry out 'immediate' (or 'desk top') informal resolutions. However, in many cases the local Inspector had suggested in his or her report to HQ that the case was suitable for IR. In one force, too, it was becoming standard practice for the Complaints and Discipline department to appoint as AO a supervisor from the same station, so that there was little difference, in practice, between a 'desk-top' IR and one initiated by Headquarters.

Of course, the appointment of an AO does not guarantee a smooth and peaceful resolution of a complaint. The complainant may be unwilling to accept IR; further discussion may reveal that the complaint is 'too serious' to be dealt with informally; and (though rarely) a complainant's strong dissatisfaction with the officer's response may lead to IR being abandoned in favour of a full investigation. Before discussing cases which were resolved, it is instructive to look at attempts to initiate IR which failed.

(a) *Failure to agree upon IR*

Among the 70 complainants we interviewed whose cases were eventually either withdrawn or formally investigated, at least 13 had discussed the possibility of informal resolution with an AO or IO. (Investigating officers would sometimes start by suggesting IR, while some investigated cases started with an AO, who was replaced with an IO when attempts at IR failed). Four of these 13 complainants had themselves put forward requests for their complaints to be resolved informally, but two had been told by the IO that the matter was too serious and one had embarked upon the process but changed his mind after hearing that the officer had flatly denied making the remarks attributed to him. (The complainant withdrew, refusing to accept that there had been any 'resolution', but unwilling to become involved in a full investigation). In the fourth case, the complainant told us that he had asked for informal resolution, but had then been informed that the officer would not agree to it, and 'would not sign the form'. He had also been led to believe that the alternative of a formal investigation would lead to a day off work for himself and his witnesses in order to 'attend a tribunal', and consequently—reluctantly—withdrew his complaint.

This last case raises the point (see also our discussion of withdrawn complaints in Chapter 7) that, despite the tiny numbers of cases which result in disciplinary hearings, complainants were frequently warned about the possibility of having to attend one—primarily it seems, as a preliminary test of the veracity of their complaint and their eagerness to pursue it further. The case also illustrates a misconception we came across several times among officers subject of complaint, and even some IOs. This is that the consent of *both* parties is needed for a complaint to be informally resolved. This is not so: it is solely the prerogative of the complainant to accept or reject the informal process (once offered by the police).

The other nine complainants had been invited to accept informal resolution. One had 'got confused with all the alternatives', so opted for a full investigation. Another had felt his complaint was too serious to be dealt with informally. Three had wanted nothing less than personal apologies from all the officers involved, and on hearing that this was unlikely, insisted upon formal investigations. A further two had declined the informal process on the grounds that they had no wish to meet the officer complained of: although this was unlikely, and certainly would not have happened against their will, they had somehow gained the impression that it was part of the process. Another said he had been told initially that informal resolution would be attempted, without a choice being offered; but it later transpired that the complaint was 'too serious' to be dealt with informally. The remaining complainant in this sub-group also said he had been given no choice, being informed that informal resolution would be carried out unless the officer denied the allegation. As no admission was made, a formal investigation was set in motion. (In fact, an admission by the officer complained against is not necessary for a complaint to be resolved informally. Indeed, as we show below, an admission was not forthcoming in the majority of cases sampled.)

The above examples illustrate not only the range of situations in which IR is offered and rejected, but some of the widespread confusion and ignorance we found among complainants, and to a lesser extent among police officers, about the process, its objectives and rules.

(b) *How consent for IR was obtained*
As described in Chapter 1, we interviewed 30 complainants, randomly selected from the records of three forces, whose complaints had been informally resolved. The majority of these cases concerned complaints of incivility, although there were also six cases of neglect of duty, three of irregular procedure and two of harassment.

How was the agreement to use the IR procedure arrived at? First, it should be remembered that AOs are appointed by Complaints and Discipline departments with the express purpose of attempting to resolve particular complaints informally, and they approach the complainant with this brief in mind. According to complainants, in most cases the AO had laid out the various options, but had clearly tried to steer them towards IR. In the great majority of these cases,

78

the AO's task had been relatively simple, little or no persuasion being needed. So what was it that appealed particularly to complainants? Their answers varied considerably. Four had simply felt that informal resolution was appropriate to the minor nature of their complaints. For example:

"I chose it simply because I didn't consider what happened was serious enough to call in others—like a headmaster telling off a little girl for being rude."

Four others had been attracted by the speed of dealing with the matter, one of these commenting:

"He thought it better for me to make an unofficial complaint because it would be dealt with quickly, and I liked that idea."

A further five had seen it as a satisfactory way of having the officer spoken to or 'ticked-off' by the AO. One man recalled:

"He said either himself or another senior officer would have a strong word, and that he'd leave him in no doubt that his behaviour had been appalling."

Most of the remainder simply took the AO's advice that this was the 'best' course of action. In four cases, indeed, complainants were not aware of any choice having been offered, and three of these were even unaware that 'informal resolution' was the procedure that had been used. For example:

"He said they'd found out who took the call and it was a civilian. 'A young girl just like you, and just in the job for three weeks. She didn't do anything about it at all, she was crying and it was her third day.' He then said, 'now do you want us to take it further?'. He also said if they caught the guy they couldn't have charged him with anything anyway. He didn't really ask me if I wanted informal resolution, it was a fait accompli."

In eight of the 30 cases, the AO had been required to work rather harder to secure agreement to IR. In three of these, this was achieved by emphasizing the possibility of their having to appear at a tribunal (clearly remote, of course, in such minor cases):

"He told me there were two methods: the informal and the fully-blown one which could go to a tribunal or to court. Of course, I was expecting that, that's why this informal way was a bit of a relief, really, because of the time it would have needed."

In other cases, the agreement was negotiated after initial resistance from the complainant. One woman claimed that it had taken six visits

79

before she could be persuaded to accept the informal procedure! She stated:

"He wanted me to accept it but I wasn't prepared to let go. In the end he pointed out he had seen the policemen and they denied it, but he said a little good might have come out of it because they wouldn't do it again."

Negotiations were equally protracted in two instances where complainants attached conditions to their eventual acceptance of IR:

"I agreed provided it was on my terms—access to all information on the file. My solicitor phoned the inspector, and he said OK, on those terms and, knowing that, I signed."

"They'd already interviewed the officers before they came to see me. I told them I knew I could have a full investigation if I wanted but I really just wanted the harassment to stop.

With just a few exceptions, then, complainants were willing parties to the process and, although certain AOs may be criticised for the ploys they used to win acceptance, only a small minority of complainants felt that they had been wrongly 'pressured' into giving their consent. Moreover, when asked how well the AO or IO had explained to them what IR entailed, three-quarters replied 'quite' or 'very' well.

(c) AOs' and IOs' comments

Twelve of the 19 IOs we interviewed had carried out at least one informal resolution, although only six had had much experience of them. Most attested both to the flexibility of the procedure—its ability to serve various purposes—and to the fact that it was rarely necessary to employ a 'hard sell': by pointing out the benefits and disadvantages of the new procedure most complainants came to see that it was the betst option for them. The following remarks illustrate these points:

"First I tell them all about the options, and then I listen to their side very sincerely and see how genuinely they feel aggrieved and what they want. I stress the time-consuming element of formal investigation, and that at the end of the day the fact that he may only get a ticking-off. Whereas with informal resolution I can give him advice. Most don't want to get the officer into trouble, they want their views aired and the officer told. Most who have informal resolution are nice, genuine people with no axe to grind."

"Many complain because the feel aggrieved about some particular course of action, but the act of making the complaint is as far as they want to go, and here informal resolution is ideal. It gives them satisfaction that someone senior has looked into it."

One Chief Inspector identified a further situation in which the procedure was suitable, although we came across no complainants who admitted that these circumstances applied to them:

"It's useful where complainants can be offered face-savers where they have made a big fuss and feel embarrassed. When they're looking for a way out—perhaps when they have been found out to be liars."

Only one of the 30 complainants we interviewed who had accepted IR could recall being told that, should he be dissatisfied with the outcome at the end of the day, then a full investigation of his complaint could take place. In theory, the complainant initially agrees only to an attempt to resolve the complaint informally. However, once embarked upon IR, AOs are naturally keen to avoid reversion to a full investigation. They tend either to tell complainants from the beginning that they may not receive an apology from the officer and that he may deny the allegation (thus pre-empting any later protest or demand for further action) or to meet any dissatisfaction by pointing out that a full investigation will achieve no more. The following examples indicate the thinking behind these approaches:

"I see the complainant and ask him what he wants. I tell them that once they've agreed on informal resolution they can't go back on it, that is, if the officer doesn't agree with them they can't revert to a formal complaint. He's got to accept it, hasn't he? You've got to tell them that there's always two sides to a story and if the officer disagrees, well, that's it."

"You don't enter into it on the basis that the officer will admit it. You can't make promises and have to make it very clear that they may get no apology or admission. You can't enter a ping-pong match going back from one to the other."

"If they're not happy then we have to do an formal investigation. But I'll ask them what they think I'm going to achieve. If the officer denies the allegation and there were no other witnesses, what can I do? The problem is if you've got some old granny. If they're truthful people, they wouldn't understand why their word can't be accepted. They can't understand that it's their word against the officers."

"I could mention the option of a formal investigation, but I'd mention the futility of it, and that someone at my level is going to spend a lot of time on it and will come to the same conclusion."

3. The Reactions of Officers Subject of Complaint
(a) *Knowledge and views of the system*
As informal resolution is a relatively new procedure, still infrequently

used in some forces, it has inevitably been prone to a certain amount of mythology among junior officers. It was regarded with some suspicion by about 60 per cent of those we interviewed, although in one of the City forces a majority were in favour. A frequent comment of the less enthusiastic was that acceptance of IR was equivalent to an admission of guilt. The following comments were typical:

"Informal resolution is like putting your hands up. If you accept it then you admit you did it."

"If I considered I'd done nothing wrong I'd want a full investigation rather than informal resolution."

"It's admitting to something you haven't done to keep them happy. As if they've got one over on you, that's my experience."

Further, several officers were certain that an informally resolved complaint was entered on their personal record—in spite of the assertion of senior officers that this is not the case:

"They're trying to tell us it's not on your record somewhere. But if it's not recorded anywhere why bother to write it down?"

Two interviewees also believed, wrongly, that any admission could be subsequently used in civil proceedings against them.

A surprisingly high proportion—over a third—seemed to think that they could refuse to accept IR and opt for a full investigation instead, simply by 'not signing the form'. For example, two officers remarked:

"It's better to have an unsubstantiated complaint than one by informal resolution. I would have turned it down had it been offered because I acted completely correctly. An officer cannot be forced to sign. It's guaranteed that it won't stick if it comes from up the road because otherwise informal resolution would not have been suggested in the first place."

"If you're guilty then informal resolution is good but if you're not guilty it's best to go back to the complainant and say you don't admit it and then if they want to, a formal complaint can be made. No-one has to sign the form."

Even some fairly senior officers were still labouring under the misapprehension that consent is needed from both sides. One experienced Superintendent noted:

"It's never a question of persuasion. It just needs the assent of both parties. But it's seldom easy to convince officers. Invariably they'll say they've done nothing wrong, and you have to say that it won't go on their record—but they don't believe that."

And an Inspector told us that one of his officers had refused to accept informal resolution, feeling that this would be an admission, and so the case had to be formally investigated. However, as one AO correctly noted:

"Sometimes they refuse, wanting a full investigation instead. I say I don't need their permission and that they're free to refuse to discuss it with me. They don't even have to sign it—that's just a matter of courtesy."

The misapprehensions referred to above probably increased the dissatisfaction several officers felt with the way they had been interviewed by the AO or IO. Two told us, for example, that their version of events had not even been asked for:

"The IO agreed the complainant was obnoxious but I wasn't given any option about it. It was a fait accompli—he said 'Don't say anything. I've got to advise you informally that this is not the way to talk to the public. Sign here'. But I hadn't insulted him. I was told off for something I hadn't done. He annoyed me, not the complainant, not being able to say anything. I wasn't even able to say I didn't want the advice because I wasn't guilty. I had no chance to explain my reaction and whether I accepted what had been said. I've got several over the years, and the points add up on my file, and I'm cross."

"It has advantages for C and D because it saves them time, but the disadvantage for us is that it's not properly looked into. I wasn't asked if I wanted to accept it. I was shown this long statement and I agreed with every word of it except at the bottom where it said I was rude. I was not asked if I had been. If it was a full-blown complaint I'd have shown I'd done my job right."

In sum, then, only a minority of officers complained against were positively in favour of informal resolution, and incomplete knowledge and incorrect perceptions about it were common. One frequent misapprehension was that signing the notification form in acknowledgement of receipt of the complaint signified an admission of the allegation. However, the fact that a much higher proportion were in favour in one of the forces suggests that attitudes may change as the 'rank and file' become more familiar with the process.

(b) *Admissions and apologies*
Only four of the 30 complainants in our sample whose cases were informally resolved had been told that the officer had admitted the allegations in full, and a further four that a partial admission had been made.[1] Sixteen of the remaining 22 had either been told or had gained the impression that the officer denied having done anything wrong,

83

and hence that they would have to 'agree to differ'. The other six could remember no further contact from the police after making their statement. In most of these last six cases, the AO had simply asked them to leave the matter in his hands, promising to see the officer and 'have a word' with him or her.

Obviously, a denial of the allegation may simply mean that the complainant had no valid reason to complain in the first place, but as over 60 per cent of the complaints in this sample related to minor incivilities, and very few of the complainants had had any previous dealings with the police, one might wonder why these people would have gone to all the trouble of making an official complaint unless some action by the officer had upset them enough to do so. (Certainly, we were generally impressed with the 'genuineness' of interviewees whose cases had been informally resolved). Thus, while it has to be recognised that there may often have been rudeness or misunderstanding on the part of the complainant, the reluctance of a majority of officers to admit *any* fault at all suggests that most junior officers simply do not yet have enough confidence in the IR procedure to be completely frank about what happened: they behave in the same way as when they risk disciplinary action under the formal investigation procedure. One factor which may have played a big part in any failure to be open about what happened, was that, according to several officers we spoke to, AOs tended to adopt a very formal tone and approach in their interviews. In sum, the spirit of frankness and conciliation which some hope will be engendered by the IR system was not evident in many cases.

Despite these obstacles, interviewees in our sample fared reasonably well as far as receiving some sort of apology was concerned. Although only five of the 30 received one on behalf of the officer concerned, a further ten said that they had been offered some form of apology by the AO on behalf of the force. AOs we spoke to were not surprised that officers rarely agreed to have an individual apology conveyed to the complainant, one remarking:

"I've never known one to agree to apologise—an apology from a policeman is a bit too much to expect. They don't do it very easily because we're not that sort of breed."

Indeed, some officers subject of an informal resolution resented the idea of an AO apologising on behalf of the force, seeing this as giving the complainant an unwelcome victory in some unseen battle they seemed to be waging with certain sections of the public:

"If I'm not sorry, I don't like the IO apologising on behalf of the force because they'd feel some satisfaction, and 99 percent of complainants don't have any cause to make a complaint."

4. Informal Resolution in Practice

(a) *The rarity of meetings between complainant and officer*

The Informal Resolution Regulations allow for a meeting to be arranged between the complainant and the accused officer if this is thought an appropriate method to effect a resolution. To many complainants, too, the term informal resolution tends to conjure up a picture of sitting round a table with the officer and a third party to discuss the incident. Yet, while 16 of the 30 complainants said that they would have liked to meet the officer(s) in such circumstances, only one actually did so. The most common reasons for wanting a meeting were a wish to extract an apology, or a desire to talk matters through and receive an explanation. Several had the notion of the AO acting as a kind of judge 'to see who was telling the truth'. There was also one who wanted to 'thump' the officer and another who wanted to see him reprimanded. Among those who did not want to see the officer were several who saw no point in a meeting, a few who thought the complaint 'too trivial' to warrant one, and two women who said they would have been 'too frightened' to come face to face with the officer again.

Only one in five of the officers we interviewed were in favour of such meetings. This was partly because about a third of the whole sample had never seriously considered the possibility before we put it to them. However, about half were actively opposed to the idea, mainly because they did not feel they had to defend themselves to individuals they generally regarded as 'stroppy', and did not see it as useful to 'trade words with a member of the public', as one put it. Despite this, over 40 per cent would have been prepared to take part if pressed.

IOs and AOs were generally doubtful about the wisdom of offering complainants a meeting with the officer. The majority view seemed to be that in most cases it would be inviting trouble. For example:

"Complainants often ask to meet the officer, but I don't have a great deal of confidence that it would be a good idea—you'd probably end up with more animosity than before. The meeting would be difficult to control and more likely to involve a further complaint."

Even so, most could recall at least one meeting that had been arranged by them, and all of these were reported to have turned out successfully. The comments of one experienced IO reflect a common view:

"This needs very careful assessment. If it seems likely that both parties will just reinforce their own views then it can do more harm than good. If

85

the complainant wants an apology and the officer is not prepared to offer one then it would be futile. But I have arranged a couple. In one the officer was able to get across to the complainants that they had been behaving badly, and they accepted this, while he was brought to account by the very people he'd upset. How better to sort it out than face-to-face with a referee?"

Coincidentally, we interviewed both the officer and the complainant who had been involved in one of the meetings we heard about. Their summarised accounts give some idea of what it feels like from both sides. The complainant in this case received a full apology:

"The IO rang again and said the officer had admitted that the information had not been given, and did I still want it to go to the Chief Constable, or would I be satisfied if he came with the officer to make an apology face-to-face. I said provided I had an apology, then I would let it go so long as he came here, and I wouldn't have to go to the station. He came up with his helmet under his arm, in full uniform, and gave me an official apology. He was very sternfaced, I don't think he was happy about having to do it. He showed signs of it having been dragged out of him. They were only here ten minutes."

Meanwhile the officer said:

"There was no point in arguing over it, you have got to admit it if you've done it. I had to eat humble pie and go and see this complainant with the Inspector. I felt very nervous about it. It went very well, very short. He just wanted an apology and an explanation. I said I had spoken to the other party and he had confirmed what the complainant was saying. He said thank you very much."

Overall, then, both AOs and officers subject of complaint were less enthusiastic than complainants about the idea of face-to-face meetings, although it was quite widely recognised that they could serve a useful purpose in selected cases. While it can mean more work for the police in setting such meetings up, mediation of this kind is in tune with the spirit of informal resolution. We feel that it is a tool that could and should be used more frequently in bringing about informal settlements. One interesting suggestion we heard was that, rather than ask a senior officer to conduct the meeting, *lay visitors* might be asked to act as independent mediators in suitable cases.

(b) *Feedback to complainants*
After the initial meeting, only 12 of our sample of 30 complainants had any further personal contact with the AO, and a further six spoke to him or her over the telephone. Most of these 18 felt that the AO had done a reasonable job and had kept them adequately informed. Among the most satisfied customers was the man who reported:

"He phoned me later that day saying the officer left 'a very frightened man', and that he would never ever bother us or anyone else in the road again and he would not stray outside his patch again. He'd spoken to him for two hours. He said he told him he'd scored an own goal and one more complaint and he'd be finished."

On the other hand, the communication was not always what they had expected or wanted. In several cases, the complainant felt that, rather than taking a neutral stance, the AO had excused or defended the officer concerned:

"The AO said the WPC was highly thought of, and when I suggested she might have made a mistake, he said 'Oh no, she wouldn't tell fibs'."

"I went to see him and the constable had admitted everything. I had to wait for half an hour for the appointment but it turned out better than I expected, but it did seem a palaver over a trivial point. The senior officer said he had been involved in the chase of my son and 'the old adrenalin flows'—he mentioned that six times—and although he'd had two other complaints against him he'd said 'I'm not going to make him apologise to you, I don't want him to apologise, but it's on his record."

Three complainants were visited at least three times, mainly to encourage them to accept informal resolution and to negotiate a settlement that would be satisfactory to both the force and the complainant. In one of these cases, the complaint concerned the disclosure to an employer of information that a relative was wanted on suspicion of a crime. Several visits were made to the complainant by a number of senior officers asking her what she wanted, and eventually she received the written apology that she had repeatedly requested.

The remaining 12 complainants, who had merely received a letter from Headquarters (or who could not remember receiving any further communication from the police), were generally annoyed about the lack of feedback. For example:

"I don't know what happened, I heard nothing for months and then I got a letter with no explanation. I was very disappointed and expected to talk it over with the senior officer who came."

"Up to the point that the senior officer said he would speak to the one I complained about he had handled it beautifully. And then I got a letter four weeks later saying that the officer had denied it. That's when I bridled because I am a man of principle. I was going to write back but I just left it. If I'd got that letter a few days after seeing the senior officer I would have taken it up again, but a month later I wanted to put it behind me because it would have been a lot of time and trouble starting it up again."

In one of the forces we studied, it was official policy to recontact complainants personally when IR was completed, but only around half those interviewed said that this had been done. AOs may think that little will be gained by informing the complainant of the officer's reaction, but failure to do so may engender more dissatisfaction than hearing, for example, that the officer has denied the allegation.

Finally, Regulation 5 of the Police (Complaints) (Informal Resolution) Regulations allows for complainants to be provided with a 'copy of the record relating to the complaint' if applied for within three months. However, not only were nearly all complainants ignorant of this fact, but even if they had requested a copy, they would have learnt very little from it. In the vast majority of cases, the record comprised little more than a short summary of the grievance. In explaining the paucity of information, one experienced AO remarked that 'the less said the better' and 'the more you write the more they'll want to have'. This minimalist interpretation of the rules seems to render the complainant's right all but valueless.

5. Levels of Satisfaction among Complainants

Despite the various irritations mentioned above by complainants who were party to an informal resolution, their overall verdict upon the new procedures tended to be positive. Substantially higher levels of satisfaction with the outcome were found among those whose cases had been informally resolved, than among those whose complaints had been withdrawn or formally investigated. Thirty per cent reported that they were 'very satisfied' with the outcome and 27 per cent that they were 'fairly satisfied' (see Table 7, Chapter 4). The main causes of dissatisfaction among the remainder were that the officer concerned had 'lied' and that no apology was forthcoming. Other reasons concerned inadequate communication and frustration that the officer had 'got away with it'. We also asked people whether, in retrospect, they would have preferred a formal investigation. Only ten per cent replied in the affirmative, and a similar proportion were unsure—for instance, acknowledging the speed of the procedure on the one hand yet disgruntled with the outcome on the other. One man reflected that:

"I didn't want the full investigation because it was a trivial complaint but in retrospect I did not like being made to look a blatant liar."

Looking back, therefore, the majority (over three-quarters) were content with their choice—although it has to be said that in several instances this seemed motivated more by dislike of what they had been led to believe were the alternatives, than for positive reasons:

"No, I didn't want to go in front of a jury, I wanted to be left alone and I've never been to a court before."

"No, I didn't want to have anything to do with the newspapers."

To sum up, informal resolution produced a reasonably high proportion of satisfied customers—and certainly much higher than that produced by formal investigations. Although apologies were received in only a minority of cases, the flexibility available to the AO allowed him to promise 'firm words' to officers, an option not open in the adversarial situation of an investigation. Few complainants wanted any more than this, and they were thus quite likely to be satisfied.

Police officers on the ground had mixed feelings about the new procedure. Negative views were reinforced by widely held false beliefs about the new procedures, such as that signing for receipt of the informal resolution notification constituted an admission of the allegation, and that cases of IR were recorded on personal files. The advantage of informal resolution to officers subject of complaint is clear where the officer has in fact committed the alleged breach of discipline, and where substantiation would be the likely result if formally investigated. As one AO succinctly put it:

"It also has advantages to the officer and to us. Before, he either had to decline to answer, tell lies or admit it and leave himself vulnerable. Now he can make an honest admission to me, he has protection—he can't be disciplined, and the complainant can get an apology."

However, in the much more common situation where the officer believes that he or she is 'not guilty'—or, at least, that there is little chance of the complaint being substantiated if a formal investigation is carried out—hostility to the idea of IR is understandably quite widespread.

Informal resolution is clearly 'here to stay', and it is important that efforts are made to 'sell' it more successfully to junior officers. This involves changing the thought process which associates the reception of a complaint with the adoption of a defensive, adversarial attitude towards the complainant—the automatic response of 'denying everything'. More positively, it involves stressing the value of attempting to understand the perceptions of a member of the public which may differ from their own. In other words, to see IR as an exercise in communication and explanation, not in investigating guilt or innocence.

It should also be emphasised that misunderstandings about IR were not confined to those on the receiving end: those negotiating a settlement, too, were sometimes confused about the rules and conditions. The training given to new IOs for both formal and informal investigation of complaints was felt to be inadequate by almost half of our interviewees.

At the time of our fieldwork, the use of informal resolution in the three forces studied was largely confined to complaints of incivility, irregular procedure and neglect of duty. In view of the relatively high level of customer satisfaction with this means of settling complaints, it is worth considering the extent to which its use might be expanded.

For instance, it seemed to be fairly standard practice that, where anything technically classifiable as an assault was alleged by a complainant, the immediate police response was to mark it down for formal investigation. We interviewed several complainants who had received minor injuries on arrest who willingly admitted that they had struggled, yet continued to feel that the actions of the arresting officer had 'gone over the top'. Although their complaints were recorded as 'assault', a more apt description might have been 'excessive use of force'. They neither wished to withdraw, nor were especially keen to have a formal investigation carried out, but would have been content with an informal resolution to 'make their point'. There are clearly dangers in channelling what might be serious abuses of police powers into a system in which the officers concerned face no risk of discipline. Moreover, at present, only Inspectors of Constabulary and, in some forces, complaints sub-committees of the Police Authority, take a relatively cursory look at the files (or digests of the files). If arrangements were made for more formal and more rigorous monitoring of informally resolved complaints by independent outsiders, we would have little hesitation in recommending much wider use of the IR machinery.

NOTES

1. It may be, of course, that the recollections of some complainants were faulty and that some admissions had been made without registering on their consciousness. However, judging by our interviews with officers, very few of whom admitted that they had been at fault in any complaint against them, as well as by accounts in casefiles we examined, it is likely that what the complainants said was correct.

CHAPTER 7

Withdrawn Complaints

As indicated in Chapter 3, over 40 per cent of all recorded complaints are eventually withdrawn by the complainants. In this chapter, we investigate the reasons behind this high rate of attrition. Is it, for example, mainly the result of 'pressure to withdraw' put upon complainants by police investigators or others (cf. Russell 1986; Brown 1987), or simply, as police officers tend to assert, of subsequent recognition by complainants that their complaints were groundless?

Our main source of data used here is our interviews with the sample of 30 people (from three police force areas) who withdrew their complaints. We shall also take into account the experiences of other interviewees with whom IOs or other police officers discussed the possibility of withdrawal, but who 'stuck to their guns', insisting upon a formal investigation. To balance the picture, we consider the views and practices of the nineteen investigating officers we interviewed.

1. Perceived 'Pressure to Withdraw' from Investigating Officers

(a) *Those who declined to withdraw*
Among the 40 complainants we interviewed whose cases had been fully investigated, 23 (58 per cent) reported efforts of varying degree by investigating officers to persuade them to make a statement of withdrawal. Seven of these described the pressure put upon them as 'strong', the remainder having been aware of various 'techniques', including 'subtle hints' and 'veiled threats'.

What forms did this pressure take? A small minority (five of the 40) reported a *quid pro quo* offered if they withdrew, including hints or assurances that charges against them would be dropped, the offer of an informal apology, and a promise to have 'strong words' with the officer. One of these complainants said she had been asked if she would accept damages for a broken window in exchange for discontinuing her complaint, while two of the most direct approaches of this kind were described thus:

"He came and suggested that it shouldn't go any further. He said, 'I'm apologising on behalf of the police force, now shall we leave it there?' But I wanted to see it through to the end."

"He basically offered to drop the charges if I withdrew. He said, 'Nothing more will come of it if you apologise.' I thought, it's you who should be apologising to me."

A further small group (three of the 40) had felt some form of veiled threat of repercussions if they did not agree to withdraw. For example:

"He told me to go away and think very carefully about it. He implied that if I continued I might get reprisals because I was putting these policemen's jobs on the line. He came back again and I told him I wanted to go through with it for that purpose alone."

And in another case, the complainant was reminded that a decision still had to be made regarding charges against his son:

"He asked specifically if I wanted to continue and then what did I want to happen to the officer. He said the officer was just a young lad who was new—just starting off. He then said he couldn't investigate my complaint until they had decided what to do about the business concerning my son. That could have been the point at which I'd crumbled. Yes, there was pressure. I thought to myself is this going to make it worse for my son . . . I think it's all part of the technique."

However, most of those who had felt some pressure to withdraw referred only to general attempts to persuade them that the matter was not worth the time and expense of an investigation, that there was little chance of a conclusive result, or that they were putting a good officer's career in jeopardy for a minor lapse. Typical examples were:

"He more or less in a roundabout way said that I was wasting my time and his. He was on about all the paperwork involved, and he tried to make me feel guilty about continuing with it. He asked me what I wanted—did I want them dismissed from their jobs? I said no, just a reprimand."

"He tried to wear me down. He kept on trying to talk the policeman out of it—'Come on, they're only trying to do their best' and all that sort of guff. I had to fight quite hard."

"He kept putting all the negative aspects—'I'll pass it on to my superiors and nothing will happen . . . not enough evidence . . . nothing will come of it.'"

(b) *Those who withdrew*

Among the 30 complainants we interviewed who had withdrawn their complaints, 21 had made the decision as a direct result of what was

Table 8: Complainants' primary reasons for withdrawing

	No.	%
Willing Withdrawers		
Objectives already attained	7	23
Informal action promised	3	10
Sub total	10	33
Reluctant Withdrawers		
Unlikely to 'win case'	7	23
Inconvenience/daunting nature of hearing	4	13
Fear of repercussions of court case/hearing	2	7
Officer would get into too much trouble	2	7
'Blinded with science'by IO	3	10
Witness to incident: 'victim' won't pursue	2	7
Sub total	20	67
Total	30	100

said at a meeting—usually their first—with the IO. Even among those who withdrew after having appeared in court on related charges (eight of the thirty),[1] the majority (six) had not made their minds up to do so until spoken to by the IO—a finding which, although admittedly based on only a small number of cases, goes against the conventional police wisdom that most complaints by people who have been arrested are solely a device to assist their defence, in which they lose all interest once their court case is over. The predominant feeling among these, as among complainants of all other kinds, was that they had been 'talked into' withdrawing, to some extent against their will.

If this is so, it is important to ask what circumstances or what arguments, precisely, tipped the balance and persuaded them to withdraw. Table 8 gives a summary of the primary reasons given by our interviewees. First of all, ten of the thirty were broadly satisfied, either with what had already been achieved by their complaint, or with assurances given by the IO that informal action would be taken and there was therefore no need to pursue the matter further. These included a man who was quite satisfied simply to have aired his grievance in person to a senior officer; a couple who thought that their complaint had helped to get their son released from custody without charge; another who received discretionary compensation from the police; a woman who received an apology from the IO on behalf of the officers complained about; a man who learned that the officer concerned had been transferred to different duties; and two separate complainants against whom, according to them, charges had been dropped in exchange for withdrawing their complaints. Also included were one man who said he had complained in the heat of the moment and had now 'cooled down', and one who admitted that his only real motive had been to help his defence in court. Police officers commonly claimed that the latter were two of the most common causes of withdrawal, but there was little evidence of this from our interviews with complainants.

The remaining 20 interviewees gave less positive reasons for their decision. Most of these were connected with the possible outcome of the complaint. Eight had withdrawn specifically upon being told that they might have to give evidence in court or at a disciplinary hearing (although, objectively, this did not seem likely). These included two who had simply found the idea daunting, two who were not prepared to give more of their time, and two who feared that a hearing would result in the officer losing his job—a consequence they did not wish to see. The other two in this group were interesting in that they had received the impression that the prosecution of an officer could somehow 'backfire' upon them. They seemed to think that there would be a court case which they would either 'win' or 'lose', and that losing would do them harm. Of course, if a police officer *were* to be charged (again, a very rare event), this would be a normal criminal case in which the complainant would merely be a witness. The complainants told us:

"He said 'You know if you do carry on it'll be sent to the public prosecutor, there's no doubt about that.' He said it would be charged and would go to the Crown Court. He then said that everything that happened from the time of the accident would be brought up in court. I couldn't understand what that had to do with the assault in the station. I got the strong impression that he was trying to say that they'd all be against me for the traffic offences and that I wouldn't stand a chance. I said 'Are you trying to blackmail me?' and he said 'Not at all, I'm just giving you the facts.' You could tell by the way he was talking that he was trying to talk me out of it, but as I couldn't have gone through with having my name in the papers, I decided to withdraw."

"He said they'd say I was struggling. Yes, I was struggling, but only to get up, I was in agony. He said the PC could sue me if it was thrown out. I wasn't confident about the result because I had witnesses when I complained before but that didn't do a lot of good."

However, the most common single reason given for withdrawing was that complainants had been persuaded (in most cases by the IO, but in a few by their own solicitor) that if it came to a court case or disciplinary hearing against the officer, there was little chance of a finding of guilt. Some were convinced by discussions about the poor quality of the evidence, while others were already disillusioned by 'lies' told in court by the officers complained against, and as a result believed there was little point in continuing with their grievances. Three examples illustrate the sorts of discussions which took place:

"The point of law was the main thing that worried us. He said that by the time it came to court, everyone would have forgotten the exact details and we could be tripped up and lose our case. He more or less said that in an arrest situation the police usually win. He suggested that the best way—although it was entirely up to us—was to leave it to him. We had a lengthy discussion, and we considered it carefully, and we decided we could trust him to do what he said and so we withdrew. Off the record he said he'd tear him from limb to limb, but we've got no proof he was punished."

"After the court case [the IO] was there. He called me into an interviewing room and he asked me what I was going to do. I remember him saying something to talk me out of it like 'Is it really worth it now?'. And then I really started to think—are they going to look at my side of the tale after my conviction? I knew it would go to court—it's the same as them prosecuting us. I think he asked me if I wanted it dealt with in the magistrates or Crown court. I was pretty fed up, it seemed to me I was going to start a losing battle, so I didn't take much convincing and said I would drop charges. He was a bit too eager to have it shut. He said 'We'll just write this down and we'll have it closed."

"I was looking forward to court, but once there, there were that many lies told I couldn't believe it. I mean they swore on oath . . . they told lies that I was swearing. They said they'd handcuffed me when they put me into the car—they never did that at all, they just gave me a good kicking. Afterwards the IO asked if I wanted to continue and I said 'Between you and me it's not worth it because I lost the case', and he agreed."

Three other complainants described meetings in which they felt they had been virtually 'tricked' or 'badgered' into withdrawing, the IO confusing them with legal points designed to show that the police had acted correctly. Although they eventually agreed to withdraw, they remained upset that the real substance of their complaints had not been addressed at all. The tone of the conversations had ranged from argumentativeness to what one complainant described as 'soft soap'. Two of these meetings were described as follows:

"Everything we said, he had an answer for. He said 'It's legal' whatever it was. He explained they were allowed to come in in hot pursuit, told us we had the law wrong. Made us feel we hadn't a leg to stand on. He said 'They are only human beings, some are good some are bad'. He wasn't concerned about the broken door or their rudeness, he just wasn't

interested. We were almost arguing with him—especially about the door."

"When he arrived he sat down and chatted for three-quarters of an hour about his family, his divorce, my 'fantastic room', and lovely outlook etc. so I ended up being sympathetic to the police. He talked about the police problems that night and got me agreeing with him. Then he whipped out my son's statement, where he'd written that he agreed he hadn't moved on when asked. I assumed that because my son had agreed he was guilty of the offence then that was the end. They throw up a lot of legal words and you become bewildered, you don't think you have a leg to stand on. It wasn't until afterwards that I realised I'd got muddled and had lost sight of my real complaint of how he was arrested and his unnecessarily long detention."

Finally, two cases involved people who had made complaints about incidents (both alleged assaults) which they had observed. In the first case, the IO showed the statement of the 'victim' to the complainant, a completely independent witness, which said that the former had no complaint about the nature of his arrest. This complainant recalled:

"I feel that a deal was definitely done, because I was shocked that he said he had no complaint about the way he was arrested. Possibly they agreed to drop some of the charges against him, or else he was too frightened to complain himself."

In his surprise, the above complainant agreed to make a withdrawal statement, forgetting that he had also complained about the rudeness of the sergeant who had arrested the victim—a complaint which he had not intended to withdraw. In the second case, the complainant said he had been told that he would be unable to continue with his complaint because his friend, the victim of the alleged assault, had declined to complain himself.

2. Satisfaction and Dissatisfaction

Despite the common feeling of having been 'manoeuvred' into withdrawing, complainants did not on the whole, with hindsight, deeply regret their decision. Levels of dissatisfaction with the outcome were not so high as one might expect: under half of those who had withdrawn (13 of the 30) declared themselves 'very dissatisfied' with the outcome and a further quarter 'a bit dissatisfied' (Table 7, Chapter 4). Indeed, when asked the main reason for their dissatisfaction, fewer were concerned about the outcome *per se* than about the manner in which their consent to withdrawal had been 'engineered'— a typical remark being:

"I was angry with how he twisted me and my son round his little finger."

Other reasons given for dissatisfaction included indignation that the officers complained against had 'lied and got away with it'; complainants' feelings that they had been disbelieved; not knowing what had happened to the officers concerned; the lack of any apology or compensation from the police: and, in one case, a complainant's anger at himself for having lost the nerve to continue. Although six had been convicted in court, only one of these gave this conviction as a reason for dissatisfaction.

Asked specifically whether they now regretted having decided to withdraw, over two-thirds answered that they did not, mainly because they felt that the complaint would not anyway have 'got anywhere'. Among those who still regretted the decision, it was interesting to find a majority saying, in answer to a later question, that they would have liked a supervised meeting with the officer concerned in order to resolve the matter informally. This supports other findings pointing to the conclusion that their desire was less for 'revenge' than for an explanation, apology, or recognition of their point of view. It also suggests that a policy among IOs, wherever possible, to steer complainants towards informal resolution rather than withdrawal might increase the general level of satisfaction.

In this respect, it is worth mentioning that some complainants were unhappy with the term 'withdrawn'. They still maintained the truth of their allegations, and spoke in terms of not having 'pursued' or 'gone on with' their complaint. Indeed, three were unaware that their complaints had been recorded as withdrawn, thinking that they had been dealt with informally or, in one case, that some form of investigation was still going on. This raises some general questions about the classifications and the terminology used in the complaints system, which we discuss further in Chapter 10. In particular, it suggests a possible change whereby all 'withdrawn' complaints are officially described in future as 'not pursued'. (Some other term would be needed to distinguish those not pursued on the decision of the *police*—for example, when investigation is impracticable or the complainant uncontactable.)

3. Investigating Officers' Views
Most of the 19 investigating officers we interviewed were well aware of their power to influence complainants' decisions, although they had varying views on whether and how often it was reasonable to set out with the objective of 'getting a withdrawal'—a phrase we heard several times in casual conversations.

97

A small minority (three of the 19) candidly admitted that this was the basic frame of mind in which they approached most complainants, because they felt that most complains were trivial, mistaken or malicious. However, even these officers were adamant that if they thought there 'might be something in it', they adopted a quite different approach.

The majority, however, claimed that they had no particular interest in whether or not a case was investigated, but in certain circumstances would suggest or, as one put it, 'guide the complainant towards' withdrawal, simply because this seemed to them the most appropriate course of action. This might be, for example, because the complainant did not seem particularly committed to the allegation, or because there seemed to be no chance at all of it being substantiated. Examples were:

"If I think it will be a waste of time, then I might try to get him round to suggesting withdrawal himself rather than me saying it. I might say 'Do you really want to go on with this?' if his heart's not really in it. Why bother if he's not that interested? Who are you trying to satisfy?"

"If I know someone is lying, do I go in there and draw him into making a false statement, or do I go in there and suggest he withdraws? It's far easier for him to withdraw rather than lying and then me proving he's lied."

"I can pick one up and tell whether or not it's going to be a runner. You can see it straight off . . . if it's a non-starter, they'd be the ones I'd try and get them to withdraw on."

"If it's a ridiculous case I'm likely to say they've not a cat in hell's chance, but I will investigate it properly if that's what they want. But if he has a genuine cause for concern then I wouldn't dream of trying for a withdrawal."

"They often withdraw at my suggestion. Regardless of the type of complaint, if he's being iffy, I will ask if his heart is really in it, and is he prepared to go to a formal hearing."

Finally, a few claimed that they never made any attempt to influence complainants, their job being simply to explain the options and procedures for complainants to make their own decisions:

"In my long experience, only about one in five have withdrawn. I have never ever suggested it myself."

The variety of approaches was also reflected in IOs' responses when asked what proportion of their recent cases had ended with the complaint being withdrawn. The answers ranged from 'nought in the past fifteen' to the 'almost one hundred per cent' reported—with a smile—by one IO from Headquarters.

In trying to account for the generally high rate of withdrawal, almost all referred at some point to the situation after a court appearance by the complainant, when any potential the complaint had possessed for assisting his or her defence no longer existed. In such circumstances, they claimed, few complainants needed any persuasion to withdraw—the 'main reason for their complaint' having disappeared. However, while 'post-court case withdrawals' certainly occurred quite often, they accounted, as we have seen, for only a quarter of all withdrawals among the complainants we interviewed. Moreover, some of the latter had in fact needed considerable persuasion to withdraw their allegations.

We also asked some of our IO interviewees if they had ever persuaded a complainant *not* to withdraw a complaint which they (the IOs) thought should be investigated. None could recall having done so, although several said that they had continued to investigate cases, after withdrawal, by means of the internal disciplinary system:

"I can continue with it in a different coloured folder. You sometimes know if a person has been mistreated even if they try and back down, especially if they are 100 per cent behind the police. I say I hope they'll assist with the internal inquiry by giving a statement later—but not a statement of complaint."

"If you know there's something in it, you go ahead and investigate it anyway—probably in fifteen per cent of withdrawals. For example, a member of the public was assaulted by another person and later withdrew, but three officers got advice for neglect of duty—they didn't stop it or help. It's not right or proper to ignore a problem because a complainant has withdrawn."

This was by no means universal practice. In the headquarters of one of the forces we studied, the prevailing view seemed to be reflected in the following statements of two IOs:

"We can't continue with the investigation internally—we kick it into touch. There's too many other pressures."

"There's plenty more in there who want to pursue their complaint without worrying about those who do want to withdraw."

Another described a particular case, of alleged assault and criminal damage in the course of a drugs raid, in which he felt certain that a full investigation would have resulted in substantiation and disciplinary action, but 'did nothing more' after the complainant withdrew. It was not quite clear why he took no action, although part of the reason seemed to be his belief that the complainants had provoked the officers and were heavily involved in crime.

4. Concluding Remarks

The general conclusion we can draw from our interviews with IOs is that it is common for them to form an early judgement upon whether or not the case is likely to be a 'runner'. If they decide that it is not, attitudes and practice vary in the extent to which they try to steer the complainant towards making the 'right decision'. Almost all admitted to gently pushing complainants in this direction at least occasionally.

It is important to emphasise at this point that in many cases there is nothing in any way 'suspicious' or untoward in a complainant's decision to withdraw, nor is it necessarily wrong for IOs to try a little gentle persuasion when there is obviously no mileage in pursuing the matter. With hindsight, some people may acknowledge that they overreacted in the 'heat of the moment'; some may be happy with the explanation offered by the IO for the officers' behaviour; and some certainly do complain solely in the hope of gaining some bargaining power in an impending court case against them. Moreover, mis-understandings about, or ignorance of, police powers may mean that the action in question was entirely legal. This has been especially true since PACE. For instance, our sample included complaints about searches made of premises without warrant, and one man complained that his son's fingerprints had been taken forcibly. The 'victims' simply did not know that both these actions had been entirely legal under the circumstances.

It is clearly reasonable for IOs to point out the legal position in the above type of case. Similarly, there is surely little harm in the practice of IOs gently 'testing the water' in any fairly minor case, to see whether the complainant really wishes to continue. However, it seems indefensible to 'badger' complainants into withdrawing—however 'silly' the complaint may seem to the IO—and equally wrong to mislead or 'con' them into dropping their complaint.

In some of the cases discussed above, there is little doubt, from the complainants' accounts, that IOs came very close to these types of approach. For example, three insisted so vehemently that particular police actions had been correct in law, that the complainants withdrew all their complaints, only to realise later that other elements of their grievance—for example, incivility during what turned out to be a legal search—had not been addressed at all by the IO. Again, not only did over a quarter of the complainants claim to have withdrawn because of a warning that they might have to attend a hearing, but several of these had gleaned the impression that the venue for this would be a magistrates' or crown court. Most such warnings were quite unnecessary, because the chances of a hearing—even should the complaint be substantiated—are minimal in all but the most serious cases.

The main comment we would make here is that, if allegations are considered serious enough to risk culminating in a disciplinary hearing or prosecution in court, it seems logical that complainants should, if anything, be *encouraged* to continue, as opposed to being either persuaded to withdraw or not discouraged from it. Conversely, if they are insufficiently serious to warrant legal or disciplinary action, then it is somewhat underhand of IOs to suggest that this is a real possibility. Moreover, if an important objective of the system is to satisfy complainants or to 'allay their grievances', strong pressure or misleading advice by IOs is unlikely to achieve this outcome. As we have shown, two-thirds of those who withdrew were dissatisfied at the end of the day, many of them more upset by the manner in which the withdrawal had been elicited from them than by the fact that their complaint had 'got nowhere'.

Two strategies suggest themselves for improving the situation. First, as alluded to in Chapter 6, it may be productive, from the point of view of complainant satisfaction, to encourage AOs and IOs to steer more people towards acceptance of informal resolution, rather than trying to persuade them to withdraw. There is a limitation here, in that over half of all complaints currently withdrawn include allegations of assault and many of these may be considered too serious for IR. On the other hand, it might be countered that if withdrawal is the only alternative, this argument loses much of its power.

Secondly, consideration might be given to changing the official term for what are presently called 'withdrawn' complaints. It might increase the level of satisfaction among complainants who decide not to go forward with a full investigation if such complaints were referred to instead as, for instance, 'not pursued'.

NOTES
1. Although 17 of the 30 had been arrested, fewer than half of these were actually prosecuted.

PART THREE

THE POLICE COMPLAINTS AUTHORITY

CHAPTER 8

Cases Handled by the PCA

1. Introduction

In Part Three, we turn to the role and effectiveness of the new independent element in the system, the Police Complaints Authority. We restrict the discussion chiefly to a set of topics specifically selected for our attention by the Authority when it commissioned the research. However, we also include the results of a postal questionnaire to a sample of complainants in cases handled by the PCA: this was not part of the official 'brief', but was incorporated later at the researchers' suggestion. As part of the PCA's task is to gain the confidence of the public, we consider the reactions of its 'customers' to be an important indicator of its effectiveness.

Our terms of reference (laid out in paras. 8.1–8.4. of the PCA Annual Report 1986, and reproduced here in Appendix 4) were, in summary, to consider:

—the nature of complaints referred to the Authority
—members' decisions on whether or not to supervise
—the effect of supervision on the outcome of cases
—the nature of supervision and variations in style
—practical problems hindering the work of the Authority.

Most of these issues were related primarily to the work of 'I' (Investigation) Division, the section of the PCA which supervises complaint investigations. We shall consequently devote relatively little attention to the work of the other (and larger) group of members, who make up 'D' (Discipline) Division. This does not reflect any intention to understate the importance of 'D' Division. On the contrary, it can be argued that its decisions are ultimately of more consequence, for the police at least, than those of 'I' Division. 'D' Division members are the final arbiters of whether there is sufficient evidence to justify disciplinary proceedings, and can, in the last resort, direct a Chief Constable to hold a disciplinary tribunal. They can also undertake some actions akin to the supervisory work of 'I' Division, such as insisting that investigating officers go back and follow up leads they have missed, even though the investigation and report have been completed. On the other hand, 'I' Division is much more in the public eye, an important part of its job being to demonstrate that there is an independent and critical eye being kept on the progress of investigations in serious, sensitive and controversial cases. This 'public relations' function is a vital one, and must be taken full account of in any assessment of the effectiveness of the PCA.

We begin our account in this chapter with a brief sketch of the kinds of cases which pass through the hands of PCA members, looking particularly at those referred to and supervised by 'I' Division (which are quite untypical of all complaints) and at 'Section 88' cases. We also discuss problems of referral and classification. In the next two chapters, we shall examine styles of supervision and the reactions of complainants to PCA involvement.

2. Cases Which Do and Do Not Reach the PCA

(a) *Cases filtered out*

Figure 1 gives a very simplified picture of the path of a year's cases (as opposed to *complaints*) through the whole system. Although constructed from statistics for 1987, this is a notional rather than a real year's cases, as the annual police returns are based upon completed, rather than newly recorded, cases (see note to Figure 1). The total cases for the year was 16,400, incorporating 28,000—or possibly more[1]—individual complaints. It can be seen that fewer than half of these cases ever crossed the desks of PCA members. About a quarter were referred to 'I' Division at an early stage for possible supervision. Nearly half of the latter—i.e. all those not subsequently withdrawn— were also seen later by 'D' Division, either after investigations were complete or when the police applied for dispensations from the requirement to investigate. In addition, we estimate that 'D' Division examined about 3,600 previously unreferred cases, of which 3,200 were reports of completed investigations and 400 applications for dispensations.

This leaves roughly 8,700 cases (53 per cent of the total) in which PCA members had no sight at all of the complaint or its outcome. About 3,900 of these had been filtered out via the Informal Resolution procedure introduced under Section 85 of PACE, the remaining 4,800 being withdrawn without any reference to the PCA.

There is little doubt that the complaints which remain unseen by PCA members are generally less serious than those they deal with. In 1987, for example, well over 40 per cent of informally resolved complaints concerned incivility, compared with only 14 per cent of fully investigated complaints. Moreover, the requirements of Regulation $4(1)$[2] should ensure that relatively few allegations of criminal behaviour by police officers are withdrawn without having been

Figure 1. Paths taken by complaints cases: approximations based on referral and completion statistics for 1987★

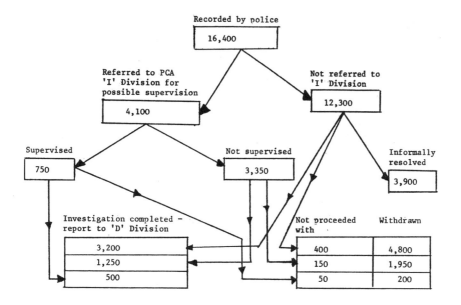

Summary of outcomes

	Total cases	(%)	Total complaints	(%)
Informally resolved	3,900	(24)	5,100★★	(18)
Not proceeded with	600	(4)	1,400	(5)
Withdrawn	6,950	(42)	10,100★★	(36)
Investigation completed	4,950	(30)	11,350	(41)
Total	16,400	(100)	27,950★★	(100)

Notes

★It is impossible to trace a full year's cases from recording to outcome. The Figure represents a notional year's cases, being built up from PCA statistics on referrals, supervision decisions and outcomes for 1987, and from police 'completed cases' figures for the same year. There are added complications, such as the use of case statistics in some sources and complaints statistics in others, requiring estimates in making conversions. However, we are confident that the Figure gives a reasonably accurate picture of the division of cases between the different 'paths'.

★★These figures are based on police returns. It is likely that informally resolved and withdrawn cases would have been deemed to contain a considerably higher number of individual complaints had they been fully investigated. The 'true' complaints total, then, could be in the region of 35,000 – although, as pointed out in Chapter 3, it anyway seems to us more sensible to analyse numbers of cases, rather than complaints.

107

referred earlier to 'I' Division for possible supervision. Typically, withdrawn cases which are not seen by a PCA member consist of complaints of incivility, oppressive conduct, irregularities in procedure, or neglect of duty—i.e. possible candidates for disciplinary, but not criminal, proceedings. However, there is an area of doubt surrounding police interpretations of when a complaint amounts to an allegation of Section 47 assault (assault occasioning actual bodily harm—'ABH'). 'I' Division members several times pointed out to us that some forces had been referring only small numbers of cases of this kind (i.e. under Regulation 4(1)) and had had to be reminded of their statutory duty in this matter. One Chief Constable responded with veiled irritation to this reminder in his Annual Report (South Wales 1988), commenting that:

"the increase in the number of mandatory referrals was directly related to the insistence of the PCA that all alleged assault injuries, including those of a trivial nature, which might technically be considered to fall within the ambit of S.47 of the Offences Against the Person Act 1861, should be referred."

The Chief Constable also noted that 'only' 7.91 per cent of referrals were selected for supervision, seeming to imply that he was being asked to waste time and resources upon a technicality.[3] From our experience of reading files and speaking to staff in the PCA and in various force headquarters, we suspect that this view is fairly widespread among police forces, and that non-referral of possible 'ABHs' is not unusual. The injuries sustained in many complaints classified and recorded by the police as 'oppressive conduct' or 'excessive use of force', for example, could on a stricter interpretation of the law fall under Section 47 of the Offences Against the Person Act 1869. We emphasize that there is no evidence of any wrongly motivated intent to conceal cases from the PCA, but it remains true that the rules on referral allow a considerable amount of leeway for individual judgement by senior police officers, and that they can be interpreted very differently in different forces.

The problem for the PCA in monitoring this situation, of course, is that, while they are empowered to 'call in' any complaint under Section 87(2), members do not know of the existence of particular cases unless they are specifically brought to their attention. Thus, the Authority is still largely dependent on media reports and on perusal of annual statistics to spot any 'under-referring' by police forces. This is one area which both Police Authorities and Inspectors of Constabulary, who have a responsibility (S.50 of the Police Act 1964) 'to keep themselves informed as to the manner in which complaints are dealt with by chief officers', might look at more closely.

At least three points for later discussion rise from the brief outline above. First, there is the issue of whether the PCA should have some form of oversight over *all* complaints, and not just the ostensibly more serious minority: for example, should the files of informally resolved and/or withdrawn cases be sent to 'D' Division for scrutiny? Or should the criteria for mandatory referral to 'I' Division be altered to draw in more cases?

Secondly, there is the fact that each year about 2,000 cases which are serious enough to be referred to the PCA for possible supervision (though not selected for supervision) are later withdrawn without further oversight. Although probably not as serious as those the PCA select for supervision, these cases almost all include allegations of assault amounting to 'ABH'. This raises the question of whether there should be some system for monitoring their fate. Any withdrawal of a *supervised* case automatically prompts a response by the PCA in the form of a letter to the complainant enquiring whether he or she is absolutely sure. This provides some insurance against the possibility of inappropriate pressure being put upon people to withdraw (Russell 1986; Brown 1987). Although it would create extra work for both the police and the Authority, this practice could be extended to cover, for example, all withdrawn complaints of assault (or, at least, all those referred to, but rejected by, the PCA for supervision).

Thirdly, it is worth considering the possible effects upon PCA members of dealing with unrepresentative sets of complaints, rather than with a full cross-section. As we show below, the in-trays of 'I' Division members are constantly filled with allegations of assault—a type of complaint strongly associated with particular circumstances and a particular type of complainant. It has to be asked whether this gives members a somewhat distorted—and hence, perhaps, jaundiced—view of complaints and complainants in general.

(b) *'D' Division*
We now provide an overview of the types of complaint referred to the Authority. We first take a brief look at the characteristics of cases sent to 'D' Division for decisions on disciplinary action.

As outlined earlier, the main task of 'D' Division is to examine the full evidence and the final report of every formally investigated case and to decide whether the PCA agrees with the recommendations for discipline proposed by the police. In 1989, members working in 'D' Division examined 5,283 reports of completed investigations, covering 11,155 individual complaints. They granted dispensations from the requirement to investigate (usually because of lack of co-operation from complainants) in an additional 2,000 or so cases (PCA 1990, Appendix Tables).

The most common categories of complaint in the investigation reports passing through 'D' Division were assault (29 per cent), incivility (14 per cent) and irregularity in procedure and neglect of duty (each 10 per cent)[4]. The proportions are similar to those shown in the police-generated statistics collected by F2 Division of the Home Office (see Table 3, Chapter 3 above), with the exception of complaints of incivility, which form 21 per cent of the total in the latter data set. The difference is explained by the absence from 'D' Division members' desks of informally resolved complaints: as noted in Chapter 3, informal resolution filters out over half of all complaints of incivility.[5] Even so, 'D' Division work clearly entails handling a wide range of complaints, not grossly unrepresentative of all recorded complaints in England and Wales—which are made by people from a broad mix of social backgrounds. As we shall see, this is not the case with 'I' Division work.

(c) 'I' Division cases

(i) Referral criteria and problems of classification

Cases referred to 'I' Division for possible supervision can be divided up as follows:

—Complaints alleging that the conduct of one or more police officers resulted in the death of, or serious injury to, some other person (Section 87(1)(a)(i)). Referral must be made (usually by telex) by the end of the day after the complaint is made, and the investigation of these cases must be supervised by a member of the PCA. 'Serious injury' is legally defined (Section 87(4)) as 'a fracture, damage to an internal organ, impairment of bodily function, a deep cut or a deep laceration', but, as discussed below, there is still some uncertainty about what constitutes a 'deep' cut. In 1989, the PCA received 398 referrals under Section 87(1)(a)(i).

—Complaints alleging conduct which, if proved, would constitute assault occasioning actual bodily harm, an offence under Section 1 of the Prevention of Corruption Act 1906(a), or a serious arrestable offence under the meaning of Section 116 of PACE (Regulations 4(1)(a),(b),(c) of Police (Complaints) (Mandatory Referrals etc) Regulations 1985, in conjunction with Section 87(1)(a)(ii) of PACE). The investigation of these complaints may be supervised at the PCA's discretion. In 1989, they received 4,449 such cases (96 per cent of them alleging assault) and decided to supervise about 330 of them.

110

—Any other complaints which the 'appropriate authority' (i.e. in most cases, the Chief Constable) deems it proper to refer to the PCA, or which a member decides to 'call in' (Sections 87(1)(b) and 87(2)). In 1989, 64 cases were referred 'voluntarily' by the police and 21 were 'called in'.

—Cases—not necessarily related to a complaint by a member of the public—in which the appropriate authority considers it possible that an officer has committed a criminal offence or an offence against discipline, if it appears that the matter should be referred by reason of its gravity or of other exceptional circumstances (Section 88). In 1989, the PCA received 76 such referrals.

We have already discussed the problem of the 'grey area' between alleged assaults which do and do not meet the criteria for mandatory referral by the police. There is also uncertainty about the borderline between cases falling under Section 87(1)(a)(i) and 87(1)(a)(ii)—i.e. between those referred for mandatory as opposed to discretionary supervision. During the PCA's initial months of operation, a 'deep cut' was interpreted as one requiring at least one stitch/suture. However, in the light of experience, the Authority decided that the threshold of two stitches was more appropriate, as a single stitch was often used in minor injuries for cosmetic purposes. They informed the Association of Chief Police Officers of this opinion, and most forces now categorise complaints on this basis. Even so, there are still some who do not (for example, one senior officer responsible for referrals from a Complaints and Discipline Department told us that he put the borderline at three stitches and another that he used his 'common sense') and PCA members quite often write back to forces asking them to reclassify complaints. Although most comply willingly, this again highlights the point that it is the *police*, rather than the PCA, who have most of the final decision on referral—a somewhat unsatisfactory position, we feel.

Members are sometimes hampered in other ways by the classification of complaints. For example, it is stated in PACE (Section 89(1)(a)) that the PCA must supervise the investigation of any complaint *alleging* that the conduct of an officer resulted in serious injury. This means that if it later transpires that the injuries are not as serious as first thought, the Authority must continue to supervise. On the other hand, efforts to avoid this difficulty can themselves run into problems. The PCA was for some time concerned that some forces were waiting for confirmation of serious injury before referring cases under S.87(i)(a)(i)—thus denying members the opportunity to commence immediate supervision if they so wished (and, incidentally, failing to meet the legal requirements of early referral). There seems to be a good case here for at least minor changes in the referral and supervision rules: perhaps, for example, the PCA should be given the right to reclassify cases themselves in the light of new information. (The police, then, could safely be encouraged to follow the principle 'if in doubt, refer'). Whether there should be more fundamental changes—for instance, removing the rules on mandatory supervision entirely—is a matter for later consideration (see Chapter 11).

(ii) *The preponderance of assaults*

We now turn to the substance of allegations referred to 'I' Division. First and foremost, as one would expect from the rules on referral, a very high proportion of the cases these members deal with include allegations of *assault*. In 1989, over 93 per cent of all cases referred for possible supervision included such a complaint. By far the most common individual complaint was that of assault occasioning actual bodily harm—appearing in 4,253 of the total of 5,008 cases of all kinds referred in that year. Among the remainder, the largest official category was complaints alleging miscellaneous serious arrestable offences (110 cases). There were also 86 cases in which corruption by a police officer was alleged (PCA 1990: Appendix Table C).

We shall show in Chapter 9 that members are much more likely to select non-assault rather than assault complaints for supervision when they have a choice. Even so, because the majority of cases which members supervise start life as Section 87(1)(a)(i) referrals, we calculate that *at least three-quarters of their supervised caseload consists of assault investigations*. This has significant consequences for the kinds of situation members typically find themselves examining, the kinds of complainant involved, and the types of evidence most commonly available.

As already shown in Chapter 3, complaints of assault have quite a different 'profile' from other categories of complaint. While most complainants in non-assault cases have not previously come to the notice of the police, and quite a high proportion have a middle-class background, the great majority of complaints of assault are made by young working-class men with criminal records and arise out of confused situations on the streets which have resulted in their arrest (see also Maguire and Corbett 1989). We have also noted that assault cases tend to be particularly difficult to prove against officers, and their substantiation rates are considerably below average. There are rarely any independent witnesses, so that, apart from the (usually inconclusive) medical evidence, decisions often have to be based on the conflicting stories of, on the one hand, the arresting officer(s) and, on the other, complainants (and perhaps their companions) lacking the ideal qualifications for credibility in a court or disciplinary hearing.

The extent to which the PCA is obliged to concentrate upon complaints of assault may well be justified in terms of its deterrent value to police officers tempted to use violence, or simply as a symbolic statement that any such behaviour by the police is seen as totally unacceptable by society, but some less desirable consequences are possible and must be considered. The necessity of devoting time to cases which, though serious, are, realistically, 'going nowhere', may result in others with higher chances of substantiation not receiving the benefit of supervision. Again, the fact that such a low percentage of cases results in any finding of wrongdoing by the police may gradually undermine public confidence in the PCA, most people being unaware of the technical difficulties of proving unjustified assault.

3. Supervised cases

Having attempted to locate the flow of cases to the PCA within the full picture of complaints dealt with by police forces, we now narrow the focus and consider the special group of cases which are supervised by members of the PCA. We shall look at the circumstances of these cases in some detail, for two reasons. First, it will provide a flavour of members' work. And secondly, it will help us discover whether the combination of the referral rules and members' decision-making (discussed in Chapter 9) achieves the objective of ensuring, as far as possible, that the PCA, with its limited resources, supervises the investigation of only the most serious complaints in England and Wales.

As described in Chapter 1, we took a stratified sample of 100 cases from PCA files, consisting of:

 (i) 40 cases supervised mandatorily under S.87(1)(a)(i)—i.e. complaints amounting to allegations that the conduct of police officers led to the death of, or serious injury to, members of the public.
 (ii) 40 cases referred under S.87(1)(a)(ii), (1)(b) or (2)[7] and subsequently selected for supervision. These include allegations of assault occasioning actual bodily harm, corruption and other serious arrestable offences (which must be referred), as well as other complaints referred voluntarily by the police or 'called in' by the PCA.
(iii) 20 cases selected for supervision after referral under S.88—i.e. matters not necessarily relating to a complaint, but which the police wish to investigate under PCA supervision.

We shall examine the nature of the cases in each of these categories in turn, finishing with a broad comparison between them.

113

(a) *Cases under mandatory supervision*

All 40 of our sample of mandatorily supervised cases included an allegation of assault. In 38 of the 40 cases, the alleged assault was directly connected with an arrest—i.e. occurring either immediately before an arrest or shortly afterwards (including in police vehicles or cells). Indeed, both of the other two cases were indirectly related to arrests: one incident occurred in court cells and the other in a police station visited by the complainant in connection with an earlier arrest.

The locations of all 40 incidents are shown in Appendix Table A. In 31 of them, an initial assault by the police was said to have taken place at the scene of an arrest—usually in the street—and in seven of the other nine, in a vehicle conveying arrested prisoners to a police station. Eight cases (20 per cent of the total) included allegations of assault within a police station, but in six of these, a prior assault had also been alleged outside.

Table 9 shows the circumstances which led up to the alleged assaults by the police, as well as the offences for which complainants (or individuals on whose behalf complaints were made) were arrested. It will be noted that the great majority of the complaint incidents arose from 'unplanned' arrests, and also that arrests for 'crime' were less common than public order arrests. Only three of the incidents followed visits to complainants' homes made specifically to effect an arrest, and three others followed 'stake outs' of premises after information that a burglary or robbery was planned. In most cases, police officers had either stopped someone in the street on suspicion of an offence of a relatively minor nature, or had been called to the scene of some form of public disorder. And in a large proportion of these, the main reason for arrest seemed to be the reaction of the complainant to the police intervention: in 19 cases (48 per cent of the total), the only offences for which arrests were made were assault on a police officer, drunk and disorderly, or breach of the peace.

It can also be seen in Table 9 that 14 of the 40 incidents were initiated by, as it were, a 'passing police officer'. These all started as fairly routine interventions and, indeed, only four of them were triggered by suspicion of a notifiable criminal offence, as follows:

1. Off-duty officers saw some boys attempting to break into a car.
2. A PC stopped a young man on a motor-bike (whom he knew) on suspicion of having stolen it.
3. A patrol car spotted a stolen car and gave chase.
4. An officer saw a man climbing through the window of a house (as it happened, his own).

Another four of the fourteen began with a driver being stopped on suspicion of drink driving or other road traffic offences. The other six

Table 9: Circumstances of arrests and alleged assaults by police: cases under mandatory supervision

| | Main offence for which complainant arrested | | | | | |
How incident initiated	*'crime'* (burglary, robbery, criminal damage)	*public order* (drunk and dis/breach of peace/assault on police)	*traffic* (drunken driving, faulty vehicle)	*other* (breach bail, etc)	*no arrest*	*total cases*
police approached complainant	4	4	4	2	–	14
complainant approached police	–	2	–	–	1	3
police called to scene	3	13	–	–	–	16
pre-planned arrest/surveillance	6	–	–	–	–	6
argument in court cells	–	–	–	–	1	1
	13	19	4	2	2	40

involved interventions by police officers alerted by miscellaneous minor incidents. In almost all cases, mutual antagonism soon escalated into a fight or struggle in which both sides alleged violence by the other. The circumstances of these last six cases were, in brief:

1. A group of teenagers walking home from a pub shouted at a police car that it had no lights and one was arrested for being 'drunk and disorderly'. He alleged that he was assaulted on arrival at the police station.
2. A PC spotted a young man in the street whom he knew to be under curfew. The man ran away and alleged he was assaulted when caught.
3. Three British Transport police officers on duty at a main line station approached a man who was under the influence of alcohol. After a struggle, he was arrested for being drunk and disorderly.
4. Two PCs on a car patrol went to a piece of waste ground and chased young motor-cyclists who were causing a nuisance. One was allegedly hit with a truncheon.
5. A man recognised by a PC while waiting at a railway station was asked what he was doing. A fight ensued, after which the complainant was charged with assault on the police.
6. A group of diners at a restaurant sitting opposite a group of off-duty policemen remarked that there was a 'smell of pork'. A fight developed, after which the diners were charged with assault on the police.

Three other cases also arose from fairly inconsequential police-public contacts, the difference being that these were initiated by the member of the public, in each case intoxicated:

1. A man under the influence of alcohol offered to assist a PC in adjusting roadworks signs, and after an altercation was arrested for being drunk and disorderly.
2. A man who had been drinking went to a police station to complain about an inadequate police response to a burglary and after an argument was arrested for being drunk and disorderly.
3. A man went to a police station to ask about a future court appearance and after an argument was allegedly thrown out of the door. (He was not arrested).

Lastly, in sixteen incidents where the police presence was in response to calls from the public, the subsequent arrests, again, rarely related to criminal offences. Three followed chases of suspected burglars, but the remaining thirteen arose from situations of public disorder. Seven of these were incidents involving crowds or

116

gatherings of people (fights outside pubs, at football matches, etc.), three were 'domestic disputes' and three were cases of perceived anti-social behaviour in individuals affected by drink or drugs. (Alcohol, in fact, was a recurring theme throughout the reports: in 17 of the 40 cases, somebody involved was clearly intoxicated, and in a further ten, consumption of alcohol was mentioned in the report—though this was disputed by several complainants.

Complainants in mandatorily supervised cases were, generally speaking, younger than other complainants, more of them had previous convictions, more were working-class, and more were male. This remained true, though not so markedly, even when just the assault cases were compared between the mandatorily and discretionarily supervised samples (see Appendix Table 8).

Virtually all (98 per cent) of the officers complained against in mandatorily supervised cases were male, and four out of five were of constable rank. Our finding from local samples (Chapter 3) that officers in their 'early middle' years of service are more likely to be complained against than those at the beginning or end of their careers, was echoed in this analysis, as was the prominence of Support Groups among their postings: 21 per cent of the PCs were in such a group. Complaints against Sergeants were also quite common in serious assault cases, although they were less likely to figure in the core complaint: just under half had been acting as custody officers, and most of these had attracted only subsidiary complaints.

A final point to make about the serious assault cases is that relatively few involved the 'one-to-one' situation of a lone complainant confronted with a single officer. In fact, there had been at least two officers present at more than nine in every ten incidents, and in over 80 per cent either the complainant had been with companions or other members of the public had been present. But while this meant that there were often witnesses to interview, most people who actually saw what happened were from one or other 'side'—a fact with important consequences for the chances of complaints being substantiated. Totally uninvolved people had been present at the scene of at least half of the relevant incidents, but in only eight of the 40 cases were any able to contribute an eye-witness account of the crucial moments. In the remainder, they were either unable to help or were not found by the police investigator.

This last point underlines a key difference between complaint investigations and ordinary crime investigations: in the latter, police officers tend to take the names and addresses of bystanders, while this is obviously rarely done at the scene of incidents which later result in complaints. It might also be significant for the chances of substantiation that complainants (and any companions) had been outnumbered

117

by officers in most cases, while in one third of incidents just one complainant had been alone with a group of officers.

In sum, it can be said that the majority of what are considered the most serious complaints against the police—those mandatorily supervised by the PCA—arise from fairly mundane policing situations. Although four out of five complainants have one or more previous convictions, only about one-third of the cases are associated with accusations against them of notifiable criminal offences. Much more often, they arise out of a confrontation—frequently late in the evening and exacerbated by alcohol—over a relatively minor incident in which the use of violence by one or both sides escalates to a major level. About one in six complaints arise from police reactions in confused—and possibly frightening—crowd scenes, but in most cases the complainant is alone or with a small group of friends, 'outnumbered' by police officers.

(b) *Discretionarily supervised cases*

Among the 40 supervised Section 87(i)(a)(ii) cases in our sample (i.e. those *selected* for supervision), only half included an allegation of assault. Twelve of these twenty cases were fairly directly 'arrest-related', occurring either at the scene of an arrest or in a police vehicle or police station. Two of the remaining eight were complaints of assaults upon prisoners on remand, but, in contrast to the mandatorily supervised cases, there were also six in which the complainant was *not* arrested. The circumstances of these six cases were:

1. A group of officers controlling a major crowd incident allegedly assaulted a television camera crew who were filming the scene.
2. An officer allegedly raped a woman in her home after visiting her on official business.
3. An officer allegedly indecently assaulted a woman, after calling to follow up a previous visit occasioned by a minor disturbance.
4. A spectator was hit with a truncheon during a football match.
5. A passer-by was hit with a truncheon during a disturbance outside a football ground.
6. A police officer was accused of corrupt dealings with a businessman. There was also an associated complaint of a minor assault.

The injuries caused in the discretionarily supervised assault complaints were, by definition, less serious than those in mandatorily supervised cases. Moreover, they seemed to us fairly 'routine' by the standards of most complaints of assault passing through Complaints and Discipline departments. As we shall show below, only two of the twenty stood out as clearly worthy of supervision on the grounds of the degree of injury alone. One must look elsewhere for the factors

118

which persuaded members to select them—a subject to which we return in the next chapter.

The other 50 per cent of our sample of discretionarily supervised cases did not involve a complaint of assault. Seventeen of these twenty cases arose from complex situations in which the complainant alleged criminal offences by police officers, mainly bribery, corruption, perjury or attempts to pervert the course of justice. A few illustrative examples are given below:

1. Two officers purported to be the complainant's solicitors in order to gain access to him while he was awaiting trial at court, allegedly in order to persuade him to withdraw his previous complaint of assault (already being mandatorily supervised).
2. A complainant alleged that an officer asked for money to drop outstanding drug charges against her.
3. Two off-duty officers involved in a traffic accident with the complainant were said to have conspired to obstruct the officer investigating the accident.
4. The complainant, an area manager of a large supermarket chain, complained that an officer tampered with price labels in an attempt to have shoplifting charges against his wife dropped.
5. An officer was alleged to have offered to replace the complainant's stolen silverware at a discount price.
6. Two officers were alleged to have perjured themselves when giving evidence about a traffic accident in which they had been involved, where the complainant's daughter had been killed.
7. An officer was alleged to have taken a 'pay off' from the complainant as part of a 'protection racket'.

The remaining three cases all included a complaint of irregular procedure, amounting to possible disciplinary rather than criminal offences. The circumstances of these were:

1. The complainant, a woman visiting her husband in prison, was strip searched for drugs by police officers.
2. The parents of a young Asian boy complained that certain irregular procedures were used following the arrest of their son.
3. The complainant, a 17 year old girl, claimed that she had been denied access to her solicitor during an interview about her knowledge of matters unrelated to the offence for which she had been arrested.

As a whole, then, the non-assault cases were diverse in character, but most commonly entailed complaints of fairly serious offences of dishonesty. Unlike the mandatorily supervised assault cases, in which investigations were usually confined to establishing what happened during a few seconds of violent activity, a number had fairly wide and complex ramifications. Direct witnesses were rarer than in assault cases: only seven of the twenty files included statements of other people present during the crucial contact between officer and complainant. However, most contained statements from a wide variety of police and other sources, and the final reports were often among the longest and most detailed of all.

The complainants were also distinguishable as a group from those alleging a serious assault. Fewer of them (half, as opposed to 80 per cent) had a previous conviction; three-quarters (in contrast to one-third) were aged 30 or over; one-third were female (compared with only five per cent); and one in six were employed in a professional or executive post (compared with one in ten). Indeed, among the various types of case dealt with by 'I' Division, these discretionarily supervised non-assault cases (which made up well under 20 per cent of their supervised caseload) were the only ones in which the complainants were anything like representative of all complainants in terms of age, sex, and social class.

Finally, the most pronounced difference between the officers figuring in these 'dishonesty' or 'irregularity' cases and the officers named in 'assault' cases, was that police constables were much less likely to be involved. Those complained against mainly comprised detective constables (18 per cent), detective sergeants (14 per cent), police sergeants (11 per cent) and other higher ranking officers (18 per cent). About a third were serving as CID officers. As one might expect from the above, the average length of service was also considerably higher: nearly 60 per cent of officers in these often complex cases had ten or more years' service, and over a third had served for more than fifteen years.

(c) *Cases referred under Section* 88

Incidents are referred to the Authority under Section 88 by virtue of their gravity or exceptional circumstances, and do not require a complaint to have been made. The Authority then has discretion whether or not to supervise: so far it has done so in 70 to 80 per cent of cases. A key feature of Section 88 cases is that the terms of reference for the police investigation can be made much wider than in straightforward complaints cases. In practice, this means that the investigating officer is able to consider matters not directly related to possible offences committed by officers. For example, in cases arising out of the policing of demonstrations or picketing, the terms of reference can go beyond the determination of whether Officer A struck Complainant B, to include questions about the deployment, tactics and supervision exercised by senior officers.

Cases were referred under this Section in varying circumstances: for example, immediately after deaths or other major incidents involving the police, even though no complaint had been made; when a complaint was withdrawn in favour of a civil action, but the police wished the investigation to continue; and following incidents which raised questions about controversial areas of police policy. Although Section 88(b) states that matters referred should not be the subject of a complaint, a fair number of the Section 88 case files we analysed did in fact contain one. Whereas in most of these an original complaint had been withdrawn or a new complaint had been added some time after Section 88 referral, we did find one or two where it seemed that the case should, strictly speaking, have been referred under a different Section, but Section 88 had been used in order to achieve a wider ranging investigation.

Police forces quite often refer cases under Section 88 even though they have no reason to suspect any police misconduct. This is simply because the involvement of the Authority is seen as beneficial to them, which is particularly true of deaths in custody and police operations that attract adverse publicity. In such cases, referral to the PCA can be a useful means of reducing any immediate pressure from the media, demonstrating that the force wishes to establish the truth and has 'nothing to hide'. Later, too, the issue of an Interim Statement, attesting to the Authority's satisfaction with the investigation, can be presented as a kind of 'good house-keeping certificate'.

As can be seen from Table 10, the main distinguishing feature of the Section 88 cases in our sample was that over half involved the death of a member of the public. Seven of the eleven deaths had occurred in police custody or shortly after release. However, only one of these carried any serious suggestion that rough handling or assault by officers had contributed to the death—this being the only one with an associated complaint. Elsewhere, the main question to be

Table 10: Characteristics of Section 88 Cases

Subject of investigation	At point arrest	Arrest-related In or after custody	No arrest	Total cases
Death	2	7	2	11
Alleged assault	2	1	1	4
Other	0	1	4	5
Total	4	9	7	20

addressed by investigators was whether there had been any neglect of duty: most commonly, prisoners had died in police cells after being detained while drunk or otherwise unwell. The remaining four deaths included two in car crashes (one following a police chase) and one thought to be suicide as police were trying to make an arrest. The last one involved failure to protect a woman from a man who was trying to kill her.

Altogether, only four of the eleven deaths attracted any significant national publicity, but most aroused some concern in the local press. Moreover, several of the investigators' reports mentioned local anger or rumours and suspicion among people who had known the deceased.

The Section 88 cases in which no death was involved constituted a very mixed bag. Although none featured prominently in the national press, and only one or two raised any local media interest, this does not detract from their potential seriousness. Unlike the deaths, seven of the nine were associated with complaints. In three of these cases, the complaint was added after an initial referral under Section 88, and in another—apparently due to an oversight—it had been made long before but not referred to the PCA. The remaining three had started as ordinary complaints, being converted to 'Section 88s' after the complainants withdrew, deciding to pursue civil actions rather than co-operate with a police inquiry (cf. Chapters 2 and 11).

There were, again, a number of assault allegations (Table 10), but investigations were also undertaken into complaints of irregular disclosure of information, harassment, mishandling of a rape investigation, and unlawful arrest. The following are illustrative of the range of cases:

1. Following the execution of a search warrant, a family complained that they had been unlawfully arrested and detained and that criminal damage had been caused to their home. They later withdrew the complaint, deciding on a solicitor's advice to pursue a civil action instead. The police then referred the matter as a 'Section 88', and the PCA agreed to supervise 'in the public interest'.
2. A police officer came under suspicion of having been working as a private investigator in conjunction with a civilian, improperly disclosing information gained from the Police National Computer.
3. Apparent blunders in a rape investigation became the subject of an internal investigation before being referred as a Section 88 case. The terms of reference included examination of the

adequacy of supervision and training for officers involved in rape investigations.

4. The case had originally been the subject of a complaint of robbery and assault by police officers. Due to an oversight, this was not referred to the PCA until a very late stage, when beginning to attract publicity. It was then referred under Section 88 'in the public interest'.

Although complaints from the general public had played a part in only a minority of Section 88 cases, individual officers were quite often under some form of investigation. Unsurprisingly, in view of the number of deaths in custody, custody officers comprised a significant proportion of these, while CID officers accounted for over a third. There were too few complainants or 'injured parties' in the Section 88 cases to allow any meaningful analysis of their characteristics.

(d) *Comparative seriousness of injuries in mandatorily and discretionarily supervised cases*

The PCA is obliged to supervise any complaint referred under Section 87(1)(a)(i) in which the resulting injury is 'serious' as defined under S.87(4)—i.e. involves 'a fracture, damage to an internal organ, impairment of bodily function, a deep cut or a deep laceration'. However, as mentioned earlier, vagueness in this definition sometimes caused the police to refer cases under what PCA members considered the wrong sub-section. Furthermore, even when members had no quarrel with the referral decision, they were sometimes irritated by having to supervise cases involving hairline fractures or small cuts in which stitches had been used. Most favoured changes in the law to allow them to dispense with supervision in such cases when it seemed unnecessary. We examined the extent of injuries giving rise to complaints of assault in our two samples, to see what differences there were in the types and seriousness of the injuries caused, and to estimate what proportion of our mandatorily supervised sample members might have chosen to supervise, had the choice been available to them.

Table 11 confirms that most complaints of assault which were supervised compulsorily involved much more serious injuries than those given discretionary oversight. However, there were several exceptions. Three Section 87(1)(a)(i) cases, originally referred as fractures, turned out after further medical examination to involve only cuts, bruises or grazing. And among the discretionarily supervised cases, one included a hairline fracture (which, strictly speaking, should have been referred for mandatory supervision) and another

123

Table 11: Range of injuries present among complainants of assault: mandatorily and discretionarily supervised cases

	Mandatorily supervised (S.87(1)(a)(i))	Discretionarily supervised (S.87(1)(a)(ii), (1)(b) or (2))
Death	1	–
Fracture	17	–
Hairline fracture	3	1
Stitches	13	–
Bodily impairment	1	–
Broken teeth	2	–
Cuts, bruises, grazing	3	16
Alleged sexual assault	–	2
Knocked unconscious	–	1
Total	40	20

entailed a man having been knocked unconscious. Two others were clearly serious in that they involved allegations of sexual assault.

We shall show in Chapter 10 that the decision to supervise is by no means always related to the degree of injury alone. Even so, it is clearly one important factor and we suggest that, in perhaps half the S.87(1)(a)(i) cases, members would have considered it a sufficient factor on its own. Arms or legs were broken in five cases, jaws or cheekbones in four, and in six others five or more stitches were necessary. Indeed, the only cases in which it might be argued that the injuries were not sufficiently serious were the six which turned out to involve only cuts and bruises or hairline fractures, and perhaps the three with broken fingers or toes.

NOTES

1. The figure of 28,000 is based on police returns. However, there is probably some undercounting in withdrawn cases, particularly, and the 'true' figure may be in the region of 35,000 complaints (see also footnote to Figure 1).
2. This Regulation (of the Police (Complaints) (Mandatory Referrals) Regulations 1985, SI 1985 No 673) requires police forces, in addition to complaints of death or serious injury (which qualify for mandatory supervision), to refer to the PCA for possible supervision all allegations which, if proved, could render police officers liable to criminal charges of assault occasioning actual bodily harm, corruption or any serious arrestable offence (see Appendix 2).
3. In fact, this proportion is only slightly below the average for 1987 of 7.6 per cent.
4. PCA Annual Report 1989 (PCA 1990: Appendix C).

5. Withdrawals also filter out a disproportionately high proportion of complaints of assault. The police statistics, it will be remembered, are based on all forces except the Metropolitan Police Department.

6. One final point of interest about 'D' Division cases is that 37 per cent of dispensations from the requirement to investigate were granted in complaints of assault. This is in accordance with a general finding we have made that complaints of assault are more likely to be withdrawn than other types of complaint (see also Chapter 3.) Our best estimate is that in 1987 there were 7,400 complaints of assault, of which 4,000 (54 per cent) were eventually withdrawn or not proceeded with. By contrast, only 7,500 (37 per cent) of the remaining 20,500 complaints were withdrawn. In terms of cases, we estimate withdrawn cases to comprise 57 per cent and 34 per cent of assault and non-assault cases, respectively (cf. Figure 1).

7. Among these 40 cases, 30 had been referred under S.87(1)(a)(ii), eight under S.87(1)(b) and two under S.87(2). Eighteen of the thirty S.87(1)(a)(ii) cases fell under Regulation 4(1)(a), two under 4(1)(b), and ten under 4(1)(c). For explanations of these categories, see Chapter 1 and Appendix 2.

CHAPTER 9

Supervision by the PCA

The feature which most obviously distinguishes the present from any former system of dealing with complaints against the police in the UK is the introduction of a 'lay' supervisory element into investigations. While critics have characterised it as mere window dressing, representing no meaningful change, this development is regarded by some policy-makers as the best compromise solution to the argument over whether investigations should be conducted by the police or by outsiders. Indeed, some even view it as the best method *per se*, combining as it does the investigative expertise of experienced police officers with the oversight of independent lay persons. We shall not in this report embark upon a discussion of this complex issue, but the findings reported in this chapter may help inform debate. We begin by examining the policies used by members in deciding which cases to supervise. We then look at what 'supervision' actually means in practice. Finally, we address the difficult question of the 'effectiveness' of supervision.

2 The Decision to Supervise

In 1987, the PCA began supervision, as is required of them by law, of 418 new cases referred by the police under Section 87(1)(a)(i). In addition, members received 3,730 cases in which the decision whether to supervise rested in their own hands. These consisted of 3,587 mandatory referrals under Section 87(1)(a)(ii) and 143 cases either referred voluntarily by the police or 'called in' by the PCA (Sections 87(1)(b), 87(2), or 88). Out of the total 3,730 cases, the six supervising members between them selected 333 (i.e. fewer than nine per cent) for supervision. In this section we look at factors which affected the decision to supervise, and note some differences between members in the proportions of cases they decide to take on. We base our discussion mainly upon interviews with members and staff, observation of members at work, and comments minuted in 60 casefiles.

The decision whether or not to supervise is seen as an important part of the Authority's work, and a considerable time can elapse before it is made. The procedure normally followed is that incoming telexes from forces are sent immediately to the Deputy Chairman, who selects some for his personal attention, leaving the rest to be dealt with by the relevant 'I' Division member. (Each member is allocated a group of forces and, unless excessive workload or other exceptional circumstances intervene, handles all the cases from these forces.) Urgent telexes are sent immediately thereafter to members's rooms, but most are assessed in the first instance by one of their support staff, who minutes his or her views on the newly opened file. The member then makes a 'yes', 'no', or 'deferred' decision on supervision and calls for further information. In the case of a 'no' decision a *caveat* is written into each reply to the force, advising that if any new information comes to light which might alter the Authority's decision, this should be passed on immediately. One such situation arose when, five months after a decision had been made not to supervise, a police witness admitted seeing the alleged assault. The Deputy Chief Constable then wrote to recommend supervision 'in light of current media attention on such assaults'. The Authority duly agreed to supervise.

'Deferred' decisions were made in about a quarter of all cases. The usual practice is for the member to call for the custody record, medical reports, photographs of injuries, or the complainant's or other witnesses' statements to be sent as soon as possible. However, this process can take some time, and PCA staff may have to contact the force several times to chase up the information. Even when it arrives, the member may call for further clarification, as occurred in a case being considered while one of the researchers was 'sitting in'. The member still felt unable to make a decision because of the omission of parts of the medical record and because the custody record had no mention of handcuffs being either on or off. (This was important since the complainant alleged he had been kicked whilst handcuffed).

Table 12: Samples of cases selected and not selected for supervision, by whether or not assault alleged

Type of sample*	Assault alleged		No assault alleged		Total	
	N	(%)	N	(%)	N	(%)
Cases selected for supervision	37	(49)	39	(51)	76	(100)
Cases in which supervision was decided against	140	(93)	10	(7)	150	(100)

*Samples taken for our postal questionnaire survey. All cases had been referred under Sections 87(1)(a)(ii), 1(b) or (2) (but not Section 88). The two types shown were separate samples and cannot be summed together.

We pointed out in Chapter 8 that over 90 per cent of cases referred to the PCA for possible supervision concern complaints of assault, but that members elect to supervise a much lower proportion of these than they do other kinds of case referred to them. Table 12 shows that fewer than half of a random sample of 76 discretionarily supervised cases included a complaint of assault, compared with 93 per cent of a sample of cases turned down for supervision. It can be calculated from this that members decided to supervise about two-thirds of the cases referred to them in which assault was *not* alleged, but under four per cent of those in which assault *was* alleged.[1]

This is a major difference, which seems to be explained to a large degree by the seriousness of many of the non-assault cases (see Chapter 9), but partly, it will be contended, by a feeling among members that the latter are more likely to give them something to 'get their teeth into' in the course of supervision. As described earlier, many complaints of assault conform to a general pattern: confused and fast-moving confrontations, often made unpredictable by drunkenness and occurring in darkness, which result in arrests and mutual accusations of violence, but following which there is rarely sufficient evidence to prove the complainants' claims. Members quickly recognise this pattern and, constrained as they are by already heavy caseloads, are unlikely to embark upon supervision of another unpromising investigation unless there is some unusual or worrying element which catches their attention. In the following section we examine some such unusual elements.

(a) *Supervision decisions in assault cases*

What, then, are the factors most likely to persuade members to supervise the investigation of a complaint of assault? From our discussions with 'I' Division members and staff, we concluded that there were four main groups of factors they considered important. These were not part of a formally agreed policy, but ideas on the subject were fairly consistent among members. The first, which might be called '*suspicious*' factors, were relatively rare, appearing in under ten per cent of our casefile sample. They included any signs of a possible 'cover-up' by police—one example being a claim that an assault had occurred at a police station in front of several independent witnesses, while the police officers present insisted that the injuries were caused in an entirely different manner. Another type of situation regarded as 'suspicious' by some members was a complaint of police violence where there was no associated arrest of the complainant.

A second set of factors likely to make members think seriously about supervision concerned the perceived '*vulnerability*' of complainants. Groups mentioned in this context were alleged victims of police violence who were either elderly or very young, who were female, or who were black. With regard to young people, one member commented:

"I take the view that two policemen arresting a fourteen-year-old boy should not cause injuries unless the boy is six foot and fourteen stone—which would be unusual. Even if he's 'resisting arrest' he really should not be injured".

A minute on another case file shows how a 'vulnerability' and a 'suspicious' factor combined to produce a decision to supervise:

"Bearing in mind the age of the complainant and the fact that neither he nor his friend were charged, I have decided to supervise"

In the context of 'vulnerable complainants', it is worth mentioning a case where a new executive officer suggested to the member that because the complainant was a Hell's Angel there was no need for the Authority to supervise. The retort from the member was that 'there's all the more reason for us to supervise'. This response reflects credit upon the vigilance of the particular member. It also raises the important issue of potential biases and stereotyping of complainants.

In Chapter 5, we have drawn attention to a certain amount of 'stereotyping' by police (including investigating) officers—for instance, a belief that almost all complaints by certain kinds of people are made purely in order to cause trouble for the police, or a tendency to treat complainants as either 'deserving' or 'non-deserving' of serious attention, depending upon their background and character (cf. Box and Russell 1975). However, despite the danger, referred to in Chapter 8, of members developing a similarly jaundiced eye, there was no evidence of this in their selection of cases for supervision. Notably, there was no difference between the mandatorily supervised and discretionarily supervised cases in the proportions of 'assaulted' complainants known to have criminal records. In other words, while members might have views about the relative importance of various 'stock' types of *incident*, they did not appear to be 'filtering out' *complainants* because of ideas about their character. On the contrary, some members and staff felt that there might be *more* reason for independent oversight in cases involving clearly 'criminal' complainants, in order to counteract any tendency among police investigators to discount their allegations as a matter of course.

A further type of 'vulnerability' taken into account was that of a person's situation at the time of the incident. PCA members were firmly of the belief that no-one should suffer any injury once in police custody and any complaints to this effect were taken seriously, even if the injuries were relatively minor. Again, if a complainant was handcuffed at the time of an alleged assault, or was apparently assaulted by more than one officer, the likelihood of supervision increased considerably.

A third factor which—with certain qualifications—seemed to increase the chances of discretionary supervision was the *likelihood of a case being substantiated*. Generally speaking, unless there was another strong reason for taking on the case, members were unenthusiastic about supervising investigations in which an obvious lack of evidence made the result almost a foregone conclusion. Similarly, most considered that a long interval between the incident and the date of complaint reduced the likelihood of evidence 'standing up' (e.g. medical evidence would be less conclusive, or witnesses' memories would have faded) and hence were less inclined to supervise. However, despite a general preference for 'provable' cases, this does not mean that they would *always* supervise those with a strong likelihood of substantiation. One member explained his thinking as follows:

"If there are no other witnesses mentioned and no serious injuries I am less likely to supervise than if witnesses are around. If it's obviously an open and shut case then the fact that I might supervise won't make any difference, and the IO will be sufficiently competent. ...But if there are witnesses, I would want to ensure that they were found and anything they said was given proper weight. So, I can see scope for supervision where there are witnesses and vice versa".

The fourth and final set of relevant factors we identified were associated with the notion of the *'public interest.'* These came into play either where an incident had already received publicity, or where the complaint was of a type likely to arouse attention later. Allegations of very serious offences were obviously important here, but we would also include among 'public interest' considerations the less easily definable 'gut feelings' of members that 'this is the kind of complaint we *should* be supervising'—perhaps because it concerns allegations that they themselves find worrying, and which, if proved, would be an affront to their core beliefs about how police officers should behave. Similarly, it was seen as important to keep an eye on some prominent recurrent problems—e.g. the possible misuse of truncheons—by means of supervising relevant cases.

The use of these four sets of criteria in decision-making does not seem particularly controversial, except perhaps the tendency—other things being equal—to choose cases in which the possibility of substantiation seems to be higher. Members were somewhat guarded on this point, and spoke in terms of not taking on 'hopeless' cases rather than of positively selecting those with a chance of a 'result'. Even so, it was clear from talking to them that, like almost anyone who

131

becomes involved in investigative work, one of the ways in which they judged their work was in terms of results. The informal use of the term 'hit rate' among 'I' Division members was one indication of this way of thinking. This is not to say that they derived any less satisfaction from helping to establish that an officer had no case to answer, but they were well aware that the ultimate *raison d'etre* of their job lies in ensuring that police officers who abuse their position of power and trust are convicted or disciplined.

Our general findings on supervision decisions can now be illustrated with a brief analysis of the twenty discretionarily supervised (but not Section 88) cases in our sample which contained allegations of assault. As mentioned in the previous chapter, two of these involved serious injuries (and, strictly speaking, should have been referred for mandatory supervision) and two others included complaints of serious sexual assault. In these four cases, the reasons for supervision were obvious. What, however, had marked the remaining sixteen cases out from the mass of assault complaints referred to the PCA? In most cases, reasons for the decision to supervise were noted on the file, while in the rest we inferred the reasons from discussions with members. The themes of 'suspicious circumstances', 'vulnerability', 'chances of substantiation' and 'public interest' were all fairly obviously present. What seemed to be 'special' about these cases was as follows:

Three had been witnessed by independent observers.
Two suggested possibilities of a 'cover-up' by police.
Two involved alleged assaults on 'innocent' bystanders.
In one the complainant was described as a 'vociferous' journalist.
One involved dog bites.
One also involved allegations of corruption.
Two had been accompanied by strong pleas—from a solicitor and from a complainant's wife—for PCA supervision.
Two related to other complaints arising from major crowd incidents, which were being supervised 'en masse', and one related to another mandatorily supervised complaint.

We could see nothing 'special' about the final case, although it may have been significant that the complainant was female.

Finally, it is worth considering the supervision issue briefly from another angle: how many of the forty Section 87(1)(a)(i) cases in our sample (which members had been *obliged* to supervise) would still have been selected by the Authority for supervision, had the choice been theirs? Again based on our interviews with those making decisions, we estimate that well over three-quarters would have been selected without hesitation. Even leaving aside the degree of injury—

which was severe in many cases (see Chapter 8)—there were numerous elements which would have attracted members' attention. Most obviously, in nine cases truncheons had been used on people's heads, nine others included allegations of assaults in a police vehicle or station, three mentioned struggles but produced no counter-charge against the complainant, and one was an incident in which the complainant's head had been 'repeatedly banged on the ground' in sight of independent witnesses. In other words, although members sometimes expressed irritation at having to supervise 'borderline' Section 87(1)(a)(i) cases, the rules on mandatory supervision are not wildly at variance with members' own notions of the kinds of case which should be taken on by the Authority.

(b) *Decisions in non-assault cases*
Cases referred under Sections 87(1)(a)(ii), 87(1)(b), 87(2) or 88 which did not contain complaints of assault were generally quite serious in nature, being made up either of allegations of corruption or other serious arrestable offences by officers, or of matters referred because the police or PCA considered them exceptional or 'high profile'. It is therefore not so surprising as it may seem at first sight that at least two-thirds were eventually selected for supervision. We found that many such decisions were taken either because of media or local community interest generated by the incident, or simply because the complaint fell into a category felt to be of particular concern. One case of the latter kind arose where, after the execution of a search warrant, the complainant alleged that a large amount of money had been taken from his house. The member commented:

"Where the raid is for drugs, you tend to worry, because there's money involved and it's usually around the place. Quite a few complaints against the drugs squad are for theft. We start with having to be a little cynical, because there's a fair opportunity for a corrupt officer to get his hands on the money".

One category of complaint about which PCA members felt particularly strongly was that of corruption. Allegations of this nature were rarely rejected for supervision, and several members thought that they should be subject to mandatory rather than discretionary supervision. Indeed, in one case in which an allegation of corruption had been made but subsequently withdrawn, the supervising member asked that the matter be referred back under Section 88, minuting that:

"I took this decision because I regard allegations of corruption as going to the heart of the public's confidence in its police".

133

On the other hand, complaints of perjury were not accorded high priority for supervision, partly because, in the words of one member:

"We're finding very frequently that we're being used as a Court of Appeal. We're reluctant to taken them on, because in effect we're usurping the power of the court".

This was almost always the line followed in cases where the defendant had been found guilty. However, other factors could tip the balance. For example, a death incidental to a complaint of perjury led to the decision to supervise in one of our sampled cases. In another, in which a complainant had been charged with numerous traffic offences over a year after the alleged incidents had occurred, the member decided to supervise out of 'intrigue' arising from the statement of the complainant's mother that none of her family could drive! And, as with any complaint, the interest of a Member of Parliament was always likely to persuade the Authority to supervise.

(c) *Consistency*

Since it is entirely the decision of individual members of 'I' Division —albeit with the advice of their administrative officers—whether or not to supervise in discretionary cases, the matter of consistency between members is an important issue. By and large, we found that members took account of the same kinds of factors, although there were differences in the relative weight they gave to each. One member, for example, felt particularly strongly about dog bites, and another thought broken teeth almost as serious as broken bones.

Equally important, there was quite a lot of variation in the proportions of cases which members decided to supervise. Based on our samples, we estimate that, while the average 'positive decision rate' for 1987 was 7.6 per cent of all cases (excluding 'Section 88s') referred for a decision, members' personal rates varied between four per cent and nine per cent.[2] In round figures, one member received 650 such cases during 1987, deciding to supervise 60 of them, while another received 600 cases but decided to supervise only 24.

Assuming that members were receiving roughly the same 'diet' of cases about which to make decisions—and there is little reason to think otherwise—this suggests that they were adopting somewhat different standards. However, it is quite likely that this was to some extent forced upon them by their differing caseloads for *mandatory* supervision. For example, at one point, the member with the lowest 'positive decision rate' was supervising about sixty Section 87(1)(a)(i) cases, while none of the others had more than forty-five. (This situation, of course, derives from variations in referral rates between the groups of forces for which each 'I' Division member is responsible). It could be that, where their mandatorily supervised caseload is especially high, members consciously or unconsciously refrain from taking on cases which they would under normal circumstances select for supervision, principally in order to avoid becoming overburdened.

Two practical changes suggest themselves if 'I' Division members are to become more consistent in their decision-making about supervision. First—rather in the way that magistrates undertake sentencing exercises—members might have formal meetings at intervals to discuss sample cases, agree a clearer policy on the acceptance of cases for supervision and establish more uniform practice. Secondly, if such policies are to be followed consistently, it would seem wise to adjust the 'mandatory' caseload of individual members more regularly, so that more uniform proportions of discretionary cases are chosen. Since our fieldwork period, we have been told that efforts are being made to even out workloads between members.

3. The Nature of Supervision

Once a decision to supervise had been made, the usual practice is to send a standard letter to the Investigating Officer (IO), asking him or her to telephone the member—or a named member of staff—as soon as possible, in order to inform the Authority of the current status of the investigation and to discuss the lines of inquiry proposed. The IO will also be asked to forward any medical reports, photographs, copies of witness statements, or other relevant documents, as they become available. Further, unless there are any matters which the IO feels should be brought to the member's attention in the meantime, he or she is normally asked to contact the PCA every four weeks to update the member on progress.

This is the formal platform from which 'supervision' is launched. However, from that point on, the progress of supervised cases becomes less predictable. It was clear from early on in our research that there were wide variations in the extent and type of attention given by supervising members to different cases, both during the investigation and after reception of the IO's report. Moreover, these variations seemed to be to some degree associated with the different kinds of referral.

In this section, we outline the range of styles of supervision we identified and the kinds of case in which each tends to be used. Our main sources of data are analysis of the files of our 100-case sample, together with notes based on interviews with members, and the experience of sitting at their elbows as they worked.

(a) *Styles of supervision*

The degree of supervision exercised during the course of investigations might be measured in a number of different ways. For instance, one could look at the numbers and types of communications (letters, telephone calls, meetings) between the Authority and the IO and other relevant parties. One could analyse remarks in files by members or staff, to see how often they merely 'note' the reception of documents from the IO and how often they make detailed or critical comments. Or, one could examine the frequency with which the Authority suggests or directs that a new or different line of inquiry should be followed.

None of these may be fully satisfactory tools of measurement on their own, but used in combination, we feel that they give a fairly good picture of the supervisory work of 'I' Division. Between them, they give an indication of the numbers of cases which attracted the three main styles of supervision we identified. We call these *'passive'*, *'active'* and *'directive'* supervision.

Passive supervision describes the minimum level, in which the member simply reads through documents (e.g. witness statements, medical reports, custody records, transcripts of interviews) as they arrive from the IO, responding if necessary, but essentially carrying out a *post facto* monitoring task rather than playing any active role in the investigation. In such cases, apart from, perhaps, an initial telephone conversation, member and IO may have little or no direct contact.

Active supervision is characterized by frequent telephone conversations, and sometimes, meetings, between member and IO, the former keeping in close touch with what is going on, and throwing in comments or suggestions as the investigation proceeds. At its extreme, active supervision shades into what we call *directive* supervision, whereby members request or even formally direct IOs to follow particular lines of inquiry.

We begin by briefly presenting four general findings about the nature of supervision. We then discuss and illustrate the different styles of supervision in more detail, before moving on to consider the central question of how 'effective' they are.

First of all, 'directive' supervision was found to be relatively unusual. We could find only eleven cases, among the 100 examined, in which members insisted that the police took a particular course of action, and only six of these concerned investigative procedures *per se*. It is possible, of course, that members sometimes gave directions in telephone conversations without recording them on file, but it is unlikely that many major points would have been put to IOs without this being noted—the files are fairly comprehensive and it is normal

136

practice to summarize all telephone calls in writing. What is much more likely, is that in many cases direction was made unnecessary by IOs agreeing to members' suggestions—even if, on occasion, privately believing them a waste of time (see later in this chapter).

Secondly, the majority of contacts between the Authority and investigating officers were undertaken by its staff—mainly civil servants from the Higher Executive Officer (HEO) or Executive Officer (EOs) grades seconded to the PCA for a fixed term—rather than by members. A large proportion of such contacts were routine, entailing the sending of standard letters or simply 'progress chasing'.

Thirdly, the vast majority of contacts were by letter or telephone. Face-to-face meetings took place in a significant minority (18 per cent) of the cases in our sample, although, as discussed below, this applied disproportionately to different types of case.

Fourthly, cases referred for mandatory supervision under S.87(1)(a)(i) tended to be handled less actively than those which had been chosen for supervision. For instance, members had personal meetings with IOs in five per cent and 28 per cent of cases, respectively (see Table 13). The difference was also apparent—though less marked—in the numbers of communications between the PCA and the police in the two types of case. Excluding standard correspondence and the passing on of evidentiary documents, fifteen or more letters or telephone calls were exchanged between PCA and IO in 23 per cent of mandatorily supervised cases and in 33 per cent of cases

Table 13: Level of supervision exercised in different categories of case

	Type of supervision		
	Mandatory: S.87(1)(a)(i)	*Discretionary*: S.87(1)(a)(ii), (1)(b) or (2)	S.88
	(N = 40)	(N = 40)	(N = 20)
Type of contact with IO	%	%	%
Meeting	5	28	25
Telephone and letter only	95	72	75
All	100	100	100
Extent of discussion between member and IO			
Considerable	15	25	20
Some	30	35	20
Little or none	55	40	60
All	100	100	100

which had been referred under the other clauses of Section 87. (The latter figure reached 40 per cent in non-assault cases). Section 88 cases showed a slightly different pattern, in that although a quarter resulted in meetings with IOs, communication was overall less frequent and there were fewer lengthy discussions about points of contention.

Table 13 also presents our own subjective assessments of the extent of non-routine communication and discussion between members and IOs in the various types of case, based upon notes in files. It can again be seen that there was more dialogue, at least during the period of investigation, in cases which members had selected for supervision. Possible reasons for this will be discussed below.

(i) *Routine, or 'passive', supervision*

We have seen that in the majority of cases it was not deemed necessary for member and IO to meet, and that in about half there was little discussion, beyond an initial telephone conversation to determine the general path the inquiry would take. In such cases, the minute sheets contained few comments, the member merely 'noting' the arrival of each fresh document.

Despite their relative seriousness in terms of injury, cases referred for mandatory supervision under Section 87(1)(a)(i) were the most likely to be investigated without any major discussions or disagreements between members and IOs. This may be partly because many of them were similar in nature (virtually all being alleged assaults on arrest) and were investigated by the police in a fairly standard fashion, fully understood and broadly accepted by PCA members. Further, unlike some of the more complex 'dishonesty' cases mentioned earlier, the investigation tended to be naturally 'bounded' by the fact that most concerned a short, discrete incident with a specific allegation—e.g. 'Officer X punched me as he placed me in the van.' In almost every such case, the usual plan of investigation—second nature to any IO—is (a) to take possession of any officer's clothing, truncheon or other article which may provide forensic evidence, (b) to obtain medical reports, custody records and photographs of any injuries, (c) to determine precisely who was present at the scene, (d) to locate and obtain statements from as many as possible of these potential witnesses (including, of course, the complainant), and (e) armed with all the above evidence, to interview the officer complained against. In most such cases, then, PCA members were unlikely to dissent in any significant way from the proposed plan of action, nor to be able to add many useful suggestions.

Where dissent and discussion did arise in such cases, it was less likely to be over the general shape of the investigation, than over the

138

way it was being carried out. For example, it was often difficult to find members of the public who were known to have been present, but whose names and addresses had not been taken at the time. (Obviously, the complainant is usually in no position to do this, and police officers make a note of witnesses of arrests only if this is likely to be necessary to support a charge.) Again, there were occasions on which it was not easy to produce a full list of all officers who had been present—or who just might have been in the vicinity. In such cases, there could be some difference of opinion between member and IO about how much effort it was worth putting into tracking down somebody who was anyway unlikely to add anything significant to the investigation.

We noted above that, although there were fewer major discussions in S.87(1)(a)(i) cases, the total numbers of IO-PCA communications were only slightly lower than in discretionarily supervised cases. This is mainly due to the high amount of 'progress-chasing' necessary in *sub judice* cases in particular: in 63 per cent of mandatorily supervised cases, investigations were delayed awaiting related court proceedings, while this affected only 28 per cent of all other supervised cases. Such delays, in fact, could be very lengthy, exceeding four months in nearly half of all cases with related proceedings. Executive officers were asked to check at regular intervals for any news on court dates or other legal developments.

(ii) *Active and 'directive' supervision*
We have established (Table 13) that supervision was fairly 'active' in about half of all cases, and considerably so in about 20 per cent— among which discretionarily supervised cases were particularly prominent. Active supervision—of which we give some examples below—was characterized by frequent telephone conversations with the IO about a case as it proceeded. It was also manifested in 18 of the 100 cases by a face-to-face meeting taking place between IO and 'I' Division member.

Meetings were arranged for a variety of reasons, but were most likely in very serious or 'high profile' cases, particularly those in which officers were likely to be prosecuted. In less serious cases, meetings usually followed correspondence or disagreements about points arising during the investigation. These included failed attempts to trace uninvolved witnesses; lack of co-opération by police witnesses; disagreement about whether an identity parade would be beneficial to the investigation; and questions about the *sub judice* status and whether an investigation could proceed. Occasionally, too, 'I' Division would begin a discussion of wider issues thrown up by the case: examples included the grading of police responses to calls from

139

the public, procedures following traffic accidents in which police officers are involved, and the question of public interest immunity for investigation documents when a complainant brings a civil action against the police.

In addition to meeting IOs, most members had occasionally 'sat in' when witnesses were interviewed (and in one case, at a meeting between an IO and representatives of the DPP where possible charges against an officer were discussed). However, although members would respond to a request for their presence, they did not make a common practice of it, partly out of a wish to avoid possible complications in any subsequent legal actions. It was also difficult, practically, for them to be present at the right time, particularly in forces some distance from London. Even so, presence at interviews seems to us a practice which should be encouraged, where possible. The Authority has noted that this is undertaken in certain cases, 'so as to assure the public of the integrity and sufficiency of the investigation' (PCA 1988a: 1.31). We would add that it might be wise for members to test this for themselves at first hand more often than they do.

Meetings, telephone calls, or lengthy correspondence may indicate complexity or sensitivity in a case, but they do not necessarily signify disagreement between member and IO. On the other hand, a 'direction' usually shows that an IO has failed to agree or respond to a member's earlier suggestions. There were six cases in which IOs were plainly told to take particular steps in investigations—the ultimate sanction, of course, being a refusal to sign the Interim Statement expressing satisfaction with the investigation. These six occasions were:

> The member directed that certain witnesses be found and statements taken (two cases).
> The IO was directed to serve Regulation 7 forms [i.e. the form—without which action cannot be taken against officers—warning them that they may be under investigation and advising them of their rights] on all officers present at the scene of the incident.
> The member insisted that particular witnesses be reinterviewed (two cases).
> The IO was told to register and investigate the original complaint which had been overlooked in the light of a subsequent S.87(1)(a)(i) complaint. He was also directed to obtain the pocket book entries of all officers on duty at the relevant time.

In an additional five cases, 'I' Division members gave other kinds of directions—for example, for the appointment of a different IO (two cases), and in connection with the transfer of an officer under

140

investigation. It should be pointed out that none of the above directions were given lightly or in an unconsidered manner. Before taking such a step, it was common practice to discuss the situation with another member or with the police advisor.

A final point to be made about 'active' supervision is that it is not usually constant throughout an investigation, but tends to appear in 'bursts' as crucial points are reached. In high profile cases there tends to be a flurry of activity by members at an early stage (starting, sometimes, within hours of the incident), in which they may be briefed about progress several times a day, and, if necessary, at night. This was common in cases involving death in custody, although in the majority of these, the issues soon became fairly clear and did not necessarily produce much discussion or close supervision at later stages. During the first five days of one such investigation, the member declined to accept the appointment of an IO from the same force, advised the IO to arrange for a third pathologist in view of a possible disagreement between two others, visited the scene of the incident and spoke to the bereaved family. Another similar case involved the member in early communications (including meetings) with an MP, the Home Office, the coroner, and solicitors acting for the police and for the bereaved family.

It is at such times that the potential of the 'amateur-professional' combination (PCA member and senior detective) as an investigative 'team' may be seen to best advantage—although whether this is the kind of relationship which the system should be aiming to foster is a matter for debate. The following recollections by an 'I' Division member of a particularly important case illustrate the kind of liaison that can occur:

"We discussed it all the time and knew what each other thought. We concluded mutually—I can't say whether it was me or him—that we ought to appeal for any other witnesses to come forward. We decided to do a leaflet which we distributed by hand to neighbouring streets—I think I probably suggested it—that sort of thing. I might have suggested that a greater emphasis was given to some point than he was considering, but I don't recall any such instances when he disagreed. He and I got on very well personally. I respected his expertise. He was more than willing to do everything that was requested. I didn't really have to 'direct' him. He became very sensitive to how the PCA should be seen by the outside world".

In these comments, too, can be seen the blurring of the distinctions between 'direction', 'suggestion', and 'discussion'. In such a relationship—assuming that the member's description of it is accurate—formal 'direction' is unnecessary. The member's respect for the IO's professional expertise, and the reciprocal willingness of the IO to listen to suggestions, make any major disagreement between them unlikely. Of course, whether or not the suggestions with which the member claims to have influenced the investigations were (a) sensible and (b) would have been thought of anyway by an experienced detective, are moot points. Moreover, it would have been interesting to hear the IO's interpretation of their relationship: did he actually carry out a better investigation as a result of the member's suggestions, or was he simply 'humouring' him? From speaking to many investigators, it is our firm impression that it would be an unusual senior detective who admitted to the former. Nevertheless, as we point out later in the chapter, it may be that the fact of supervision— particularly of the active kind we have described—'concentrates the mind wonderfully' and ensures that the investigator gives the case his or her full and scrupulous attention.

(b) 'I' Division responses to IOs' reports

When an IO believes that an investigation is complete, he or she prepares a report and submits it to 'I' Division for consideration. It is read first by an EO or HEO, who then passes it, with comments, to the relevant PCA member. It seems to us an important finding that in 25 per cent of cases in our sample, the member asked for additional information or documents, or for further interviews to be conducted, before issuing an Interim Statement. As Table 14 shows, contrary to the situation *during* investigation (Table 13), members were much more likely to request further action on receipt of reports in

Table 14: 'I' Division responses to investigation reports

	Type of supervision		
	Mandatory:	*Discretionary*:	
	S.87(1)(a)(i)	S.87(1)(a)(ii), (i)(b) or (2)	S.88
Percentage of cases in which:	(N = 40) %	(N = 40) %	(N = 20) %
Additional inquiries and/or re-interviewing requested	43	18	5
Lack of rigour noted in investigation	13	3	5
'Bias' noted in interpretation of evidence	18	5	0
One or more of above responses	48	23	5

S.87(1)(a)(i)—i.e. mandatory supervision—cases than in other kinds (in 43 per cent as opposed to 13 per cent). The explanation may lie in the tendency to supervise this kind of case less actively during the investigation stage.

A similar pattern was evident in comments about the way reports were written up. In 15 of the 100 cases, the file contained critical notes by 'I' Division members or staff concerning lack of rigour or possible bias in the IO's presentation of evidence. Again, such criticisms were more frequent in mandatorily supervised cases (28 per cent) than in others (seven per cent). In most cases, members did not convey their dissatisfaction to the IO, but simply 'noted' it on the file. Their comments, of course, would be read and taken account of later by 'D' Division when the disciplinary outcome was being considered.

The following two examples illustrate the kinds of criticisms made. In the first case, which included allegations of assault in a police station, the member passed the report, with queries, to the PCA's police advisor, who noted that the IO had failed to consider a possible case of neglect of duty. The member wrote back, asking this to be added to the report. He also commented in the file on various 'biases' in the report, including the IO's unquestioning acceptance of a police witness statement that 'Mr X is a persistent drunk and a romancer'. It was noted that no evidence at all had been provided for this allegation.

In another case of alleged assault on arrest, the member wrote back to ask why, if the complainant was apparently 'violent, aggressive and struggling', he had been left alone and not handcuffed. Moreover, although the IO had sent a photograph of the 'injured side of the face', commenting that 'there is nothing to see', the member was not satisfied and asked for the full-face photograph. On hearing that this was not available since it was 'double-exposed', the member became suspicious—and said so in his reply. The IO replied that he found no significance in the fact that the full-face photo had been spoiled. The member's feeling was that the significance lay in the fact that a swelling was more likely to be apparent in a full-face father than a side-view photograph. However, he took the matter no further.

Finally, despite the vigilance demonstrated above, it should be underlined that it is all too easy to miss weaknesses in the large and complex files which accumulate, and that the more people who read a report, the more omissions or unjustified conclusions will be noticed. Thus, while 'I' Division staff or members raised queries or criticisms in a quarter of the 100 supervised cases we sampled, 'D' Division still noted a lack of thoroughness in six other investigations with which the supervising member had pronounced himself or herself fully satisfied. Naturally, unless any errors or omissions noted at this stage are exceptionally serious, the member considering discipline is inhibited by the existence of the Interim Statement from asking for the investigation to be reopened.

4. The Effectiveness of Supervision

We have concluded that supervision by the PCA can be (though by no means always is) very active, even directive, in nature, and that if members consider a particular line of inquiry to be important, they have no hesitation in ensuring that it is pursued. However, questions remain about the overall effectiveness of supervision.

Before assessing 'effectiveness' in any context, it is necessary to define precisely the goals of the activity in question. Where the PCA is concerned, this is not a straightforward exercise, not least because of the existence of several 'audiences' for its work—individual complainants, various pressure groups, senior police officers, officers complained against, the media, and the public in general—all of which need to be convinced that the Authority is not only doing an unbiased job, but one which meets their own particular idea of an effective one.

We now look at the evidence we have regarding the effectiveness of the PCA from a number of alternative points of view. We begin with a brief summary of the views of two interested parties—investigating officers and complainants—about how well 'I' Division does its job (more detailed expositions of their views are provided elsewhere in the report). We then consider findings relating to the outcomes of cases from both our main samples, to see whether any association can be found between supervision and the substantiation (or other results) of cases. However, we emphasize that such an association cannot be taken as proof of cause and effect. Finally, we consider miscellaneous other ways in which supervision might be considered effective, the most important—though data here are limited—being its possible impact upon the faith of the general public in the complaints system.

(a) *The investigating officer's perspective*

We interviewed altogether nineteen investigating officers in three forces. These were either of superintendent or chief inspector rank and were working in Complaints and Discipline departments or 'on division'. Only twelve had direct experience of supervision by the PCA, but all held fairly informed views about the PCA, irrespective of their personal experiences.

We asked all IOs what value, if any, they saw in supervised investigations. Opinions varied considerably. About a third felt that the main value was to reassure the public of the integrity of the investigation—some alluding to this as 'useful for PR purposes'—another third believed that supervision might be useful to them in a high profile case to divert media attention away from themselves (though none had had direct experience of this kind of case). The remaining third could see no value at all in supervision, one referring to it, for example, as 'a complete and utter waste of time'.

None of those who had been supervised felt that this had ever made any difference to the result, nor—except in unimportant respects— to the lines of inquiry they had pursued. One had even found the experience anti-climactic:

"I was quite pleased to have the opportunity of being supervised, to see what would happen. In fact nothing did—it was another myth exploded."

Further, few would accept that they raised their own standards of investigation in supervised cases—a typical remark being, 'I always take a pride in my work, whoever's watching or not'. Nevertheless, it seems revealing that most felt that supervision might act as a safeguard against complacency in *other* IOs' investigations. Again, when we began talking about actual instances of supervision, it became clear that they had not been able to treat the PCA as a distant 'rubber stamp'—they were acutely aware of its presence, as an irritant if nothing else.

Only two had been directed to pursue a particular strategy and both had experienced it as a slight upon their professional abilities. One was annoyed that 'they teach you to suck eggs', and another commented: 'A prisoner was injured and I was asked to interview all officers on duty, whether or not they were in the station at the relevant time. I pointed out that that would be a waste of time'.

More often, however, PCA involvement did not reach the stage of direction, because IOs were generally willing to go along with member's suggestions without argument, however unnecessary or even foolish they privately thought them to be. This attitude is illustrated in the two comments below:

"In one case I disagreed with their first tack, but I would have felt inhibited saying that it wouldn't be fruitful, because I wouldn't want them to think I wasn't being thorough"

"I've had no arguments with them, though you have to bite your tongue sometimes".

145

The perception of supervision as characterized by 'overfussiness' was echoed by several other IOs, the following remarks perhaps summing up their view:

"You need to dot every 'i' and cross very 't' for the PCA"

"You just do everything by the letter to keep them off your back."

Of course, while IOs find this irksome, the above remarks confirm our impression from files and research with members that members and staff are quick to spot any omissions or 'corner-cutting' by investigators. In other words, the PCA want investigations carried out 'by the book' and IOs are aware of this. Most agreed that the department and the IO appointed were 'on their mettle' in supervised cases and gave them priority over other investigations—although, of course, as most are serious complaints they would be quite likely to receive special attention anyway.

The general view of IOs, both from their own experiences and from what they had heard, was that PCA members would not be capable of leading or conducting investigations themselves, but that they were learning, and some had a 'good knowledge of the system'. One member was praised by two IOs for grasping 'amazingly quickly the essentials of investigations'. When asked whether they thought it would be easy for IOs to 'pull the wool over the eyes' of the Authority if they so wished, over half replied that this would be 'difficult'. Others considered it 'possible, although very dangerous'—again demonstrating that the PCA is not dismissed lightly as a group of toothless amateurs.

In sum, in spite of the rather dismissive attitude expressed by a minority of IOs, and the unanimous belief that supervision has no effect on the outcome of cases, at the same time most were mindful and respectful of the Authority's power. IOs' impressions of the members themselves, of their knowledge of the police organization, and of their ability to understand the procedures involved in investigations, were varied, but fairly favourable on the whole. Moreover, impressions were particularly favourable among the four IOs who had met members personally. One of these recalled that he had been 'surprised how good he was' and that he had found the member 'down to earth' and 'a man of the world'. This may be an argument for more frequent face-to-face meetings in order to disabuse IOs of the negative stereotypes some of them hold. On the other hand, some members put the counter-argument that they should not 'get too close' to the police and, while not opposed to introductory meeting with newly appointed IOs, were cautious about the idea of frequent visits to forces. We take this point, but believe that there would be value in members showing their faces during investigations more often than currently occurs.

(b) *The complainants' perspective*

One of the most important viewpoints on the effectiveness of supervision belongs to its consumers—those who have had complaints supervised by the PCA. As described in Chapter 1, we carried out a postal survey of 232 complainants whose cases had been supervised and 150 whose complaints had been referred, but not selected, for supervision. A total of 186—125 and 61, respectively—replied. Their responses to questions relating to 'effectiveness' are shown in Table 15. In interpreting these, and other responses, it must be borne in mind that 46 per cent failed to reply, which may have affected the results to some degree. (A more comprehensive picture of complainant's views will be presented in Chapter 10.)

Table 15: Responses to questions relating to the effectiveness of supervision

	Status of case		
	Supervised*		Not supervised*
	Mandatory (Total N = 79) %	Discretionary (Total N = 46) %	(Total N = 61) %

Q. When you heard that the PCA would be supervising the investigation, did that make you feel

Much more confident	7	12	–
A little more confident	24	31	–
Less confident	30	12	–
Made no difference	40	45	–

that it would be dealt with fairly?

Q. How seriously did the officer who investigated your complaint appear to treat the matter?

Very seriously	25	27	15
Fairly seriously	29	42	37
Not very seriously	29	16	27
Not at all seriously	16	16	22

Q. Generally, how well were you kept informed about what was happening?

Very well informed	4	7	5
Fairly well informed	26	22	10
Not very well informed	34	31	39
Very badly informed	36	40	46

Continued overleaf

147

Table 15—*Continued*

	Supervised*		Not supervised*
	Mandatory	*Discretionary*	
	(Total N = 79)	(Total N = 46)	(Total N = 61)
	%	%	%

Q. Did the investigating officer ever suggest that you might withdraw your complaint?

Yes, tried to persuade me	25	22	36
Mentioned the possibility	32	18	33
No	43	60	31

Q. Overall, is it your impression that the police investigators:

Really tried hard to get to the bottom of the matter?	7	16	2
Did quite a thorough job?	16	18	16
Just went through the motions, making no real effort?	40	44	48
Deliberately went out of their way to avoid the truth?	30	16	26
Don't know	8	7	8

Q. Leaving aside the actual result, how satisfied would you say you were with the way the investigation was conducted?

Very satisfied	3	9	7
Fairly satisfied	21	21	10
Fairly dissatisfied	21	19	35
Very dissatisfied	55	51	48

Q. Having experienced it, have you now more faith or less in the whole complaints system than you had when you first complained?

A lot more faith	3	4	2
A little more faith	4	7	2
A little less faith	8	13	3
Much less faith	66	64	73
No difference	20	11	20

*Based on responses from 125 complainants whose cases had been referred and supervised under S.87 (79 of them supervised mandatorily and 46 at the PCA's discretion), and from 61 whose cases had been referred but not accepted for supervision. Blank or unclear replies have been excluded.

148

The overall message from these responses seems to be that, while the level of faith in the complaints system is generally low, the fact of supervision increases it a little. First of all, over one third of complainants whose cases had been supervised stated that the news that the Authority would be involved had initially boosted their confidence in the fairness of the investigation (though almost quarter said the opposite). At the end of the process, too, those who had experienced supervision were generally happier than those who had not. For example, higher proportions of the former group believed that the IO had treated their case seriously, that he had been thorough in his investigation, and that they had been kept well informed about what was happening. Overall, 26 per cent were very or quite satisfied with the way the investigation had been conducted, compared with 17 per cent of those whose cases did not receive the Authority's over-sight. (Figures on satisfaction with the *outcome* in relation to super-vision will be discussed in Chapter 10).

It may also be significant that fewer respondents in supervised cases reported that the IO had tried to persuade them to withdraw their complaint. This could simply be a function of the greater seriousness of these cases, or it may indicate that the watchful eye of the Police Complaints Authority deters some investigating officers from attempting to 'get a withdrawal'—a phrase we heard several times in casual conversation in Complaints and Discipline depart-ments. This issue will be discussed further below.

Only a tiny proportion of respondents reported that, having experienced it, they had more faith in the complaints system than before. Those with supervised complaints were more likely than the rest to feel this way (eight per cent compared with three per cent), but this does not offset the rather disturbing finding that, even among those whose confidence in the system had initially risen on hearing that the PCA was going to supervise, three in five reported 'much less' faith in it at the end of the day.

Finally, we asked all respondents to 'give in your own words your general impression of the Police Complaints Authority—how inde-pendent they are and how effective'. Sixteen failed to reply, leaving a total of 170 responses. The tone of the replies—examples of which will be given in Chapter 10—was largely negative. Sixteen (nine per cent) of the 170 made comments to the effect that they thought the PCA was, or tried to be, independent. Three of these respondents and only a further nine (together making five per cent of the total) gave replies which indicated a belief that the Authority was at all effective, however they interpreted this question. There was no discernible difference here between those involved in supervised and unsuper-vised cases.

In sum, only a limited amount of comfort can be gleaned by the PCA from these results. Supervision appears to have produced a slightly higher proportion of complainants satisfied with the handling of their cases, but this 'good news' is overshadowed by the prevalence of negative reactions. The generally low levels of satisfaction (with the *process* as well as the result),[3] the belief of a quarter of all complainants that the investigators had 'deliberately gone out of their way to avoid the truth', and the evaporation of faith in the system among many initially hopeful complainants, all present a major challenge to the PCA—as well as the police—to find more successful ways of convincing complainants of the fairness, independence and effectiveness of investigations.

(c) *Outcomes*

We turn now to the difficult question of whether supervision affects the *outcomes of cases*. It is important to emphasize at the outset that there are serious doubts about whether substantiation rates or analogous measures should be regarded as indicators of effectiveness at all. This point was put forcefully by several—though by no means all—members of the PCA. The production of a higher 'hit rate', they insisted, is not a goal to which the PCA should aspire: the Authority is, ultimately in the business of *establishing the truth*, not of trying to prove a complainant's case or to initiate proceedings against as many officers as possible. Moreover, they argued, if a case is simply not provable by the demanding standard of 'beyond reasonable doubt', there is nothing a member can do to alter the situation. While conceding these points, we would argue that such statistics should at least be considered, if only because the question is central to the debate about the desirability of appointing independent investigators to look into complaints. Proponents of this proposal often point to the low substantiation rates produced by the present system, assuming that these are a result of biased investigations inevitably arising from the fact of the police 'investigating themselves' (cf. LSPU 1987). If this is the case, one might predict that, the more independent elements are involved in the system, the more complaints will be substantiated. This whole issue will be considered further in Chapter 11.

Statistics on the outcomes of complaints are among the most confusing and misleading of all figures associated with the police complaints system. They can be based on the proportions of individual complaints substantiated, or of cases which include a substantiated complaint, or of officers charged with (or, alternatively, found guilty of) criminal or disciplinary offences, of officers given advice (including or excluding advice on matters not directly associated with

150

the complaints recorded, and including or excluding advice resulting from unsubstantiated complaints), and so on. We have no wish to venture deeply into these labyrinths, but it is necessary to examine briefly the main differences between statistics produced by the police, the PCA and our samples of cases.

As mentioned in Chapter 3, of 29,312 complaints against the police completed in 1989, only 765 (under three per cent) were eventually substantiated. Of course, large numbers were withdrawn, not proceeded with, or informally resolved, and if these are excluded from the calculations, it emerges that eight per cent of investigated complaints were substantiated.

If one looks at the situation in terms of *cases* rather than complaints, and *'action'* rather than 'substantiation', a slightly different picture emerges. According to the 1989 PCA Annual Report (PCA 1990: 25), 664 of the 5,283 cases completed by 'D' Division in 1989—that is, 12.6 per cent—resulted in some form of action against a police officer. But cases which had previously been supervised by an 'I' Division member were shown to have an 'action' rate of nearly 19 per cent, compared with a rate of only 12 per cent among those which had not been supervised.

The majority of the 'actions' referred to above consisted of 'advice' given formally to police officers by a senior officer (others being admonishment and criminal or disciplinary charges.) Moreover, it is probable—based on calculations from our analysis of casefiles—that in about two-thirds of the cases in which advice was given, no complaint was substantiated.[4] If one looks only at the more serious outcomes—criminal or disciplinary charges brought against officers —the difference between supervised and unsupervised cases is seen to be even greater: about ten per cent of the former produced such a result, compared with only two per cent of the latter.

At first glance, the above figures seem to suggest that supervision substantially increases the chances of a complaint resulting in action against officers. We shall show in a moment that matters are not so simple as this. First, however, we look at data from our samples of PCA cases, in which can be observed differences in outcomes between different types of complaint.

In analyzing our postal questionnaire sample, we weighted results to reflect the actual balance between mandatorily and discretionarily supervised cases[5]. On this basis, we concluded that 18 per cent of all cases had led to some form of action against a police officer. This is a rather higher proportion than the 13.8 per cent of 1987 cases suggested in the PCA's Annual Report (PCA 1988), which may reflect a different method of counting. (It should also be noted that our sample included cases completed in 1986 as well as 1987—though there was little difference between the years). Unlike the PCA, we included advice given to officers which was not directly related to the complaint or complaints recorded, such as when the investigation threw up incidental errors in pocket book entries, or a custody officer had been slow to arrange a medical examination.[6] This difference of approach was also reflected in our own findings on the results of supervised and unsupervised cases: we found the respective 'action' rates to be 33 and 17 per cent (weighted data), compared with the PCA's figures of 22 and 13 per cent for 1987.

Among the 382 cases selected for our postal questionnaire sample, one factor in particular was associated with variations in the outcomes: the presence of an allegation of *assault*. Assault cases were more than twice as unlikely as all others to end in a prosecution or disciplinary hearing (see Table 16 below), and a lower proportion also led to advice being given to officers.

Findings on outcomes from our PCA casefile sample have to be treated with more caution, owing to the smaller number of cases, but they suggest that the *arrest of a complainant* may further lower the chances of a 'result'. In this sample, action (including 'unrelated' advice) was taken in 28 per cent of assault cases in which there had been an arrest, but this was greatly surpassed in cases without an arrest, where eight out of twelve resulted in substantiation, advice or a court case.

Returning now to the questionnaire sample, we present in Table 17 findings which may throw a little more light on the difficult question of whether *supervision* has any influence on the results of cases. As stated earlier, the sample included 150 cases which had been rejected by members of 'I' Division for supervision, as well as 156 supervised mandatorily and 76 by choice. The Table demonstrates

Table 16: Outcomes of cases, by presence or absence of a complaint of assault

| | | *Outcome of cases* | | | |
Main element of complaint	Criminal or disciplinary charges %	Advice, admonishment, etc. %	No action %	All %	(N)
Assault (S.87(1)(a)(i))	5	26	69	100	(152)
Assault (Reg. 4(1)(a))	6	12	82	100	(177)
Other	13	30	57	100	(53)
All	6	20	74	100	(382)

152

Table 17: Outcomes of supervised and unsupervised cases

Type of case	*Outcome* *Advice given:* Prosecution or discipline %	related to complt %	unrelated to complt %	No action %	All %	(N)
Supervised:						
Mandatory supervision						
—assault alleged	5	10	16	69	100	(152)
Discretionary supervision						
—assault alleged	19	5	8	68	100	(37)
Discretionary supervision						
—no assault	13	13	21	54	100	(39)
All supervised						
cases	8	9	16	67	100	(232)
Unsupervised:						
—assault alleged	3	4	7	86	100	(140)
All unsupervised						
cases	4	5	7	83	100	(150)

that, not only did a higher proportion of supervised than unsupervised cases result in action against an officer, but this remained true when the comparison was restricted to assault cases only.

Unfortunately, these findings—impressive as they may look—do not constitute 'proof' that supervision has any effect on the outcome of complaint investigations. As pointed out earlier in this chapter, it is quite possible—indeed, we would say likely—that members select cases for supervision partly according to the likelihood of a 'result', in which case one would *expect* a higher substantiation rate among cases they choose to take on, compared with those they reject. This interpretation is supported by the major difference in outcomes we found between *mandatorily* and *discretionarily* supervised cases involving complaints of assault: among the 'mandatory' group (where, obviously, the element of selection for supervision was absent) the proportion of cases which resulted in criminal or disciplinary charges was only five per cent, only marginally different from that of unsupervised assault cases. By contrast, the equivalent rate for the 'discretionary' group stood at 19 per cent.

On the other hand, if one looks not at prosecutions and disciplinary charges, but at the proportions of cases in which *advice* was given, there is rather more support in Table 17 for the contention that supervision has an effect. This rate was much higher among supervised cases, including—significantly, we feel—those supervised mandatorily. In addition to being free of any 'selection bias', mandatorily supervised cases are generally considered by IOs to have low chances of 'results' owing to the types of situation and characteristics of complainants typically involved. This being so, it was striking to find that advice had been given to officers in a quarter of such cases, compared with only one in eight of unsupervised cases of all kinds.

Taking this further, perhaps the most convincing argument for the claim that supervision has an effect upon outcomes is provided by the finding (Table 17) that *'unrelated'* or *'incidental'* advice (to officers interviewed as witnesses, as well to those subject of complaint) was much more common in supervised than unsupervised cases. While the element of selection may greatly affect substantiation rates, it is unlikely to affect in any dramatic way the proportions of officers under investigation who have committed incidental breaches of police regulations. A more plausible explanation for the differences would seem to be the influence of supervising members on the amount of attention paid by IOs to such breaches.

Certainly, this fits in with comments made by several 'I' Division members that they sometimes had to prompt IOs concerning the scope of investigations. For example, there might be a mention in a complainant's statement that he or she had been denied certain rights under PACE in a police station, but this had not been registered or investigated as a separate complaint (an alleged assault being considered more important). In such cases, members were likely to insist that the subsidiary allegations be investigated fully, and covered in the final report.

At the same time, it has to be said that, with this important exception of 'unrelated' advice, we were unable in our close reading of 100 PCA casefiles to identify any clear instance of actions by an 'I' Division member having made a difference to the final outcome of a case. The various suggestions, requests and directions described earlier—that more evidence be gathered, witnesses re-interviewed, IOs' 'prejudices' ignored, and so on—may have helped produce more thorough or balanced reports, but none seemed to us to have significantly influenced either DCCs' recommendations or 'D' Division's eventual conclusions regarding substantiation and/or disciplinary action. The additional inquiries did not appear to have thrown up any useful new information or evidence.

This is not to say that supervision *never* makes a significant difference to the outcome of a case—although we would assert that this is a rare event. Indeed, interviews with 'I' Division members largely supported this conclusion. When asked whether they could recall any cases in which their intervention had affected the outcome, none claimed more than a 'handful' of such instances, and only two quoted actual examples. It should be emphasized that this is not an adverse judgement of members—after all, if IOs (most of whom are Superintendents with CID experience) do their job conscientiously, one would hardly expect civilians working at a distance from the investigation regularly to produce a crucial 'breakthrough'. On the other hand, it does take us back to the key question of what precisely the PCA is attempting and is able to achieve through supervision, and whether, if it is wrong to judge the effectiveness of supervision in terms of 'hit rates', the success or failure of 'I' Division's work can be demonstrated in other ways. We conclude this chapter with a brief consideration of five other points which might be taken into account in any general assessment of their effectiveness. Some of these have been discussed earlier, but bear repetition in order to draw the threads together.

(d) Other indicators of 'effectiveness'

(i) Reduced withdrawal rates?
We have already presented in Chapter 8 (Fig. 1) our estimate that over 60 per cent of cases rejected by 'I' Division for supervision were eventually withdrawn or not proceeded with, whereas investigations were completed in around two-thirds of supervised cases. Of course, supervised cases generally entail more serious allegations, and it may be that this in itself causes more complainants to 'stick to their guns'. We have also shown (Table 15) that fewer complainants in supervised cases had perceived any 'pressure' (subtle or otherwise) put upon them by IOs to withdraw. This, again, could be partly a reflection of the greater seriousness of supervised cases, more IOs feeling that it is important, from the police point of view, that the matter is investigated. However, our interviews and conversations with IOs suggested that the fact of being supervised by the PCA was an important factor in its own right in the decision of investigators whether or not to 'try for a withdrawal'. Even if they considered the complaint to be a 'complete no-hoper' or a false allegation, they were unlikely to risk any form of 'comeback' by saying so strongly to a complainant. As one put it when we pressed this point:

"When the PCA's involved, you do treat it a bit differently. Quite often if there's obviously nothing in the complaint you can go in saying "Come on, what's all this about?" and so on. But, yes if you've got someone looking over your shoulder, obviously you tend to do everything by the book."

155

He then qualified his answer, putting a point stressed by many IOs:

"But that's not to say I agree that I ever put 'pressure' on people. I explain the system to them and I try to find out whether they still really want to pursue the complaint, now they've had time to think about it. If they do, I accept that, whatever I may think about it personally."

It should be mentioned here that several IOs argued that it is perfectly legitimate to attempt to save time and money through a little 'gentle persuasion', so long as (a) there are doubts about the genuineness or the 'sustainability' of the complaint (an example of the latter being a complaint about minor injuries caused on arrest when the complainant admits he was violently resisting the arrest) and (b) it is understood that, if, after the IO has 'tested the water', the complainant remains determined to proceed, this wish is respected and a thorough investigation is carried out without further question.

If one accepts these arguments, one might be forced to conclude that, even if it could be shown beyond doubt that supervision by the PCA prevented withdrawals, this should not be seen as an indication of 'effectiveness'. However, evidence from our interviews with complainants, together with earlier evidence from Russell (1986) and Brown (1987) suggests that 'pressure to withdraw' may not always be as gentle or as justified as IOs tend to claim, and can on occasion be interpreted by complainants as a form of intimidation. On the assumption that it is more important to prevent one genuine complainant from withdrawing than to save money by curtailing several 'unnecessary' investigations, we would argue that the reduction of withdrawal rates can legitimately be regarded as one indication of the effectiveness of supervision by the Police Complaints Authority.

(ii) *More thorough investigations and reports?*
Although we were unable to identify any cases in which specific suggestions, requests or directions to IOs by supervising members had clearly affected the outcome, it is nevertheless possible that the effect of supervision *per se* was to put investigating officers 'on their mettle'—the result being a more thorough report than might otherwise have been compiled, and consequently perhaps, in some cases, a different outcome. This effect might also be produced in a more indirect manner by the *selection of higher quality IOs* to investigate supervised cases.

Clear evidence on these points is again difficult to obtain. As discussed earlier, the general verdict of IOs was that supervision made no substantive difference to their investigations, although most were willing to concede (a) that it might 'sharpen up' the work of *other* IOs, if not their own and (b) that a supervised case would usually be given priority in their own or their department's current workload—if only because of its seriousness. Moreover, although most began by giving the stock response that they took a professional approach to all investigations and report-writing, whatever the circumstances, a fair number were prepared to admit subsequently (in informal conversations, if not always in formal interviews) that they personally would take extra care to ensure that every possible witness had been interviewed, all the documentary evidence was in the file, and so on. Even so, it was consistently claimed that any apparent increase in thoroughness this produced was superficial—it made no significant difference to the investigation or its outcome.

Another factor which is sometimes affected by supervision—and one which we believe is equally as, if not more important than, the IO's reactions to being supervised—is the choice of investigating officer. In supervised cases, no IO can be appointed without the approval of the PCA, and although local forces' recommendations were 'vetoed' only occasionally (in just two of the hundred cases we examined), it was clear from our research with local forces that in such cases it was common practice to put forward the best investigators available. Once again, it has to be pointed out that as these are mainly the most serious cases, one would anyway expect an experienced IO to be appointed, but, even so, the desire to 'make a good impression' with the PCA was obviously strong, and special attention was paid to selection in supervised cases.

A final indication that supervision may have some influence on the quality of reports comes from our interviews with 'D' Division members and staff. Although by no means all agreed, some said that they had noticed a difference in thoroughness between supervised and unsupervised cases. This was reflected, for example, in the comment that 'I can't remember the last time went back [to the IO] in a supervised case.' However, once again, the difference may be only indirectly related to the fact of supervision—i.e. it could be a function of the selection of IOs, or of greater care taken due to the seriousness of the allegations. Taking all the above into account, along with the finding that 'unrelated' or 'incidental' advice to officers was a more frequent outcome in supervised than unsupervised cases, it seems fair to conclude that supervision does have some 'sharpening up' effect on investigations, reflected—if only occasionally—in more thorough reports. Although this may make little or no significant difference in the vast majority of cases, and may sometimes involve IOs in 'unnecessary' extra work, it is clearly a desirable consequence of supervision, and hence one which can be put forward as an indication of the effectiveness of the PCA.

(iii) *Quicker investigations?*
One of the most common criticisms of the police complaints system over the years has been the length of time it takes to complete inquiries. Unfortunately, there is no clear statistical evidence as to whether supervision expedites or delays investigations. We found that supervised cases in general took longer to reach a conclusion, but this seemed to be largely due to a combination of their greater seriousness and/or complexity. The picture is further complicated by delays due to related proceedings and the attendant *sub judice* rules. For what it is worth, the files on 67 per cent of unsupervised cases and 55 per cent of supervised cases were closed within twelve months of the complaint being registered at the PCA. Investigations of complaints of assault—despite their more frequent delays for related proceedings, were more likely than others to be completed quickly (57 per cent of files in supervised assault cases were closed within one year, compared with 49 per cent in supervised non-assault cases).

The qualitative evidence we have from reading files and speaking to interested parties suggests that supervision does tend to speed up investigations. Admittedly, some investigations were prolonged by the insistence of members on extra interviews, searches for witnesses, or other courses of action considered unfruitful by IOs. However, this aside, the whole thrust of supervision was towards keeping up a good pace in investigation. In cases affected by *sub judice* considerations, IOs were encouraged to do as much as they could prior to the relevant court case and, indeed, members often argued successfully that the matter complained about was sufficiently distinct from the charges against the complainant to make a delay unnecessary. In addition, IOs were routinely asked to report on progress every four weeks, and 'progress chasing' was a regular feature of the PCA staff's work. And as already discussed, IOs tended to give supervised cases priority over their other commitments.

(iv) *More public confidence in the system?*
A final test of whether the PCA can be said to be 'effective' lies in whether it has led to increased public confidence in the fairness of investigations. Past failures to achieve this have already been described in the introductory section of this paper. Some evidence about the current situation can be obtained from the answers to questions we inserted in the 1988 British Crime Survey.

Respondents from a random sample of households were asked, 'If you were to make a complaint against the police, how thoroughly do you think it would be investigated?' A total of 46 per cent answered either 'very' or 'fairly' thoroughly, but there was a substantial minority (25 per cent) who thought the opposite, the remainder being unsure. Similarly, when asked how happy they were with the present system, only 36 per cent declared themselves 'very' or 'reasonably' happy. And to the question of who they thought *should* investigate complaints, under one in six replied that they were content to leave it to the police: the most frequent response was 'an independent lay body'. The above questions drew negative answers from significantly higher proportions of black and ethnic minority respondents than of white respondents.

In the absence of comparable data from the period before the creation of the PCA, it is impossible to tell how much difference, if any, this development has made to the level of public confidence. However, some of the survey responses may be relevant. Under ten per cent of the full sample of householders said that they knew of 'an independent organization which supervises the way police investigate complaints', only one in five of these could name it correctly, and, even when the name was put to them, only 38 per cent of the full sample claimed to have heard of the PCA. It will also be remembered that many complainants were fairly hazy about the Authority's role. All of this suggests that the PCA has some way to go before it can claim to have made a major impact upon public perceptions of the fairness of the system.

NOTES

1. This estimate is based upon figures in Table 3 and paragraph 4.9 of the 1987 Annual Report. If 250 cases were supervised discretionarily (excluding S.88s), about 125 of a possible 192 were 'non-assaults', and 125 of a possible 3,457 were assault cases.
2. One member had supervised 33 per cent of our sample of 76 discretionarily supervised cases, but had rejected only 24 per cent of the sample of 150 cases which had not been supervised. At the other extreme, the corresponding figures for another member were 18 per cent and 33 per cent, respectively.
3. Satisfaction with outcomes is discussed in Chapter 10.
4. The PCA itself makes no reference to 'substantiation'. This is because their task under the Act is restricted to deciding whether or not disciplinary charges are to be preferred.
5. In our sample, the 'mandatory'–'discretionary' division was 156–76, whereas in 1987, 'I' Division members began supervision of 418 mandatory and 252 'discretionary' cases ('discretionary' here excludes S.88 cases). When weighting our sample, we have adjusted it to reflect the latter proportion.
6. The information that advice had been given was not normally conveyed to complainants. For discussion of this point see Chapter 10.

Supervision by the PCA: Complainant's Views and Reactions

The chief source of data for this chapter was our postal survey of complainants whose cases had passed through 'I' Division (see Chapters 1 and 9; the questionnaire is reproduced in Appendix 5). 125 of the 186 who responded had experienced PCA supervision of their case (79 mandatory and 46 discretionary). All cases had been fully investigated, none being withdrawn or dispensed with. 82 per cent of respondents were male, 54 per cent aged under 30, and nine per cent were non-white. 154 had complained of assault, the remaining 32 of other matters. Although we did not collect more detailed information about the cases in this particular sample, it can be safely assumed from our analysis of 100 casefiles (see Chapter 8) that the majority of complainants had been arrested before, during or after the incident in question—mainly for relatively minor 'public order' offences—and that the majority had at least one previous conviction.

In Chapter 9 we have already summarised some of the responses relevant to the effectiveness of supervision by the PCA, noting differences of viewpoint between complainants in supervised and unsupervised cases. Our general conclusion was that respondents whose cases had been supervised were slightly happier than the remainder, but that the overall levels of confidence and satisfaction were uncomfortably low. Here we enlarge upon those findings, considering respondents' early expectations about the way their complaint would be handled, and the extent to which these expectations were actually fulfilled. We also examine their accounts of their original aims in complaining, and of what, if anything, they felt they had achieved.

We then consider the issue of communication between the PCA and complainants, analysing the views of the latter on how well they had been kept informed, what they thought of the tone and clarity of the letters they received, and what general impressions they had formed of the Authority and its work. We conclude with a few findings concerning complainants' impressions of the investigating officer, the effect of their experiences upon their opinion of the police, and their general views about the complaints system and how it might be changed.

1. Expectations, Experiences and Levels of Satisfaction

(a) *The time factor*

It was clear, first of all, that complainants' expectations of the length of time it would take to deal with their complaint had been over-optimistic. Fifty-eight per cent had believed that it would be dealt with within six months and only two per cent had expected it to take longer than one year. As stated in Chapter 9, nearly half the cases in our sample eventually took more than a year to complete, so it was not surprising to find that over 70 per cent of respondents felt that the period had been too long. (Indeed, 45 per cent felt that it had been 'much too long'.) Supervision by the PCA did not seem to have affected complainants' views on this point. Levels of satisfaction with the time-scale were related to the time actually taken, rather than to whether the case was supervised or the extent to which complainants were kept informed of progress.[1]

(b) *Expectation of a 'fair deal': how much fulfilled?*

Respondents' expectations in a more general sense had been lower than among our interviewees in local force areas (Chapter 4). Only nine per cent of the PCA sample stated that, when first making their

Table 18: Complainants' expectations and ultimate satisfaction of dissatisfaction with the investigation*

| | *Expectations: how confident initially in fairness of system* | | |
| | Very or fairly confident | Not very or not at all confident | All |
How satisfied with the way investigation was conducted?	%	%	%
Supervised cases:			
Very satisfied	7	4	5
Fairly satisfied	29	17	21
Fairly dissatisfied	17	21	20
Very dissatisfied	46	58	54
	100 (N = 41)	100 (N = 76)	100 (N = 117)
Unsupervised cases:			
Very satisfied	6	7	7
Fairly satisfied	13	9	10
Fairly dissatisfied	31	36	34
Very dissatisfied	50	48	48
	100 (N = 16)	100 (N = 42)	100 (N = 58)

*Eleven 'don't knows' and non-responses excluded.

162

complaint, they had felt 'very confident', and 22 per cent 'fairly confident', that it would be dealt with fairly. As shown in Chapter 9, the news of supervision by the PCA had made about one-third feel more confident on this score, although almost a quarter said that it had actually made them *less confident*.

Table 18 shows the original optimism or pessimism of complainants whose cases were supervised by the PCA, in relation to their eventual satisfaction or dissatisfaction with the way the case was investigated. It can be seen that, among those who embarked upon their complaint in an optimistic frame of mind about the system, nearly two-thirds finished up being dissatisfied. Disappointing as this sounds from the PCA's point of view, the situation in unsupervised cases was worse: here, 13 of the 16 initially 'confident' complainants (81 per cent) ended up dissatisfied.

Conversely, among those who had originally been pessimistic about the chances of a fair deal, about one in five had been pleasantly surprised and ended up fairly or very satisfied. Again, supervised cases produced this reaction slightly more often than unsupervised cases. Yet, such 'bright spots' apart, the overall message for the PCA from Table 18 is a negative one. The majority of complainants had not expected their cases to be dealt with fairly, and afterwards remained unimpressed with the way the investigation had been conducted. Over half of the whole sample declared themselves 'very dissatisfied' and a further quarter 'fairly dissatisfied'.

(c) *Satisfaction with outcomes*

It will be noted that the measures of satisfaction quoted above refer to satisfaction with the *investigation*. Earlier, we had asked respondents to state their level of satisfaction with the *outcome* of the case. Perhaps not surprisingly, considering the low proportion of cases substantiated, levels of satisfaction here emerged as even lower. Only four per cent of the whole sample were at all satisfied with the outcome, while 85 per cent said that they were 'very dissatisfied'. Moreover, there was no major difference between respondents in supervised and unsupervised cases (see Table 19).

What was a little surprising, however, was that satisfaction with the outcome remained low even in cases in which officers had been found to have acted wrongly. According to PCA files, in 24 (13 per cent) of the 186 cases, at least one officer was found to have been at fault expressly in the matter complained about (seven of these cases had resulted in findings of guilt in court or at a tribunal, and the other 17 in 'advice').[2] Yet only five of the 24 complainants in these cases stated that they were satisfied with the outcome (see Appendix Table C).

Table 19: Levels of satisfaction with the outcomes of cases

	Supervised %	Unsupervised %	All %	(N)
Very satisfied	2	0	1	(2)
Fairly satisfied	2	4	3	(5)
Fairly dissatisfied	11	11	11	(19)
Very dissatisfied	85	86	85	(152)
All	100	100	100	(178)*

*Eight respondents who answered 'don't know' or failed to respond have been excluded from the Table.

Part of the reason for this may be that some complainants remained unaware of, or had misunderstood, the result of their case. (Brown 1987 found a similar picture pre-PACE.) To explore this, we compared the official result of each case (from PCA files) with respondents' answers to our question, 'What was the result of your case—was it found that any officer had done wrong?' The results are shown in Table 20.

We analysed the answers of the 166 respondents who answered this question.[3] Based on the results shown in the official files, we would have expected 18 of these 166 to reply in the affirmative. In the event, 17 replied 'yes', but we were surprised to find that nearly half of these should not have done so—their complaints had not been substantiated and no advice had been given! Apart from total misunderstanding on the complainant's part, the only explanation we can offer is that, in some of the final letters in these cases, the Authority implied

Table 20: Actual and perceived outcomes of cases

	Official result				
	court/trib (guilty)	advice given	unrelated advice	no action/ not guilty	All
Result according to complainant					
Officer found to have done wrong	5	3	1	8	17
No officer found to have done wrong	0	6	16	92	114
Don't know	0	4	2	29	35
Total replies	5	13	19	129	166

that his or her story had been believed, even though the evidence was insufficient to support action—this being interpreted as a finding that 'the officer had done wrong'.

More important, several complainants whose cases had resulted in some form of blame being attached to an officer seemed to be unaware of this. As one would expect, all five whose cases had ended in a finding of guilt at a court of disciplinary hearing knew about it. On the other hand, among 13 cases in which advice had been given to officers on a matter directly related to the complaint, only three complainants seemed to be aware of this fact—or, at least, associated the term 'advice' with blame having been attached to the officer. This, of course, raises the general issue of complainants' understanding of the official terminology of the complaints system, and the success of the PCA in clarifying its complexities to them. We comment on this further below.

The above mentioned confusion about outcomes almost certainly had some negative effect upon complainants' levels of satisfaction. However, it is not the whole story. For, even when we limited our attention to *perceived* outcomes, looking only at the 17 cases in which the complainant believed that an officer had been found to have done wrong, we still found a majority expressing dissatisfaction with the outcome: only six of these 17 'case winners' were very or fairly satisfied, while eight very *very* dissatisfied.

How can this be explained? The only conclusion that can be drawn is that complainants' satisfaction with the outcome depends on factors beyond it being proved or accepted that an officer has done wrong. To investigate this further, we looked through the questionnaires returned by the eleven 'case winners' who were dissatisfied, seeking clues as to the sources of their dissatisfaction. The principal reasons to emerge were as follows:

—Four had wanted charges against themselves dropped, but the complaints investigations had not had this result. (In two of the four cases, however, they appear to have been mistaken about the official outcome.)
—Two felt that the officers had not been sufficiently punished for their actions (one had received 'advice', while the other case had in fact been unsubstantiated).
—Two stated that they had felt disbelieved by the PCA despite some blame having been attached to the officer.
—One was angry that he had not been told what had happened to the officer (he only knew that a tribunal had found the officer guilty).
—One had wanted financial compensation once his complaint had been substantiated.

165

—One had wanted changes in police procedure, not the punishment of an individual officer.

Although the reasons varied, as a group they make the important point that the satisfaction of complainants against the police—at least, in the more serious types of case referred to the PCA—is no simple objective to achieve. Even those who had (or thought they had), as it were, 'won their case' were still likely to be dissatisfied with the outcome, because they had been looking for something more from the system which it is not at present designed to give. While it is clearly not possible to satisfy many of these wishes, it is at least desirable that those who deal with complaints are aware of them. In the next section, we look at complainants' statements about their aims in complaining.

(d) *What complainants really wanted*
All respondents were asked:

"Below are a number of aims you might have had in mind when complaining. Could you show which of these come closest to explaining what you most wanted?"

They were given the list of possible aims shown in Table 21, and asked to state which of them they had had in mind when complaining, and in what order of importance they placed them. As the Table shows, three aims stood out, being mentioned by around three-quarters of all respondents. These were:

—to have the officer punished.
—to have it 'proved that what you were saying was true'
—to 'stop it happening to someone else'

The first point to stress is that these responses are different in one important respect to those we received in interviews with complainants in local force areas, most of whose complaints had not been referred to the PCA (see Chapter 4). The majority of interviewees there did not want to see the officer punished, their most commonly stated aims being to receive an acknowledgement that misconduct had occurred, to bring it to the attention of a senior officer to stop it happening again, and to receive an apology (see also Maguire and Corbett 1989). One likely reason for the difference is that cases referred to the PCA, especially those eventually supervised, tend to involve serious injuries and allegations of conduct which complainants are less able to 'forgive'. Another factor may be the relatively high proportion of complainants with criminal records to be found among cases dealt with by the PCA, who might be expected to feel more than average hostility towards the police. This point is reinforced in Table 21, in the clear difference in the degree of

166

Table 21: Frequency and rank order of complainants' aims in complaining

	Type of complaint			
	All cases		*Assault*	*Other*
	per cent mentioning	% ranking first	% ranking first	% ranking first
Wanted to stop it happening to somebody else	78	22	22	21
Wanted the officer(s) punished	75	26	30	7
Wanted it proved that what you were saying was true	74	30	28	43
Wanted to express how angry or upset you felt	54	5	5	7
Wanted an apology	45	6	6	7
Wanted money in compensation	36	3	3	4
Wanted an explanation	33	1	1	4
Wanted the officer(s) to get a ticking off	25	3	4	0
Wanted the police to drop charges against you	25	2	2	0
Other	8	2	1	7
		100	100	100
	(N = 186)	(N = 169)	(N = 141)	(N = 28)

importance attached to punishment by complainants in assault and non-assault cases. Punishment of the officer(s) was seen as the 'number one' priority by 30 per cent of those complaining of assault, compared with only seven per cent of the remainder.

There were only two other significant differences between assault and non-assault cases in responses to this question. One was that, as one would expect, complainants alleging assault (most of whom had been arrested) were more likely to mention a desire for charges against them to be dropped. Even so, the proportion of them mentioning this aim (25 per cent) would be thought low by many of the police officers we spoke to, who took the cynical view that this was the principal reason for complaints of assault being made at all. But the finding accords with our general impression that most complainants, even those in conflict with the law, are motivated by a genuine conviction that the police have acted wrongly, and that purely instrumented or bogus complaints are in a minority. (It should be remembered, too, that most complainants, even among those with criminal records, are 'first-time complainants'.) The second difference was that those complaining of assault were more likely than the remainder to want money in compensation—though few respondents put this aim first.

Perhaps the most important finding to emphasize from Table 21, however, is that the aim put in first place by the highest proportion of complainants was what one might call the *'desire for justice'*—for it to be 'proved that what you were saying was true'. This also came across to us strongly in interviews with complainants, even when the matter complained about seemed objectively to be relatively trivial. Whether or not their anger was justified, a high proportion of the complainants we spoke to were clearly genuinely angry and upset about the way they had been treated, and some were burning with a sense of injustice. While, if the matter was serious enough, complainants might also wish to see officers punished, their chief desire was an official acknowledgement that their complaint had substance. This being so, the wording of the letter they received from the PCA could be an important factor in the dissipation (or not) of their sense of grievance.

Lastly, fourteen respondents mentioned other aims they had had in complaining, in addition to ticking boxes on the list we provided. These included wanting the officers concerned to be dismissed from the force (four people), getting the incident publically known (two) and getting property back (two).

(e) *What complainants felt they had achieved*
One other area of light which can be shed upon the reasons for complainants' dissatisfaction with the outcomes of their cases comes from the 'free' responses to our question:

"Looking back now over the whole affair, what if anything do you think you achieved by complaining?

Table 22 classifies the responses according to whether they were totally negative or contained some positive comments.

As elsewhere in the questionnaire, a clear majority of responses were uncompromisingly negative. By far the most common reply (made by 60 per cent of respondents) consisted or words to the effect that 'nothing at all' had been achieved, quite often accompanied by cynical remarks such as:

"Only that the police could get away with manufacturing evidence in my case".

"I achieved the knowledge that police investigating police is a farce".

In addition, ten per cent of respondents referred to damaging consequences for themselves or their families, most commonly stress

168

Table 22: What if anything do you think you achieved by complaining?

	Number	Per cent
Negative answers		
Nothing at all	111	60
Brought trouble upon self	8	4
Ill-health/worry	7	4
Other negative	5	3
Sub total	131	70
Some positive element in answer		
Might restrain, make think twice	18	10
Superiors will watch officer(s) in future	7	4
Personal satisfaction that seen it through	6	3
Civic duty/exercising right to complain	4	2
Other positive	5	3
Sub-total	40	22
No response/other unclassifiable	15	8
Total	186	100

or ill-health and feelings that they had been harassed or 'marked' by the police. Examples of such replies were:

"Nothing achieved, a wasted two years of heartache to myself and my family, waste of money".

"Nothing apart from worry, anxiety and disappointment in realising that what I was told, previous to making the complaint, was true, i.e. that nothing would come of it'".

"I've achieved getting more summons and fines for things I haven't done and got myself a lot more trouble than I thought".

"I have caused the police to take a particular interest in me since—not good!".

(Where stress and ill-health are concerned, it is interesting to note that this reaction, like perceptions of the system as remote, bureaucratic and secretive (Chapters 4 and 5), was shared by complainants and police officers alike.)

Among the more positive replies, the most common points made were that it was likely that the officer(s) involved would think twice before behaving in a similar fashion again, and that senior officers would keep an eye upon them in the future. For example:

"I hope I have achieved in making the police officer think twice before taking the law into his own hands, and to take the more serious side of his job!".

"Nothing at all, except that this particular P.C. will have to take more care, more complaints would prove me right".

"A closer look at the officer, by his superiors, maybe?".

A small number of complainants wrote in a more abstract way about the importance of carrying the matter through—whatever the result—as part of their 'civic duty', and others referred similarly to a sense of personal satisfaction in having persevered to the end. Examples were:

"At least I know I tried and didn't just leave it after the court case".

"Peace of mind, knowing that I have at least tried to get something done about it".

"Nothing, but satisfaction in knowing that I had at least tried".

"It is our civic duty. At least it keeps the police aware of the public and I am sure, makes them hesitate, even if the PCA declares them innocent".

"Nothing from the case, but now I know that the PCA are there to help you and try".

Finally, it should be put on record that two of the 186 respondents went right against the flow, expressing total satisfaction with both the investigation and the outcome. The reasons they gave for their satisfaction were:

"It was proved that the officers assaulted me and that what I said was true".

"A thorough investigation".

(f) *What more the PCA 'could or should have done'*
In order to encourage respondents to come up with constructive criticisms, we asked them what more the PCA could or should have done in their case. About two-thirds gave an answer. The most common suggestion (made by about 40 per cent of those who responded) referred to possible improvements in the thoroughness of the investigation. Whether or not the complaint had been supervised made little difference to the answers here. Examples are:

"Yes, they could have spoken to every witness who was on the scene when the assault took place".

"Insisted that the original inspector was interviewed, also made sure that discrepancies in police statements were explained. Contradictory statements were made by police officers".

"They should have questioned the officers in question a lot more closely, and then they'd get the truth".

Another 17 per cent commented to the effect that the evidence should have been tested publicly with both parties present. This accords with the quite common feeling we picked up during our interviews with complainants (and, interestingly, from some of the officers complained against) that there should be more openness in the system, with more access by each side to what has been said by the other, as well as clearer explanations of reasons for decisions. Examples were:

"They should have let a jury decide, not take the view that in their opinion there was insufficient evidence".

"Yes, I should have asked that the police charged me with the crash with the police car. This would have ensured that the case was dealt with in open court and then my injuries would have to have been explained".

"I should have been interviewed with the accused at the same time with my solicitor present".

"They should have taken it to court and had it tried in front of the jury, as they would if a police officer got hurt".

Other comments were less easily classifiable into groups, although the following points were each made by five or more respondents:

—Statements should be taken by non-police investigators.
—The PCA should accompany IOs on investigations and/or sit in with them during interviews.
—The process should be quicker.
—The complainant should be involved more in the complaint process.
—The officer should have been charged, dismissed, or suspended.

2. Communications from the PCA

We now move to the question of respondents' reactions to the information, explanations and other communications they received from the PCA. The most important communication is normally the final letter, which is sent by 'D' Division members to all complainants in whose cases formal investigations have been completed. Although recognizing that its primary purpose is to convey a quasi-legal assessment of the case, members placed great emphasis upon the 'public relations' aspects of this letter, and some spent a great deal of time and care in trying to make it both informative and 'personal' or 'unbureaucratic' in tone.

We asked respondents about the tone of this letter, and how clear and informative they had found it. The results are shown in Table 23.

The tone was interpreted as 'friendly' by fewer than one in ten of all respondents, and by only six per cent of those who had complained of assault. On the other hand, only 15 per cent had found it 'unfriendly', the vast majority describing it as 'neutral' in tone.

Members seem to have been reasonably successful in producing English that ordinary people can comprehend. Just under two-thirds had found the letter 'simple to understand'. On the other hand, while only eleven per cent overall had found it 'very difficult to follow', it seems worthy of attention that this proportion rose to nearly 20 per cent among respondents with complaints other than assault. This may reflect the greater degree of complexity in such cases, and suggests a need for extra attention to clarity when letters are written to the complainants. Finally, although the majority of respondents understood the contents of the letter well enough, almost half felt that it had not adequately explained the reasons behind the decision, and a further quarter stated that there had been 'no explanation at all'

Table 23: Reactions to final letter from the PCA

	%	(N)
Tone of the letter		
Friendly	9	15
Unfriendly	15	25
Neutral	77	132
	100	172*
How simple to understand?		
Simple to understand	64	108
Bit difficult to follow	26	44
Very difficult to follow	11	18
	100	170*
How fully did the letter explain the reasons behind the decision?		
Very fully	8	13
Quite fully	19	33
Not fully enough	49	85
Not at all	24	41
	100	172*

*Non-responses are excluded (the total questionnaire return was 186).

for the decision. Overall, under ten per cent were prepared to describe the explanation as 'very full'.

To explore this problem further, we may look at the answers received to one of our 'free response' questions:

"Is there anything more you would have liked to know from the Police Complaints Authority? (If so, what?)".

Table 24 shows the range of responses among those whose cases were supervised—these being chosen because there is more opportunity for communication with the complainant. The majority answered in the affirmative. About a quarter expressed a desire simply to know more about how the investigation was carried out, and/or how the final decision had been arrived at. Some examples were:

"How they go about investigating the policemen concerned'.

'What they were doing, who they were investigating, what witnesses they were talking to'.

"An explanation into how they drew the reasons for their conclusions, that is to say, what made them draw the conclusions they did from the evidence given".

"I would like to know how they came to their conclusions and how much more they believe a policeman because he is a policeman".

"How they arrived at their conclusion, when there was already pictorial evidence".

"The reason why he got away with breaking my nose".

Table 24: What else complainants wished to know from the PCA

	(Supervised cases only)	
	Number	Per cent
Nothing/no reply	50	40
Wished to see police statements or reports	15	12
How outcome is decided, reasons behind decisions	15	12
How investigation is done/information about procedures	14	11
What happened to the officer(s)/why not punished	7	6
Why witnesses not interviewed/other leads not followed	6	5
Who are the PCA?	5	4
Other	13	10
	125	100

The remainder gave more specific replies. About one in seven wanted to see copies of police statements or the IO's report. For instance:

"They decided there was enough evidence to warrant an investigation, therefore they should send a copy of their report to the person complaining".

"Yes, why I was not allowed to see the statements of other people (police and witnesses), and not allowed to challenge evidence in the presence of the PCA. The PCA simply behaves contrary to established laws and rules of justice".

Smaller groups wished to know why particular witnesses had not been interviewed and what precisely had happened to the officer(s) concerned. Finally, confusion about the identity of the PCA was reflected in the answers of five respondents who wanted to know more about the Authority and its members—a stark example being the simple comment 'Who are they?'.

We end this section with an account of the general impression that respondents had received from the letter, both of the attitude of the PCA towards them and of the Authority's independence. We asked first whether, *leaving aside the formal outcome of the case*, they felt that the PCA had 'believed their story' (see Table 25(A)). There were differences here between complainants, those with discretionarily supervised complaints being the most likely, and those with mandatorily supervised complaints the least likely, to think that the PCA had believed their story. These differences are perhaps not surprising when it is remembered (a) that the decision to supervise is often based on members' worries or suspicions about particular aspects of cases sent to them, and (b) that mandatorily supervised complaints are most likely to be made by complainants with a criminal record. However, the general finding that well over half of all complainants thought that the PCA had disbelieved them totally, gives serious food for thought about how to communicate the negative decisions which, under an adversarial system with strict rules of evidence, will inevitably constitute the great majority of outcomes, without at the same time conveying an unsympathetic impression of the PCA and its allegiances.

This point is emphasized again in the responses to our final question about the letter, in which we asked whether it had given respondents the impression that the PCA was basically 'anti-police', 'independent and unbiased' or 'on the side of the police'. As Table 25(B) indicates, despite the efforts made by PCA members to convey their neutrality and independence, relatively few respondents

174

Table 25: Impressions of the PCA created by the letter

A. Whether PCA appeared to believe complainant's story despite the official result

	Believed story %	Doubted some of it %	Didn't know whom to believe %	Didn't believe at all %	All %	(N)
Not supervised	18	7	20	55	100	(56)
Discretionary supervision	24	18	18	39	100	(38)
Mandatory	14	2	18	66	100	(73)
All	17	8	19	56	100	(167)*

B. General impression created of PCA allegiances

	Anti-police %	Independent & unbiased %	On the side of the police %	All %	(N)
Not supervised	2	12	87	100	(52)
Discretionary supervision	0	23	77	100	(39)
Mandatory	0	16	84	100	(75)
All	1	16	83	100	(166)*

* Non-responses are excluded (the total questionnaire return was 186).

felt that the letter had imparted an independent and unbiased impression of the Authority. Only one person thought it had indicated anti-police sentiments, while a large majority thought the letter had conveyed the message that the PCA was on the side of the police.

3. General views about the PCA

The closing remarks of the previous section lead us appropriately into the final lap of our exposition of research findings, in which we discuss findings relating to the general image which complainants had acquired of the PCA, of investigating officers and of the complaints process as a whole, as well as any suggestions they had for improving the system. We confine our attention here to responses to our postal questionnaire (to complainants whose cases had passed through 'I' Division of the PCA), although, of course, other findings on this subject (from our local complainant interviews) have already been presented in Chapter 4.

Our questionnaire, which is reproduced in Appendix 5, contained several 'free response' questions (i.e. unlike the majority, in which they were asked to tick one of a number of alternative replies). One of these, already referred to in Chapter 9, read:

"Could you give in your own words your general impression of the Police Complaints Authority—how independent they are and how effective?"

We begin with some examples of the replies to this question. (We shall use answers from the full sample, not just those whose cases were supervised.)

Let us look first at the minority—around one in eight—of the responses which were in any way positive. First of all, the small number who were unreservedly enthusiastic about the PCA tended to refer to its 'independence' or 'impartiality'. For example:

"Overall, I think that this is a good example of an independent service that is very reliable and reassuring".

"In my case I am satisfied that they carried out a fair and impartial inquiry".

Secondly, those who awarded the PCA, as it were, 'marks for trying' tended to feel that the Authority's independence and effectiveness were compromised, either by the fact that investigations were carried out by the police, or by the close links between the PCA and the police. For example:

"They seem on the surface to be independent from the police, but the person appointed to do the investigation has a past and present connection with the police force, therefore they cannot be totally independent".

"I can't help but think the PCA is connected to the police".

"I feel that the PCA try to be unbiased, but because much of their information comes through the police they are prone to deception".

In a rather higher number of replies, concern about links with the police was expressed in a more suspicious fashion, including doubts about the motives and loyalties of PCA members. For example:

"I have no evidence that they are independent and are suspicious that they are not".

"Not very independent. I wouldn't be surprised if they were ex-police officers".

The largest proportion was quite adamant that the Authority was not independent. The only encouraging finding here from the PCA's point of view—confirming the results of the precoded question used in Table 25B—was that an unmistakably negative opinion was expressed more often among those whose cases had not been supervised (about 70 per cent of those who answered) than among those who had experienced supervision (about 50 per cent). Typical examples of negative views are:

"They are totally biased, and cover up the truth to protect their police".

"The PCA is an extension of the police force itself ".

"They sit in their office in London and let the police investigate themselves. They should appoint an independent person to follow and indeed sit with the senior officer doing the investigation, not sitting in an office waiting for his report about one of his friends. They are not independent".

Negative views were sometimes combined with misunderstandings about the identity of PCA members. Several respondents seemed to believe that the Authority was a branch of the police, and others thought that the IOs were members of the PCA. For instance:

"They still are police and not independent".

"PCA are not an independent body, they are completely biased towards the police. If a policeman gave them a statement it was believed without question. I myself was constantly questioned and harassed by the PCA to drop my complaint".

As discussed in Chapter 4, such confusion about the identity of the PCA was also evident among our local interview sample.

Statements specifically about the effectiveness of the PCA likewise exhibited a high degree of scepticism, a fairly representative set of comments being that the Authority is 'all bark and no bite', 'a waste of time and money', 'very slow', 'powerless' and 'not worth a light'. Very few indeed considered it able to affect police actions in any way.

We asked respondents to describe in their own words the general attitude of the investigating officer towards themselves and their complaint. Overall, more than one-third gave a positive response, although this varied considerably according to the type of case. Those whose cases had been discretionarily supervised were the most favourably impressed (45 per cent giving positive responses) and those with unsupervised cases were the least impressed (18 per cent positive). This finding supports the point made in Chapter 9 that IOs may be more attentive towards complainants in supervised cases, if only because they contain more serious allegations (and perhaps because the IOs selected are more experienced). It is also worth stressing the finding that IOs created a favourable impression among 34 per cent of respondents in mandatorily supervised cases. Considering the negative stereotypes held by many police officers of complainants of assault (most of whom are 'known to the police'), it speaks well of the professionalism of IOs that they impressed a third of such complainants with their attitude towards the investigation.

Many of the favourable comments referred to the general 'sincerity' or 'pleasantness' of the IO, or to his or her willingness to listen to what the complainant had to say. Examples of positive views about the IO's attitude included the following:

"He called at our home at tea-time, but was polite and funny".

"Very understanding and was sorry about what had happened".

"He was very fair, thorough and courteous".

"Very good, and interest shown in all conversations and for once we thought someone believed our complaint".

"Confident, understanding and reliable".

Even so, although the number of comments of this kind was strikingly high in relation to the overwhelmingly negative responses we received on most aspects of the complaints system, it remains true that over half the comments made were negative. The only exception here was the responses of complainants in discretionarily supervised cases, 28 per cent of whom made negative comments about the IO. Negative remarks about two particular aspects of IOs' behaviour were fairly common, these being that they had put pressure on complainants to withdraw, and that they had been merely 'putting on an act'. For example:

"He said I would "pay the consequences" if I took it further".

"He could not care less but pretended to go along with me".

"He pretended not to condone the fractured wrist ... but I suspect, however, that he was more sympathetic to the detective, whom he apparently knew".

However, the most frequently expressed criticisms were that the IO's attitude had implied disbelief of the complainant or a lack of concern about what had happened.

"He tended to make me feel that I had no right to waste his time".

"Amusement and disbelief, off-handedness".

"He made me feel guilty and that I was not telling the truth, and as if it was all my own fault".

"Totally disbelieving that this could happen".

"He didn't seem at all interested".

(It is possible, as one senior officer claimed, that such impressions are sometimes created *deliberately* by IOs, using interview techniques designed to test the veracity of complainants. But if that really is the case, it serves to underline the fundamental problem that the formal demands of the disciplinary system tend to squeeze out the kind of sympathetic response which is likely to satisfy complainants.)

We also asked complainants whether and how their experience of the investigation and its outcome had changed their general view of the police. Over two-thirds replied that they had changed their view for the worse. As one would expect from earlier replies, those whose cases had been supervised discretionarily were again the least likely to report a negative change—56 per cent compared with 70 per cent of those in unsupervised cases. Only one in twenty of all respondents reported that their view of the police had improved. Thus, rather than the complaints procedure 'making good' any damage to complainants' views of the police which had been caused by the incident, most complainants seemed to emerge from the process more disillusioned about the police and the PCA than they had been before embarking upon it.

What improvements, finally, would they have liked to see in the procedure? We have already mentioned wishes emerging from responses to other questions—such as for fuller explanations of the procedures and outcomes, for more 'openness' in decision-making, and for unambiguous apologies when any wrong-doing is discovered. However, it is quite clear that the overall experiences and views of most complainants were so negative that the only way they could be satisfied would be through radical changes in the system. At the end of the questionnaire, we asked the following basic question:

'*Which of the following statements do you most agree with:*
  (*i*) *The police should investigate complaints themselves*
  (*ii*) *The police should investigate complaints themselves, but under the supervision of an outside body*
  (*iii*) *The whole investigation should be carried out by someone other than the police.*'

Nearly 90 per cent replied that the whole investigation should be carried out by someone other than the police. Only two respondents believed that the police should investigate complaints themselves without any external oversight, the remainder (about ten per cent of the total) supporting the present arrangement. Those whose cases had been supervised discretionarily—who were, we surmise, the least likely to have started out with an 'anti-police' attitude[4]—were the happiest with the current system, but even here the vast majority were in favour of fully independent investigation (82 per cent compared with 92 per cent of those in mandatorily supervised or unsupervised cases).

NOTES

1. Those whose cases had been supervised mandatorily were the most content on this score (33 per cent considering the time taken to have been 'reasonable'), but complainants in discretionarily supervised cases were less satisfied (24 per cent) even than those in unsupervised cases. (Mandatorily supervised cases tended to be completed more quickly than unsupervised cases, which in turn were completed more quickly than discretionarily supervised cases).

2. In 19 other cases, officers had been given advice, but this had been on other matters not directly related to the complaint.

3. Due to a misprint on the first batch of questionnaires sent out, only 166 of the 186 respondents had a chance to answer this question.

4. The group contained a lower proportion of assault complainants, who, we found in our other samples, were more likely to have previous convictions (see Chapters 3 and 8).

CHAPTER 11

Summary and Implications of Findings

The two research reports which form the basis of this publication were commissioned by organizations concerned with the practical problems of dealing with complaints, and consequently were aimed primarily at eliciting detailed empirical material on matters with clear relevance to policy and practice. We have made only a modest attempt here to go beyond this and place our findings within the broader framework of the history of the police complaints system and of debates about its fundamental principles and purposes. We have begun this task elsewhere (Maguire 1991) and hope to publish more reflective discussions on the subject in the future. In this concluding chapter, we shall do no more than draw some of the threads together and identify aspects of the system which appear from our research to demand attention. We shall not go so far beyond our 'brief' as to formulate firm proposals on fundamental issues, such as the desirability or otherwise of creating a fully independent system of investigation.

1. Summary of Findings

We begin with a summary of the previous ten chapters. In Chapter 1, we provided a brief history of developments in the complaints system, ending with the passing of the Police and Criminal Evidence Act 1984 and the creation of the PCA. This followed a period of intense debate about police powers and accountability, in which numerous calls were made for independent investigation of complaints. The present arrangements, we pointed out, represent a compromise between opposing views on this central issue: PCA members 'supervise', but do not actually carry out investigations.

We then considered the objectives of complaints systems in general, noting that in many commercial organisations their primary purpose is simply to 'keep customers happy': hence firms will readily apologise or offer small sums in compensation. However, the situation with the police is more complex. Police officers have the almost unique right to use force, where necessary, to uphold the law, and the complaints system represents an essential safeguard against abuse of this power. Inevitably, at least in serious cases, the complaints system is bound up with the disciplinary system, and the rigidity and formality of the latter (necessary to protect officers, whose careers may be at risk, from false accusations) tend to work against the goal of 'keeping the customer satisfied'. We identified four main objectives which, ideally, the police complaints system should aim to achieve, but which were sometimes in conflict with each other: the maintenance of 'discipline in the ranks' (including the removal of seriously offending officers); the satisfaction of complainants; the maintenance of public confidence in the police; and the provision of 'feedback from consumers' to police managers for use in instigating change.

In the final part of Chapter 1 we outlined the research methods used, describing the various samples we extracted from files, both in three local force areas and in the offices of the PCA.

In Chapter 2, we set out the basic procedures used to deal with complaints, beginning with the complexities of recording, classification and referral to the PCA. We then described the normal investigative procedures, also drawing attention to the problem of cases becoming *sub judice*, and to the question of at what point 'Regulation 7' forms should be issued. Finally, we outlined the decision-making process which determines criminal or disciplinary outcomes, covering the role of the 'Chief Officer', the PCA, the Director of Public Prosecutions and the Chief Constable.

In Chapter 3, we looked at statistical and other material concerning the nature and frequency of complaints. It was noted that complaints statistics are both complex and subject to variations in recording practice, particularly in the enumeration of separate complaints. The unit of the 'case', which refers to an incident involving any number of police officers, complaints or complainants, seemed to provide the best base for measuring trends. We found that the national total of cases had remained fairly steady over the past decade, although—at least until 1987—the Metropolitan Police District (which contributes the highest number) showed a decreasing pattern, in contrast to gradual increases in most other forces. Contrary to what might have been expected, the advent of (official) 'informal resolution' did not appear to have pushed up the totals. It had, however, contributed to a fall in the proportion of all complaints which are substantiated, which stood in 1989 at under three per cent (or eight per cent of all complaints which went to a full investigation).

It was found that well over half of all complaints entail allegations of assault, incivility or oppressive conduct, and about one-third of all cases include a complaint of assault. We then presented an analysis of the circumstances of a random sample of 264 cases from three police force areas, which involved 347 individual complainants and 685 police officers. About half the relevant incidents had occurred during night shifts, and as many as 20 per cent between 10.00p.m. and

2.00a.m. on Friday or Saturday nights; 46 per cent took place on roads or in the street, 24 per cent at private houses and 18 per cent within police stations. The kind of officer most likely to be the subject of a complaint was a male constable in his early middle years of service), especially when on duty with an operational support unit. Complainants came from all sections of society, but three-quarters were male and almost half were under 30. The great majority were complaining for the first time in their lives.

We identified certain kinds of case with recurring features. Most obviously, almost all complaints of *assault* arose from incidents in which the complainant or others had been *arrested*. Typically, it was claimed that police officers had used excessive force in effecting the arrest on the street, sometimes with subsequent assaults in a vehicle or a police station. Most of the arrests were 'unplanned', made during confused or fast-moving incidents, often at night, and consumption of alcohol was mentioned in the report in over 50 per cent of the cases. Although several potential witnesses might be present, it was usually difficult to trace them subsequently, the investigators having to rely on conflicting accounts of police officers on the one hand and the complainant and his or her companions on the other. A clear majority of complainants (and many of the witnesses) in these cases had criminal records, which was regarded by investigators as devaluing their versions of what happened. Moreover, the outcome often turned upon the slippery concept of 'reasonable force' in effecting arrests. The substantiation rate in such cases was lower than in all other kinds.

A second common type of case was '*driving related incivility*' arising usually when a vehicle was stopped by a patrol or traffic car. The complainants here tended to be older, and many more were middle class people with no previous adverse contact with the police. Typically, there was a pattern of escalation from a trivial argument or misunderstanding to a loss of temper on one or both sides. Over half of all complaints of incivility came about in these circumstances.

A third readily identifiable kind of case was a perceived *inadequate response to a request for service*—for example, failure to follow up a report of a crime. Such complaints were less common than the other two, and were often motivated by a desire to 'get something done' rather than to see an officer punished.

In Part Two (Chapters 4–7), we looked at the operation of the system, and the views of the main participants, in three police force areas. In Chapter 4, we explored the complainant's perspective. We began, though, with a discussion of the 'dark figure' of people who feel they have cause to complain but do not do so formally. Evidence from the 1988 British Crime Survey (where it was found that 20 per cent of respondents had been 'really annoyed' by the behaviour of a police officer within the past five years) indicated that only about one in five of those who seriously consider complaining actually attempt to do so and that, even among these, only a very small proportion end up with a recorded complaint. Over 30 per cent of our sample of complainants reported that police officers had tried to deflect them from their intention, while Inspectors informed us that over half the people who arrived in their offices wishing to complain left without any recourse being made to official procedures—their grievance having been 'informally allayed'.

It was our firm impression that most officially recorded complaints come from people who, whatever the merits of their case, genuinely feel a sense of grievance. Although a proportion are 'tactical', made largely in the hope of escaping a criminal conviction, most of the complainants we interviewed were clearly upset or angry about what had happened. In serious cases, a majority of complainants expressed a desire to see the officer punished, but this was much less frequently the principal motivation behind the much larger number of minor complaints. Almost as many interviewees gave as their main aim the prevention of similar behaviour in the future by bringing it to a senior officer's attention, and a substantial minority (indeed, 50 per cent of those whose cases were informally resolved) simply desired an apology.

About half had been optimistic, when complaining, that the matter would be treated seriously and fairly. However, satisfaction with both the outcome and the handling of complaints was generally low. Among those whose cases had been fully investigated, 90 per cent declared themselves 'very' or 'fairly' dissatisfied. Dissatisfaction was less common among those who had withdrawn their complaint (67 per cent) and those who agreed to the system of informal resolution (43 per cent). The main reasons given for dissatisfaction were the time taken to resolve the complaint, the lack or inadequacy of explanations of the decision, and the absence of an apology. We noted that part of the problem may lie in poor communication: 80 per cent said that they had not been adequately informed about the progress of the investigation, and many seemed to misunderstand the letter from the Police Complaints Authority informing them of the outcome of the inquiry. Rather like the crime victim in relation to the criminal justice system, many complainants felt that after their initial input they had been excluded from the process. While there was considerable praise for the manner of investigating officers during the initial interview, the majority said that the experience as a whole had changed their view of the police for the worse, and only about half would complain again in similar circumstances. Over 85 per cent were in favour of independent investigators and many would have preferred a 'hearing' with themselves and the officer present.

In Chapter 5, we explored police views, based largely upon interviews with a sample of 50 officers who had been the subject of a complaint. Their general image of complainants was negative—they were seen either as 'professional trouble-makers' or as people hoping to escape punishment for criminal behaviour. Nevertheless, they recognised that certain officers (not usually themselves!) tended to attract complaints through insensitive behaviour or short temper. Most said that they had never altered their conduct through fear of receiving a complaint, although about one in five claimed that experience of the complaints system had had the (to them) negative effect of causing them to 'back away from' some difficult or potentially violent situations, when they felt the correct course of action was to 'go in hard' or to make an arrest. Most had no fear of the outcome of complaint investigations, but found the experience of being put 'under the spotlight' by a senior officer uncomfortable, particularly in regard to possible misdemeanours incidental to the complaint (such as failings in pocket book entries). It was clear, too, that—especially for inexperienced officers—the whole procedure could produce considerable stress. Like complainants, police officers felt excluded and alienated from the investigation, did not like the delays, and were dissatisfied with the amount of information they received. Almost half would have preferred an independent investigator, albeit for different reasons: such a person would be unable to 'pull rank' in the manner of a Superintendent, and thus would have less 'clout' to press them to answer questions.

The nineteen investigating officers we interviewed were generally in favour of retaining the present system, their main argument being that as 'insiders' they were in a stronger position than civilians to obtain evidence and admissions. On the other hand, they felt that too much of their time was taken up with 'rubbish'—minor or blatantly unjustified complaints. Several criticised Inspectors for failing to deal with minor complaints informally, adding unnecessary work for investigators. There was a general feeling that complaints were a useful management tool—as one put it, a lever to give certain officers a 'kick in the pants'. They also pointed out that complaints generated a considerable amount of informal disciplinary activity 'behind the scenes': as another insisted, 'I'm a complaints *and discipline* officer'. One complaint they themselves had about the system was a lack of feedback about the quality of their reports—they felt unrewarded when they had done a good job.

In Chapter 6, we looked at the system of informal resolution (IR). It was noted that recourse to this option varies widely between forces (ranging from 12 to 48 per cent of complaints in 1989). In 13 of the 70 cases we analyzed in which informal resolution had not been used, the possibility had been mooted but rejected for a variety of reasons. A certain amount of ignorance about the process was evident among officers as well as complainants, and this had sometimes contributed to failures to use it. Complainants who had accepted informal resolution had been attracted mainly by the speed of the procedure, a belief that the offending officer would get a 'ticking off', or the fact that they would not have to attend any formal hearing (which, of course, was anyway unlikely).

Police officers were less enthusiastic, many seeing informal resolution as tantamount to an assumption of guilt. They also believed that, despite assurances to the contrary, a record would be kept and might be held against them in future applications for transfers or promotion. Officers disputed the facts of the case in 26 out of 30 informally resolved complaints, and very few agreed to apologise, although 10 of the 30 complainants received something akin to an apology on behalf of the force. Informal resolution was sometimes treated by Appointed Officers as an adversarial procedure, akin to a formal investigation: this tended to produce the result of 'agreeing to differ' rather than an amicable resolution. Meetings between complainants and those complained against (in order to discuss the incident in the presence of a third party) were rare, and few officers (though many complainants) were in favour of such a practice. However, it should be borne in mind that these were still 'early days' in the adoption of the system. In the three years since our fieldwork was conducted, attitudes appear to have mellowed in some forces at least, and IR is becoming more generally accepted, or even preferred, as an alternative to the full investigation of complaints.

Finally, we reiterated in Chapter 6 that complainants' satisfaction levels were reasonably high, and certainly much higher than in investigated cases. Where apologies were offered or promises made to 'have a word with the officer', complainants generally felt they had achieved what they wanted. Dissatisfaction was caused mainly by failure to receive adequate feedback from the Appointed Officer, and by absolute denials by officers of the substance of complaints.

Chapter 7 dealt with withdrawn complaints. Over half the 40 complainants interviewed whose cases had been fully investigated, said that they had experienced some pressure to withdraw, mainly from the investigating officer (IO). In most cases this was described as a fairly 'friendly', but persistent, attempt to persuade them that there was little point in continuing. Similarly, of those who *had* withdrawn, over two-thirds had done so as a result of discussing the case with the IO.

One third of the 'withdrawers' remained content with their decision, feeling that they had achieved all they could (had 'made their point', etc). The remainder had been somewhat reluctant withdrawers, but had done so mainly because the IO had convinced them that they had no chance of 'proving their case' due to lack of evidence, or because they feared too much trouble or inconvenience (there was a common belief, apparently fostered—or, at least, not discouraged—by some IOs, that complaints were likely to result in a requirement to attend court or a disciplinary hearing as a witness). A small number of the IOs we interviewed agreed that they actively solicited a withdrawal in cases they regarded as hopeless, but most said that they simply put the options in a neutral way. Differences in approach may help to explain considerable differences between IOs in the proportions of investigated and withdrawn complaints among their caseloads. Finally, one in three of all 'withdrawers' said that they would have accepted informal resolution, had this been offered and fully explained to them.

In Part Three, we turned our attention to the Police Complaints Authority. In Chapter 8, we showed that only about half of all recorded complaints are seen by members of the PCA, the remainder being either informally resolved or withdrawn without prior referral to 'I' (Investigation) Division. Generally speaking, the 'unseen' half are less serious, although differences in the interpretation of the referral regulations may mean that some potentially serious complaints of assault do not reach the attention of the PCA.

While 'D' (Discipline) Division's caseload covers a broad cross-section of both complaints and complainants—albeit, due to the use of informal resolution, with an under-representation of complaints of incivility and of older and middle-class complainants—we found that of 'I' Division to be quite untypical of complaints as a whole. We calculated that over 90 per cent of cases initially referred to 'I' Division members, and three-quarters of those they actually supervised, contained allegations of assault. By contrast, only about one-third of all cases recorded by local police forces include a complaint of assault.

We distinguished three types of case supervised by the PCA. Those supervised mandatorily (S.87(1)(a)(i)) were, by definition, complaints of assault causing serious injury. Nearly all these complaints arose from situations in which the complainant had been arrested, most commonly in the course of incidents on the streets after police officers had intervened in, or had been called to deal with, some form of disorderly behaviour.

Many of the arrests and charges, in fact, related to behaviour alleged to have occurred after the arrival or intervention of the police (assault on police, breach of the peace, drunk and disorderly, etc). Although as many as 80 per cent of the complainants in mandatorily supervised cases—two-thirds of whom were males under 30—had at least one previous conviction, very few faced serious criminal charges following their current arrest. As in our findings from the local samples (Chapter 3), the majority of the alleged assaults by the police took place at the scene of the arrest, although there were complaints of assault in police vehicles in 20 per cent of cases, and in police stations in 18 per cent. Again, four out of five of the officers complained against were PCs, virtually all were male, and those in their 'early middle' years of service (7–9 years) were most likely to be involved. Moreover, 21 per cent had been on duty at the time with a Support Group.

Complaint cases supervised at members' discretion were of two main kinds. About half were 'assault' cases similar in character—but with less serious consequences in terms of injury—to those referred for mandatory supervision. They were, however, less likely to be arrest-related. The other half were quite different. They tended to be complex affairs containing allegations of bribery, corruption, perjury or other serious offences of dishonesty. Both the complainants and the officers involved had different characteristics from those in assault cases. The complainants were older as a group, included more females and people from middle-class backgrounds, and fewer (though still half) had previous convictions. The officers were more likely to be in the CID or of senior rank.

Finally, cases supervised after referral under Section 88 constituted a mixed bag, although nearly half related to deaths in (or shortly after) police custody. 'Section 88s' were the most likely cases to have attracted press attention. Some included complaints against individual officers, but most were general inquiries into incidents giving rise to police or public concern. The terms of reference for the investigation were often wider than in complaints cases, a feature seen as an advantage by PCA members, who were thus free to make broader statements than usual about matters of police policy which concerned them.

We ended Chapter 8 with a brief comparison of the seriousness of injuries in mandatorily and discretionarily supervised assault cases, concluding that, while there was a fairly clear difference between them in most cases, there was also a significant 'grey area'. This was evident particularly where small lacerations and hair-line fractures were concerned, there being differences of view between police forces about what constituted a 'deep cut' or 'broken bone'. On occasion, members found themselves having to supervise cases which they themselves would not have classified as falling under S.87(1)(a)(i).

188

In Chapter 9, we looked first at 'I' Division members' decisions on which of the cases referred to them to supervise. Where assault cases were concerned, we identified four factors—'suspicious' elements, special vulnerability of the complainant, the likelihood of substantiation, and public interest—which seemed particularly important in this decision. We calculated, however, that only about four per cent of cases referred in accordance with Regulation 4(1)(a)—i.e. potential offences by officers of 'assault occasioning actual bodily harm'—were selected for supervision. By contrast, about two-thirds of those referred under 4(1)(b) or 4(1)(c)—i.e. allegations of serious offences other than assault—were selected for supervision. Here, the 'public interest' factor was often uppermost in members' minds. They thought it particularly important to supervise complaints of corruption.

We then discussed the nature of supervision, distinguishing what we called 'routine' or 'passive' supervision from a more 'active' or 'directive' approach. We found that members only rarely gave direct instructions to investigating officers: we could find only 11 cases in 100 where this had happened, and only six of these concerned investigative strategies *per se*. On the other hand, 'active' supervision —frequent telephone (and sometimes face-to-face) discussions with IOs about progress and plans—was evident in about half of all cases. This was particularly so in non-assault cases, which were generally more complex.

Somewhat ironically, supervision in mandatorily supervised cases was often seen by members as the most straightforward. These cases tended to involve discrete incidents with limited numbers of witnesses (often police witnesses on the one hand and the complainants' companions on the other, giving opposing versions of who had struck whom) and, while it was very difficult to arrive at the truth, the basic shape the investigation should take was frequently clear and uncontroversial. Supervision therefore tended to consist of routine responses to evidentiary documents as they arrived (combined sometimes with 'progress chasing'). However, there were often more queries here than in other types of case in the final stages of supervision—i.e. when the IO's report was scrutinized prior to the issue of an Interim Statement—mainly concerning the IO's interpretation of evidence or the tone of the report.

Generally speaking, we were impressed with the care with which both members and their staff scrutinized casefiles and picked up omissions. However, this in itself does not answer the question of whether or not supervision is *effective*, which we took up in the final part of the chapter.

We addressed this question from a variety of angles. First, we presented the views of various interested parties. Beginning with the perspective of the IOs we interviewed, we found that about one-third thought supervision by the PCA 'a complete waste of time', one-third found it useful, strategically, to the police, and one-third thought it effective to some extent in reassuring the public of the fairness of the system. None, however, believed that it made any significant difference to the conduct or outcome of investigations: it was seen mainly as an irritant, sometimes compelling them to waste time on trivialities or irrelevancies. The most they would concede was that the very fact of supervision could put less conscientious IOs 'on their mettle' and thus produce a more thorough job. On the other hand, those who had met PCA members had usually been impressed by their knowledge and abilities, and most were mindful of the Authority's power.

Brief mention was made next of the complainant's perspective, although most findings on this were reserved for Chapter 10. The general message to emerge from responses to our postal questionnaire was that complainants considered the PCA ineffective in producing a fair investigation, and most had finished up more disillusioned than when they started. Nevertheless, satisfaction with the system was evident among a higher proportion of those whose cases had been supervised than among the remainder.

We then turned to the difficult question of whether supervision affected the *outcomes of cases*. We emphasized, first of all, that the production of a higher 'hit rate' is not necessarily a goal to which the PCA should aspire or by which its effectiveness should be judged: the Authority is, ultimately, in the business of establishing the truth, not of trying to prove cases against as many officers as possible. Moreover, if a case simply is not provable under the demanding standard of 'beyond reasonable doubt', there is nothing a member can do to alter the situation. Even so, the matter is of considerable interest, as the argument for independent investigators is often predicated on the assumption that this would lead to more complaints being substantiated.

We also made the point that measurement of outcomes is itself difficult. It is complicated, for example, by differences between the total numbers of cases, complaints, complainants and officers; by the fact that advice given to officers can be either directly or indirectly related to complaints; and by the existence of both substantiated complaints and unsubstantiated complaints with advice. Nevertheless, categorising cases in our questionnaire sample according to the criterion of whether any officer had been charged with criminal or disciplinary offences or had received 'advice' directly related to the complaint, we found that this had occurred in 17 per cent of the supervised cases, compared with 9 per cent of the unsupervised cases. Again, using the criterion whether of action of *any* kind (i.e. including advice on matters only indirectly related to the complaint) had been taken against any officer, we found that 33 per cent of the supervised cases, compared with 17 per cent of the unsupervised, had resulted in 'action'. Even when we restricted the comparison to assault cases only (complaints of assault being much less likely than others to be substantiated), the difference remained roughly the same.

Although these findings superficially suggest that supervision has a considerable effect on outcomes, it has to be remembered that the element of selection in S.87(1)(a)(ii) cases may account for much of the difference: members may simply be picking those with the best chance of substantiation. However, what does seem likely from our analysis is that supervision—perhaps by reason of its attention to detail—leads to more *subsidiary* or *incidental* action: for example, advice to custody officers who have technically breached PACE requirements or to PCs with errors in their pocket book entries.

We concluded Chapter 9 with some comments about other ways in which 'effectiveness' might be assessed. There was some evidence to suggest, first, that supervision may reduce the likelihood of complaints being withdrawn; secondly, that it may encourage the selection of higher quality IOs and the production of better reports; and thirdly, that it may expedite investigations a little. Finally, we offered a few findings from the 1988 British Crime Survey on the important question of the effectiveness of the PCA in persuading the general public of its own independence and of the fairness of the system as a whole. While the evidence was limited—and no comparable data from the pre-PACE era exist—the indications were that there was still a long way to go before the Authority could claim to have made a major impact upon public confidence. Only 36 per cent of respondents (and a lower proportion of ethnic minority respondents) declared themselves 'very' or 'reasonably' happy with the present system; equally important, only a minority even knew of the PCA's existence.

Chapter 10 was devoted almost entirely to responses to our postal questionnaire to complainants in cases serious enough to have been referred to the PCA for possible supervision. The respondents included people with and without experience of supervision. Among the whole group, expectations of a fair and thorough investigation had been generally low at the outset. Moreover, among the minority who had started out in a reasonably optimistic frame of mind, nearly two-thirds finished up dissatisfied with the way the investigation had been conducted. Altogether, over half the sample declared themselves 'very dissatisfied' and a further quarter 'fairly dissatisfied' in this respect.

Dissatisfaction with the outcome was even greater: around 85 per cent were 'very dissatisfied'. Surprisingly, however, the degree of satisfaction did not seem to depend upon the actual outcome of the case. It emerged that a high proportion of complainants were in fact ignorant of, or mistaken about, the outcome. Only three of thirteen whose complaints had directly resulted in 'advice' seemed to know that any blame had been attached to an officer. This may reflect problems in communicating outcomes, especially in the use of terms like 'advice', which, although familiar to police officers and PCA members, have a different meaning for most ordinary people. Yet even where people knew, or believed that, they had 'won their case', this did not necessarily imply that they were satisfied: 11 of 17 such respondents still had other reasons for feeling disgruntled. This illustrates the point that reasons for complaining are complex, and go beyond wanting to see an officer disciplined.

To explore the latter point further, we looked at replies to questions about our respondents' initial aims. While the desires to 'have the officer punished' and to 'have it proved that what you were saying was true' were among the most prominent (both mentioned by about three-quarters of the respondents), there were also other commonly expressed aims, such as the desire for an apology, for an explanation, for compensation, to 'stop it happening to somebody else', or simply to express anger, which were not necessarily achieved solely by the disciplining of, or giving of advice to, an officer. All this suggests that the clarity and the tone of communications from both the police and the PCA to complainants are important to levels of satisfaction.

Twenty-two per cent of complainants felt that they had achieved something by complaining, most of these being hopeful that they had restrained future behaviour of a similar kind. The majority felt that nothing had been achieved. Asked what more the PCA should have done, 40 per cent of the two-thirds who replied stated that it should have ensured a more thorough investigation. About one in six wanted to see more openness in the system, with access to statements or a chance to argue their case and cross-examine the officers in the presence of a senior officer.

In the final section of Chapter 10, we discussed complainants' perceptions of the letter they had received from the PCA informing them of the outcome of their case. Some were unhappy with the 'tone', and only a minority thought it had adequately explained the reasons behind the decision. When asked what impressions of the PCA's attitude they had received from the letter, a majority thought that the Authority had disbelieved them entirely (although this fell to 39 per cent among those whose cases had been supervised discretionarily) and a large majority thought that the PCA was basically 'on the side of the police'. Similarly, when asked to give in their own words their general impressions of the PCA, most replied to the effect that it was 'biased' and not independent of the police. Nevertheless, positive opinions were more common among those whose cases had been supervised than among the remainder. A further important finding here was that misunderstandings about the role and identity of the PCA were quite common. For example, despite explanations in the standard leaflet given to complainants by the police, as well as in enclosures in the final letter, several complainants believed that the Authority was staffed by senior police officers.

Respondents' impressions of the IO who had interviewed them were more frequently positive, ranging from 18 per cent positive replies among complainants in unsupervised cases to 45 per cent of those in discretionarily supervised cases. One third of complainants in mandatorily supervised assault cases had something good to say about their IO—a high proportion, considering the anti-police attitudes and dissatisfaction they tended to display in other replies. This underlines the importance of *personal communication* in any attempt to satisfy complainants: IOs we interviewed often stressed that they achieved more in terms of 'PR' by listening to complainants and answering their questions fully than by investigating their complaints.

Finally, we presented the responses to a question about who should investigate complaints. Nearly 90 per cent replied that this should be the task of a body outside the police.

2. Concluding Comments

This has been a complex report, with a great many detailed findings—itself a reflection of the complexity of the system we set out to describe and evaluate. It is difficult to put the results of the study 'in a nutshell', but it may be helpful to preface our concluding remarks with a very brief summary of what appear to us to be the findings which provide on the one hand, the most encouragement and, on the other, the greatest challenge, to supporters of the present complaints system.

On the positive side, we were generally impressed with the commitment and the abilities both of police investigators and of PCA members. Where IOs were concerned, many had been 'promoted into' Complaints and Discipline departments and these, particularly, seemed anxious to do a thorough, professional job in their first middle management post. We found PCA members, all of whom had had successful careers in other fields, independent-minded, conscientious and well informed about police practice and procedure. The Authority was also increasingly winning respect from police officers responsible for complaints and discipline. At its best, the combination of an experienced detective and an alert and closely involved PCA member, backed up by civil service staff, appeared to constitute a powerful investigative weapon, potentially providing the 'best of both worlds'—insider knowledge and a firmly independent viewpoint.

The other positive finding we would single out is the promising start made by the 'informal resolution' procedure, which was valued by police managers as a cheaper and less unwieldy way of dealing with less serious complaints, and at the same time was more likely than a full investigation to satisfy the complainant.

The most important negative findings, we suggest, are the following. First, every way we measured complainant satisfaction, in relation to every category except informally resolved cases, indicated an overwhelming majority of 'dissatisfied customers'. Secondly, high proportions of both complainants and officers complained against expressed the following criticisms of the system: that they felt excluded from it; that it was too secretive and 'bureaucratic'; that investigations took too long; that they were not kept informed of progress; that they received inadequate explanations of decisions; and that, in some cases, it brought them or their families a great deal of anger or stress. Thirdly, the (admittedly limited) evidence we have on public views of the complaints system and the PCA, suggests not only that ignorance and misunderstandings predominate, but that only a minority of the population feel confident that, if they made a complaint, it would be investigated fairly.

The police complaints system has developed over the past 25 years from a somewhat haphazard and totally internally operated system, into a set of procedures quite tightly controlled by Statutes, Regulations and Instructions to Chief Officers. It has also incorporated new, and now quite substantial, independent elements. These changes go right across the board, from recording and classification to investigation and disciplinary tribunals (with the exception of punishment in non-criminal cases, which remains firmly the prerogative of the Chief Constable.) There has also been a move away from the traditional inextricable link between complaints and discipline—represented by the introduction of informal resolution, whereby complaints can be settled without officers facing any risk of discipline. All the above developments may be regarded as the gradual adaptation of an antiquated system to modern demands for openness, accountability and 'consumer satisfaction'.

The present shape of the system is essentially three-tiered: investigations into the most serious complaints are supervised by outsiders; 'medium serious' complaints continue to be investigated in the

194

traditional manner (with the addition of external scrutiny of the final report); and minor complaints are increasingly dealt with informally. This appears to be a logical development, in that more attention, more resources and more external scrutiny are devoted to the more serious cases. However, even if one accepts the principle, there remain many questions about the appropriate extent of external involvement in each 'tier', and about the criteria by which individual cases should be judged suitable, for example, for supervision or informal resolution.

We shall structure the discussion in terms of the four objectives we identified in Chapter 1 as the main purposes which the complaints system should be aiming to serve: maintaining discipline, satisfying complainants, gaining public confidence, and providing managers with information they can use to make improvements. We shall comment, in the light of our findings, on the extent to which the current system seems to meet these objectives, and on possible implications for reform.

Where the first objective—maintaining discipline—is concerned, it should first be said that, in an ideal world, the formal complaints and discipline system would act only as a rarely needed long-stop to the 'front-line' supervision carried out day-to-day by Sergeants and Inspectors. However, we have argued elsewhere (Maguire 1991) that weaknesses in front-line supervision—due, among other factors, to greater administrative pressure upon Sergeants' and Inspectors' time—have meant that the complaints system, with its deterrent threat of disciplinary sanctions, has become more important within overall strategies for preventing misconduct. It is therefore valid to ask whether the possibility of receiving a complaint acts as a deterrent to, for example, rudeness or aggressive behaviour.

First of all, for such sanctions to be effective, they must be applied frequently and consistently enough to constitute a genuine deterrent. But, as we have seen, the proportion of complaints which end in substantiation is extremely low, and most officers, although disliking the process of being investigated, know that there is little chance of a complaint of any but the most blatant misconduct leading to any action against them. Certainly, senior officers sometimes apply informal sanctions, such as 'sideways moves', after complaints which, though unsubstantiated, give them some cause for concern; and officers who accumulate numerous complaints over a short period are sometimes warned that their behaviour is being watched closely. However, such sanctions have their limitations, and are not backed up by the ultimate threat of dismissal. As the Chairman of the PCA pointed out in the Authority's 1988 report, once officers have completed their probationary period, it is extremely difficult to

195

remove them from the force, however unsuitable they later turn out to be.

The underlying problem in such cases is that the standard of evidence required to prove a disciplinary charge is higher in the police service than in any other professional organisation: cases have to be proved, as in the courts, 'beyond reasonable doubt', not, as in disciplinary systems elsewhere, 'on the balance of probabilities'.[1] While it may be defensible to demand the highest standard of proof when an officer's career is at stake, there is a much weaker case for this in less serious complaints, where the only sanction risked is a reprimand or formal advice.

The difficulty in substantiating even minor complaints undermines the effectiveness of the system not only in helping to maintain discipline, but also—the second of the four aims defined above—in satisfying complainants. Complainants who are simply informed, many months later, that their complaint has been unsubstantiated through lack of evidence, often feel that the exercise has been totally in vain. While some complaints were clearly trivial, malicious, or based on a misunderstanding of police powers or procedures, and in others the complainant's own conduct had provoked the police behaviour they objected to, we were generally impressed by the genuineness of the sense of grievance expressed by the complainants we interviewed—an impression confirmed by several of the IOs we spoke to. Most were making the first complaint against the police in their lives, and a large minority told us that it had taken some courage to do so: as one put it, 'It's like walking up to a six foot man'. They were incensed by what had happened, and expected some form of redress, if only an apology, a full explanation (at the very least, of why, precisely, their complaint was considered unjustified), or an assurance that steps would be taken to prevent a recurrence. The 'black-and white' nature of the outcome—the response to the complainant being totally dependent upon whether or not a breach of the disciplinary code could be proved against a named officer—meant that none of these wishes were met in the great majority of cases, and satisfaction was rare. (And even in some cases where advice was given to officers, this was either not communicated to complainants or it was not clearly enough explained that receiving advice was regarded in the police force as a significant penalty.)

Some of these problems have been ameliorated by the introduction of informal resolution, although the procedure is still not used as often as it could be. 'D' Division of the PCA, too, has made efforts to provide fuller explanations of the reasons behind decisions in investigated cases, but responses to our postal questionnaire indicate that few complainants consider these adequate. (There are, it should be said, sometimes legal reasons why the PCA is unable to disclose certain facts to complainants, although there is clearly room for the release of more information than is currently passed on.)

In sum, as long as the complaints system remains so closely interlinked with the disciplinary system—and, in serious cases, it is difficult to see how it could be uncoupled—there is limited scope for making responses more akin to those provided by other, more 'consumer-oriented' organisations (where satisfaction of the complainant is accorded high priority). The position of the complainant against the police remains rather like that of the victim of crime in relation to the criminal justice system: he or she provides the initial input into a large impersonal system, which then takes over the case and processes it largely to meet organisational goals rather than in the interests of the individual.

Perhaps the most difficult problem of all, however, is that of meeting the third aim we have defined—winning general public confidence in the complaints system. The key to this, almost certainly, lies in the handling of serious complaints which attract media attention: it was such cases, not 'run-of-the-mill' complaints, which stirred up the controversy which led ultimately to the establishment of the PCA and the mechanism of supervision.

Whether or not PCA supervision 'works', in the sense of making the conviction of guilty officers more likely, is impossible to answer with certainty, although we concluded that its very existence has probably had some 'sharpening up' effect upon IOs, if only in matters of detail. (There was also some evidence that it helped to expedite some investigations and that it marginally increased complainant satisfaction). However, what is equally important is that it is carried out in a conspicuously active style, sufficient to convince outsiders that it is ensuring a thorough and unbiased investigation. Passive supervision achieves little more than the *post hoc* monitoring of reports. And even very active supervision, although possibly influential (and certainly, in our experience, rigorous and conscientious), does not always appear to be so to outsiders. We read several files in which it was obvious that the member had put in an immense amount of work, yet none of this was known to the complainant or to anyone outside the police, PCA and DPP. To achieve a higher public profile and to gain more credit for what it does, it seems, the Authority needs to find ways of 'blowing its own trumpet' harder.

The greatest hope for convincing a wider public of the PCA's effectiveness appears to lie in what might be called 'intensive', or 'participant', supervision—a level of involvement at present achieved in a very small minority of cases. This involves, for example, visiting the scene, meeting complainants, sitting in on interviews, answering questions from the press or concerned groups, and so on.

Unfortunately, under present conditions there is little scope for expanding the number of cases in which this kind of supervision takes place. The reality remains that is comparatively rare for members even to meet IOs in person. One of the main practical problems is the size of caseloads. At the time of our research, each member was dealing on average with about 80 cases at any one time (although, admittedly, a fair number of these were *sub judice* and hence not yet 'live'). Moreover, the PCA has only one office, in London, so that meetings with IOs are made difficult by long travelling distances.

These obstacles might eventually be overcome by expanding the membership of the Authority and opening regional offices. However, given the current restraints, the practical question for the near future is whether members should continue to 'spread themselves thinly' or should concentrate upon the intensive and publicly visible supervision of a much smaller number of carefully selected cases.

The latter course seems attractive from many angles, not least that of reducing the counter-productive effect of raising expectations among complainants (and, indeed, IOs), only to disappoint them. On the other hand, the issue of selection would be likely to cause difficulties. If it were left entirely to members, the indications are that, in addition to cases which 'hit the headlines', they would tend to choose unusual or complex cases that they could 'get their teeth into', as well as those with particularly vulnerable categories of complainant. This might lead to the exclusion of some of the complaints of assault, now subject to mandatory supervision, which arise from injuries to 'known offenders' sustained before, during or after arrests: such cases are often more straightforward in terms of investigative strategy and offer low chances of substantiation.

The case can certainly be argued for abandoning S.87(1)(a)(i) and giving members a free choice on supervision, encouraging them to take on fewer cases, which they then would have time to supervise more actively. On the other hand, complaints of assault, in whatever circumstances they occur, can be argued to be among the most serious of all. This is not only by dint of the injuries caused, but because, if genuine, they represent an abuse of the crucial power which marks off the police from the rest of society—the right, where necessary, to use force to uphold the law. Moreover, there is a strong argument, articulated very firmly by one PCA member, that groups such as 'known offenders' have a greater need than other groups for an independent presence in the investigation of their complaints: if IOs are affected by any prejudices in their work, it is in this kind of case. We stress, again, that we have no evidence that personal feelings ever caused IOs to carry out a less thorough investigation. But 'stereotyping' of such complainants as, for example, 'time-wasters' or 'liars' was not unknown in their reports—several instances having been noted by PCA members on the files we analysed—and in casual conversation with us, IOs quite often made it clear that they disliked having to investigate complaints made by people they variously described as 'yobboes', 'villains' or even 'the scum of the earth' (for a discussion of what they call 'discrediting the complainant', see Box and Russell 1975). There is also the possibility (though, again, we have no evidence of this) that such cases might be excluded by members on occasion, through a feeling that 'he got what he deserved'. In sum, in implementing a 'free choice' system of supervision as outlined above, one would have to sacrifice the symbolic (and perhaps, on occasion, practical) value of mandatory supervision in all such cases, for the advantage of conspicuous involvement by the PCA in a small number of high profile cases.

The last of the four objectives of the system we identified—managers' use of 'lessons' from complaints to improve police conduct—was one to which, at the time of our research, few forces appeared to be paying much attention. On the other hand, there were exceptions even then and, in the light of recent attention to complaint patterns by HM Inspectors of Constabulary, many more forces are now beginning to look at them more seriously.

We would argue, first of all, that crude statistics on the numbers—or even the categories—of complaints in any given area are of very limited value, owing to the vagaries of recording practices described in Chapters 3 and 4. Moreover, a rise in complaints can signal an increase in police misconduct or, conversely, greater faith in the investigative system. On the other hand, *qualitative* information from complaints files can be much more useful for management purposes. Among the more effective uses we saw of such material was the circulation by a Complaints and Discipline department of a monthly bulletin to all divisional managers, in which a digest was given of points arising from recent complaints. These might include information about trends (e.g. an unusually high number of complaints about damage in home searches), reminders about procedural failings (e.g. failures to record consent to fingerprinting on custody records) or advice on dealing with complainants (e.g. for Appointed Officers to re-contact complainants after seeing the officer). This seemed to us an excellent model for other forces to follow.

Another possible use of complaints data not yet fully exploited is for training purposes. For example, judiciously selected casefiles in which complainants and witnesses describe the circumstances leading up to a complaint make excellent material for courses. One feature we noticed from reading numerous files was the frequency with which a simple misunderstanding, combined with one or other of the parties being under some form of stress, started off a chain of reactions and counter-reactions leading to either a scuffle or a verbal explosion. For example, a driver, blinded by lights and rain, misunderstood a police instruction and drove into a set of cones at the scene of an accident. A young officer, already upset by dealing with some serious injuries, rushed up to the car and screamed at the driver, who in turn reacted angrily, the incident resulting in a scuffle and a complaint. The reactions of both are fully understandable, but the escalation could have been stopped by more professional behaviour by the officer. There are many educative examples, too, of officers over-reacting to provocation by teenagers on the street: these make good material for group discussion of how the matter could have been better handled. Yet at present, the only people who see most of these files are the IO, the C&D managers and the CPS and/or PCA.

One further useful practice might be to circulate to divisional managers a proportion of the full files relating to cases in their division, so that they had a clearer picture of what had happened: brief summaries are often misleading. In sum, while recognizing the constraints of confidentiality, we would support the wider circulation of information about the substance and genesis of complaints. We would stress in particular the value of getting officers to understand the totally different perceptions of incidents which are held—in good faith—by many complainants: what appears to the officer a fairly trivial altercation can take on great significance for a member of the public.

Finally, in this context, we would pick out the related theme of the importance of comment by an independent body, not just about the circumstances of particular major cases, but about lessons to be learned from either individual cases or series of cases. The PCA has done this to some extent (for example in recommendations for making officers individually identifiable in large-scale operations), but could go further, particularly if the Authority were permitted to widen the scope of investigations beyond the question of the guilt or innocence of individual officers when they considered it in the public interest to do so. The wider 'briefs' permitted by S.88 referrals already give a precedent.

In this concluding section, we have drawn attention to many of the shortcomings of the current system, and have also suggested some possible reforms. The central question, however, detailed discussion of which is beyond the scope of this report, is whether most of the problems we have identified would be solved by the radical step of creating a fully independent system of investigation. It may be, of course, that political pressure and criticism of the current arrangement—fuelled by new cases of public concern and by the growing tendency of people with serious grievances to resort to civil actions rather than the complaints system (Clayton and Tomlinson 1987)—will eventually force such a move upon the government. If this were to happen, we speculate, there might be a gain in terms of public confidence in the system, although it is by no means certain it would be more effective in other ways. If outsiders were to investigate *all* complaints, the resource implications would be enormous, and one might simply be replacing one unwieldy bureaucratic system with another. If, as seems the most practical solution, outsiders were to investigate only the most serious cases (as, for example in Toronto, where the independent Police Complaints Commission can take over the investigation of any case it chooses—see McMahon 1988), the difficult problem of selection would remain. Above all, experience in other countries suggests that independent investigation would fail to make any significant difference to the outcomes of cases (McMahon 1988, Loveday 1989), so problems of credibility and complainant dissatisfaction would still rear their head when only small proportions of complaints continued to be substantiated. Bad news remains unpalatable, whoever delivers it.

In conclusion, if satisfactory and lasting solutions are to be found, it is necessary to find an alternative to the reactive approach to reform which has prevailed in the past, whereby change has occurred largely in response to crisis. What is needed is a return to first principles: consideration of the fundamental aims and priorities upon which a complaints system should be based, of the different kinds of case it has to deal with, of the practical problems it faces, and of the interests and attitudes of those involved on all sides. Equally important, as the Association of Chief Police Officers has clearly recognised (ACPO 1990), effective responses to complaints are only one piece of the jigsaw which is needed to change poor police attitudes and win the full confidence of the public. Without improvements in training, supervision, police-public consultation and other broader mechanisms of accountability, whatever way complaints are handled will make little difference to these fundamental aims.

NOTES

1. For example, in the Fire Brigade, which has its own disciplinary code, the standard used is the civil standard. This was established in law in the case of *R—v—Hampshire County Council ex parte Ellerton*, 1985. However, shortly after this case, new Police Regulations based on PACE went through Parliament without attracting much attention, explicitly stating that a criminal standard of proof is required (see Lustgarten 1986).

Bibliography

ACPO (1990). *Strategic Policy Document: Setting the Standards for Policing: Meeting Community Expectation* London: Metropolitan Police District.

ALVES, E and SHAPLAND, J. (1985). *Legislation for Policing Today: The Police and Criminal Evidence Act.* Issues in Criminological and Legal Psychology, No. 7. Leicester: British Psychological Society.

BITTNER, E. (1974). "Florence Nightingale in pursuit of Willie Sutton: A theory of the police", in Jacob, H. (ed.), *The Potential for Reform of Criminal Justice*, Beverley Hills: Sage.

BOX, S. and RUSSELL, K. (1975). "The politics of discredibility: disarming complaints against police". *Sociological Review*, Vol. 23, no. 2, 315–346.

BROWN, D. C. (1983). "Civilian review of complaints against the police". HORPU Study no. 19. London: HMSO.

BROWN, D (1987). *The Police Complaints Procedure: A Survey of Complainants' Views* Home Office Research Study No. 93 London: HMSO.

CHRISTOPHER, S. and NOAKS, L. (1989). *Assaults Against the Police* Unpublished Report to Home Office.

CLAYTON, R. and TOMLINSON, H. (1987). *Civil Actions Against the Police* London: Sweet and Maxwell.

COHEN, B. (1985). "Police complaints procedure: why and for whom" in *Police: The Constitution and the Community* (ed. Baxter, J. and Koffman, L.) London: Professional Books.

CORBETT, C. (1991). 'Complaints against the police: the new procedure of informal resolution" forthcoming in *Policing in Society*, Summer issue, Vol. 2 (1)

COX, B., SHIRLEY, J. AND SHORT, M. (1977). *The Fall of Scotland Yard* Harmondsworth: Penguin Books.

EMMENT, L. E. (1984). "An analysis of complaints received from members of the public by the Thames Valley Police between 1 January and 31 March 1983". Kidlington: Thames Valley Police Force (unpublished)

FREEMAN, M. (1985). *The Police and Criminal Evidence Act* 1984 London: Sweet and Maxwell.

GOLDSMITH, A. (ed. 1991). *Complaints Against the Police: The Trend to External Review* Oxford: Oxford University Press.

HOBBS, D, (1988). *Doing the Business: Crime, Culture and Detective Work in East London* Oxford: Oxford University Press.

HOME OFFICE (1985). *Guidance to Chief Officers on Police Complaints and Disciplinary Procedures* London: Home Office.

IRVING, B. and MCKENZIE, I. (1988). *Police Interrogation: The Effects of the Police and Criminal Evidence Act* 1984 London: Police Foundation.

JEFFERSON, T. and GRIMSHAW, R. (1984). *Controlling the Constable* London: Frederic Muller.

KEMP, C. and MORGAN, R. (1989). *Behind the Front Counter: Lay Visitors to Police Stations* Bristol: Bristol and Bath Centre for Criminal Justice.

LOVEDAY, B. (1984). *Police Complaints Procedure: An Overview* City of Birmingham Polytechnic, Department of Government and Politics, Occasional Paper No. 11. Birmingham: Birmingham Polytechnic.

LOVEDAY, B. (1989). "Recent developments in police complaints procedure: Britain and North America." *Local Government Studies* May/June 1989 pp. 25–57.

LSPU (1987). *Police Complaints: A Fresh Approach* Police Monitoring and Research Group, Briefing Paper No. 4 London: London Strategic Policy Unit.

LUSTGARTEN, L. (1986). *The Governance of Police* London: Sweet and Maxwell.

MAGUIRE, M. (1988). 'Effects of the 'P.A.C.E.' provisions on detention and questioning: some preliminary findings" *British Journal of Criminology*, Vol. 28, No. 1. Winter 1988.

MAGUIRE, M. (1991). "Complaints against the police: the British experience" in Goldsmith, A. (ed.) *Complaints Against the Police: the Trend to External Review* Oxford: Oxford University Press.

MAGUIRE, M. and CORBETT, C (1989). "Patterns and profiles of complaints against the police" in Morgan, R. and Smith, D. (eds), *Coming to Terms with Policing*. London: Routledge.

MAGUIRE M. and POINTING, J. (1988). *Victims of Crime: A New Deal?* Milton Keynes: Open University Press.

MARSHALL, G. (1979). "Police accountability revisited" in *Policy and Politics* (Butler, D. and Halsey, A. eds.) London: Macmillan.

MCMAHON M. (1988). "Police accountability: the situation of complaints in Toronto" *Contemporary Crises*, 12: 301–22.

PCA (1987). *Police Complaints Authority, Annual Report* 1986 London: HMSO.

PCA (1988). *Police Complaints Authority, Annual Report* 1987 London: HMSO.

PCA (1988a). *Police Complaints Authority, Triennial Review* 1985–1988 London: HMSO.

PCA (1989). *Police Complaints Authority, Annual Report* 1988 London: HMSO.

PCA (1990). *Police Complaints Authority, Annual Report* 1989 London: HMSO.

PEAY, J. and MANSFIELD, G. (1988). *The Director of Public Prosecutions* London: Tavistock.

POLICE STAFF ASSOCIATIONS (1990). *Operational Policing Review* Surbiton, Surrey: Joint Consultative Committee.

REINER, R. (1985). *The Politics of the Police* Brighton: Wheatsheaf Books.

ROYAL COMMISSION (1908). *Report of the Royal Commission on the Powers and Duties of the Metropolitan Police.* London: HMSO (Cmnd 4156).

ROYAL COMMISSION (1929). *Report of the Royal Commission on Police Powers and Procedures.* London: HMSO (Cmnd 3297).

ROYAL COMMISSION (1981). *Report of the Royal Commission on Criminal Procedure* London: HMSO (Cmnd. 8092).

RUSSELL, K (1976). *Complaints against the Police.* Leicester: Milltak.

RUSSELL, K. (1986). "Complaints against the police which are withdrawn". Leicester Polytechnic: Reprographic Unit.

SCARMAN, LORD (1981). *The Brixton Disorders* London: HMSO (Cmnd. 8427).

SELECT COMMITTEE (1834). *Select Committee on the Policing of the Metropolis.* London: HMSO.

SHAPLAND, J., WILLMORE, J. and DUFF, P. (1985). *Victims in the Criminal Justice System* Aldershot: Gower.

SKOGAN, W. (1990). *The Police and Public in England and Wales: A British Crime Survey Report* Home Office Research Study 117. London: HMSO.

TUCK, M. and SOUTHGATE, P. (1981). *Ethnic Minorities, Crime and Policing: a Survey of West Indian and White Experiences* Home Office Research Study No. 70. London: HMSO.

WILLIAMS, G. (1985). "Letting off the guilty and prosecuting the innocent" *Criminal Law Review* pp. 115–123.

WOLFF OLINS (1988). *A Force For Change* London: Wolff Olins.

ZANDER, M. (1985). *The Police & Criminal Evidence Act* 1984 London: Sweet and Maxwell.

Appendix 1

Sampling and Research Methods in Local Forces

As stated in the text, our samples of complainants for interview were drawn from consecutive cases in batches of recently completed complaints files (different cases than used in the casefile analysis) in three police force areas. However, as contacting and interviewing complainants turned out to be more time-consuming than originally envisaged, we were forced to alter our plans and interviewed fewer complainants in the two City forces than in the County force. Appendix Table 1 shows the samples taken and the response rates finally achieved.

In the County force, we took a sample of 119 complainants (from 114 cases). Just over half of these had had their cases fully investigated, about a third had withdrawn their complaints, and the remainder had agreed to informal resolution. The strategy adopted was for the head of the Complaints and Discipline Department to send a letter to all the complainants, informing them about the research project. In this letter, it was stated that, unless he heard back from them within a week, he would assume that they had no objection to taking part and would permit the researchers to contact them to arrange an interview. The advantages of this strategy were, first, that it protected the police from the charge that they had allowed outsiders to use complainants' names and addresses without the latter's permission and, secondly, that it constituted a rather effective kind of 'inertia selling' for the research. Very few people wrote back to the police with an outright refusal; and when we contacted the remainder, we were able to mention the letter from the police and consequently ask 'when' rather than 'whether' they would be free for an interview.

The above strategy was tried mainly because the otherwise excellent study of complainants by Brown (1987) had suffered through low response rates. In addition, we made special efforts to find and contact people in our samples, including follow-up letters, telephone calls and visits. We found that a considerable number had changed addresses (including several who were now in prison) and we also wasted a number of journeys when people failed to keep appointments. Altogether, this interviewing proved to be a very time-consuming exercise. However, the extra effort paid dividends, in that, of the 109 complainants in the County force area who had a chance to respond

207

Appendix Table 1: Interviews with complainants: samples and response rates

Type of Case	Force Area County	City	City II	All
Investigated				
Moved—no address	5	–	–	5
Did not reply	12	–	–	12
Refused	4	–	–	4
Interviewed	40	–	–	40
Total sample	61	–	–	61
Response rate*	71%	–	–	71%
Withdrawn				
Moved—no address	3	2	1	6
Did not reply	11	3	0	14
Refused	6	1	0	7
Interviewed	20	4	6	30
Total sample	40	10	7	57
Response rate*	54%	50%	100%	59%
Informally resolved				
Moved—no address	2	2	1	1
Did not reply	2	6	1	9
Refused	3	1	2	6
Interviewed	11	15	4	30
Total sample	18	24	8	50
Response rate*	69%	68%	57%	67%
All cases				
Moved—no address	10	4	2	16
Did not reply	25	9	1	35
Refused	13	2	2	17
Interviewed	71	19	10	100
Total sample	119	34	15	168
Response rate*	65%	63%	77%	66%

*Those who had moved, leaving no address, are excluded from this calculation, as they had no opportunity to respond. If they were included, the overall 'response rate' would be 61%.

(i.e. excluding the ten whose letters were returned marked 'gone away', with no forwarding address) we managed to interview 71—a response rate of 65 per cent, or 61 per cent of the full original sample. This is more than double the rate achieved in Brown's study, where the researcher was unable to follow up the initial requests for interview.

The negative side was that the slow progress in the County area caused the project to fall behind schedule. We therefore decided to reduce the size of the samples we had planned to take in the City areas. Here we abandoned investigated cases entirely, taking samples only of withdrawn and informally resolved cases (two categories at which we had planned to take a special look). Our new plan was to contact enough complainants to provide us with a final total of 30 interviewees in each of these categories. We thus needed another 29 interviews in all; these were achieved eventually after attempts to contact 49 complainants. While the overall response rate for complainants in informally resolved cases was similar (67 per cent) to that in investigated cases (71 per cent), the rate in withdrawn cases was somewhat lower, at 59 per cent. This is partly due to the relatively high proportion (14 out of 51) who failed to reply to our letters and were not contactable by telephone. This may be because after withdrawing they were simply not interested in the complaint, or it may be because they had left the address but nobody had bothered to return their letters to the sender. ('Withdrawers' as a group were younger than other complainants, more likely to have previous convictions, and more likely to have been arrested during the 'complaint incident': it is therefore likely that a higher proportion of them lived in short-term rented accommodation.)[1]

This difference in response rates, together with the fact that the total sample is unbalanced in terms of the forces studied, gives some pause for thought about the representativeness of our interviewees. Appendix Table 2 shows some of the measurable differences between those who did and did not respond. Non-respondents were considerably more likely than respondents to be young, to be unemployed, and to have previous convictions. They were also (though not to the same degree) more likely to have been complaining of assault and to have been arrested shortly before, during or after the incident which led to the complaint. Taken together, these differences suggest that, if there is a general 'bias' in the findings from our interviews, it will be in the direction of showing more satisfaction with the system and more 'pro-police' attitudes than actually exist. Nevertheless, any such bias is unlikely to be large, as people's reactions to the way their complaints were handled did not vary greatly according to their personal characteristics.

It is a further limitation of the study that all the interviewees in fully investigated cases were drawn from one police force area. Some caution is therefore called for in generalising from the findings. However, they are similar in many respects to the results of our postal survey based on PCA cases, which covered the whole country. (Although the latter cases were much more serious than average, the reactions of

Appendix Table 2: Selected Characteristics of Interviewed Complainants and Non-Respondents

	Interviewees (N = 100) %	Non-respondents (N = 68) %	All (N = 168) %
1. *Sex*			
Per cent male	68	72	70
2. *Occupation*			
Per cent unemployed*	12	27	18
Per cent manual*	36	41	38
Per cent non-manual*	41	15	31
3. *Age*			
Per cent aged under 30*	31	58	41
4. *Previous convictions*			
Per cent with one or more convictions**	32	58	41
5. *Type of complaint*			
Per cent complaining of assault	29	48	37
6. *Arrest*			
Per cent arrested in complaint incident	42	54	47
7. *Outcome* (investigated cases only)	(N = 40)	(N = 21)	(N = 61)
Per cent who had a complaint substantiated	13	19	15

*Percentages based on 159 cases (nine with missing data excluded)
**Percentages based on 157 cases (eleven with missing data excluded)

complainants to the way they were handled did not differ fundamentally from those of the complainants we interviewed.) Moreover, there were no obvious major differences between the responses of complainants in the City and County areas where informally resolved and withdrawn cases were concerned. There was also nothing to suggest that the substance or seriousness of the complaints varied widely between areas.

Finally, it has to be conceded that 100 interviews constitute a relatively small sample, and that some caution must be exercised in generalising from the findings, especially those deriving from analysis of the major sub-groups, such as complainants in informally resolved cases, where the sample used shrinks to 30. Again, however, this problem is to some extent offset by the availability of comparative and corroborative evidence, both in the PCA sample and in Brown's (1987) study. This, together with the consistency of responses in many areas of questioning and the general 'feel' for the subject (as well as for the veracity of complainants) which we got from long interviews, often lasting for over an hour and a half, makes us confident that, despite the above weaknesses, the findings give a sound general picture of complainants' experiences, reactions and attitudes.

NOTES

1. Among our full interview sample of 168 (see Appendix Table 2), 52 per cent of those who withdrew were under 30, compared with 33 per cent of those who did not; 55 per cent had previous convictions, compared with 46 per cent of those whose cases were investigated, and 23 per cent of those whose cases were informally resolved; and 63 per cent had been arrested in the 'complaint incident', compared with 54 per cent and 20 per cent, respectively, of the remainder. (The above figures exclude cases with missing data).

Appendix 2

Referral and Supervision: Relevant Statutes and Regulations

The Police and Criminal Evidence Act 1984—*Part IX*

S. 87. (1) The appropriate authority
    (a) shall refer to the Authority—
        (i) any complaint alleging that the conduct complained of resulted in the death of or serious injury to some other person; and
        (ii) any complaint of a description specified for the purposes of this section in regulations made by the Secretary of State; and
    (b) may refer to the Authority any complaint which is not required to be referred to them.
  (2) The Authority may require the submission to them for consideration of any complaint not referred to them by the appropriate authority; and it shall be the appropriate authority' duty to comply with any such requirement not later than the end of a period specified in regulations made by the Secretary of State.
  (3) Where a complaint fails to be referred to the Authority under subsection (1)(a) above, it shall be the appropriate authority's duty to refer it to them not later than the end of the period specified in such regulation.
  (4) In this Part of this Act 'serious injury' means a fracture, damage to an internal organ, impairment of bodily function, a deep cut or a deep laceration.

S. 88. The appropriate authority may refer to the Authority any matter which
    (a) appears to the appropriate authority to indicate that an officer may have committed a criminal offence or an offence against discipline; and
    (b) is not the subject of a complaint,
if it appears to the appropriate authority that it ought to be referred by reason
    (i) of its gravity; or
    (ii) of exceptional circumstances.

213

S. 89 (1) The Authority shall supervise the investigation

    (a) of any complaint alleging that the conduct of a police officer resulted in the death of or serious injury to some other person; and

    (b) of any other description of complaint specified for the purposes of this section in regulations made by the Secretary of State.

(2) The Authority shall supervise the investigation

    (a) of any complaint the investigation of which they are not required to supervise under subsection (1) above; and

    (b) of any matter referred to them under section 88 above, if they consider that it is desirable in the public interest that they should supervise that investigation.

The Police (Complaints) (Mandatory Referrals) Regulations 1985

Mandatory referrals

4. (1) Without prejudice to section 87(1)(a)(i) of the Act of 1984 (requiring reference to the authority of any complaint alleging that the conduct complained of resulted in the death of or serious injury to some other person), the appropriate authority shall refer to the Authority any complaint to which these Regulations apply, being a complaint alleging conduct which, if shown to have occurred, would constitute–

    (a) assault occasioning actual bodily harm; or

    (b) an offence under section 1 of the Prevention of Corruption Act 1906(a); or

    (c) a serious arrestable offence, within the meaning of section 116 of the Act of 1984.

(2) Where a complaint is required to be referred to the Authority under paragraph (1) above, notification of the complaint shall be given to the Authority not later than the end of the day following the day on which it first becomes clear to the appropriate authority that the complaint is one to which that paragraph applies.

Appendix 3

'Regulation 7' form

To:

A report/allegation/complaint has been received from:

It is alleged that:

The purpose of this Form is to provide you with notice of the nature of the allegation made against you. IT DOES NOT NECESSARILY IMPLY THAT DISCIPLINARY PROCEEDINGS WILL BE TAKEN, BUT IS SERVED TO SAFEGUARD YOUR INTERESTS. Please acknowledge service by signing below.

As required by Regulation 7 of the Police (Discipline) Regulations, 1985, I hereby give you notice that:

(a)   You are not obliged to say anything concerning the matter, but that you may if you so desire, make a written or oral statement to the Investigating Officer or to the Deputy Chief Constable.

(b)   If you make such a statement, it may be used in any subsequent disciplinary proceedings.

(c)   You have the right to consult a friend at all stages of the investigation.

(d)   You may be interviewed in due course by the Investigating Officer and he may serve upon you a further notice when the full extent of the issues are known.

Date ....
(Signature of Investigating Officer)

Notice served by ....
(Signed)

I acknowledge receipt of this Notice

Date ....
(Signed)

215

Appendix 4

Terms of Reference for Research Commissioned by the PCA
Our 'brief' for the Police Complaints Authority was described in the
1986 Annual Report (PCA 1987: paras 8.1–8.4) as follows:

1. Complaints and other matters referred to the Authority by police
   forces in accordance with Sections 87(1) and 88 of the Police and
   Criminal Evidence Act 1984. The report should distinguish cases
   referred under Section 87(1)(a)(i) from those referred under
   Section 87(1)(a)(ii), as read with the Police (Complaints)
   (Mandatory Referrals Etc) Regulations 1985, and from those
   referred at the chief officer's discretion under Section 87(1)(b)
   and 88. It should study the nature of the complaint, where there
   is one, and the seriousness of the alleged misconduct and, where
   the Authority has discretion to supervise the investigation of the
   matter, the process of assessment within the Authority and the
   reasons for their decisions to supervise or not.
2. The effect that supervision of the investigation has on the
   outcome of cases.
3. The extent and nature of supervision exercised by members of
   the Authority over investigations of complaints and the reasons
   for variations in the style of supervision in different types of
   complaint.
4. Practical problems hindering the work of the Authority with an
   assessment of whether such problems arise from the broad nature
   of police investigative procedures or from weaknesses in legisla-
   tive provision.

Appendix 5

Questionnaire to Complainants in Cases Referred to PCA

COMPLAINTS AGAINST THE POLICE

Oxford University Questionnaire   Our ref:......

IT WOULD HELP US GREATLY IF YOU TRY TO ANSWER ALL
QUESTIONS

---

1. Immediately after you made your complaint,
how confident were you that it would be dealt
with fairly?

PLEASE TICK ONE
Very confident ......
Fairly confident ......
Not very confident ......
No confidence at all ......

2. When you first made your complaint,
how long did you think it would take to
deal with?

PLEASE TICK ONE
Less than a month ......
1–3 months ......
4–6 months ......
7–12 months ......
longer ......

2a. Do you think the time it actually took was . . .

PLEASE TICK ONE
Reasonable ......
A little too long ......
Much too long ......

3. We assume that your complaint was investigated by a senior police officer –
probably a superintendent or a chief inspector. If so:

(a) Could you describe his (or her) general attitude towards you and your
complaint? ....
....

(b) How seriously did he appear to treat the matter?

PLEASE TICK ONE
Very seriously ......
Fairly seriously ......
Not very seriously ......
Not at all seriously ......

219

(c) Did he ever suggest that you might withdraw your complaint?

PLEASE TICK ONE

Yes, tried to persuade me ......
Mentioned the possibility ......
No ......

(d) If so, what was your reaction? ....

....

4. Overall, is it your impression that the police investigators:

PLEASE TICK ONE

Really tried hard to get to the bottom of the matter? ......
Did quite a thorough job? ......
Just went through the motions, making no real effort? ......
Deliberately went out of the way to avoid the truth? ......
Don't know ......

5. Generally, how well were you kept informed about what was happening?

PLEASE TICK ONE

Very well informed ......
Fairly well informed ......
Not very well informed ......
Very badly informed ......

6. What was the final result of your case – was it found that any officer had done wrong?

PLEASE TICK ONE

Yes ......
No ......
Don't know ......

6a. How satisfied were your with the outcome of the complaint?

PLEASE TICK ONE

Very satisfied ......
Fairly satisfied ......
Fairly dissatisfied ......
Very dissatisfied ......

7. Leaving aside the actual result, how satisfied would you say you were with the way the investigation was conducted?

PLEASE TICK ONE

Very satisfied ......
Fairly satisfied ......
Fairly dissatisfied ......
Very dissatisfied ......

8. Overall, would you say that the investigation and its outcome:

PLEASE TICK ONE

Changed your view of the police for the worse? ......
Made no difference to your view? ......
Gave you a better opinion of the police than you had before? ......

9. After your complaint had been investigated, you will have received a letter from the POLICE COMPLAINTS AUTHORITY ("PCA"), telling you what the investigation had found and what the final outcome of your complaint was. Please ring one answer in each line below:

THE TONE OF THE LETTER WAS ... friendly .. neutral .. unfriendly

THE LETTER WAS ...   simple to   .. a bit difficult .. very difficult
                      understand   to follow   to follow

THE LETTER EXPLAINED THE REASONS BEHIND THE DECISION...

very fully   ..   quite fully   ..   not fully enough   ..   not at all

WHATEVER THE OFFICIAL RESULT, YOU FELT THEY...

believed   ..   doubted some   ..   didn't know   ..   didn't believe
your story   of your story   who to believe   you at all

THE LETTER GAVE YOU THE IMPRESSION THAT THE PCA IS BASICALLY...

anti-police   ..   independent and unbiased   ..   on the side of the police

10. Could you give in your own words your general impression of the Police Complaints Authority – how independent they are and how effective?

....

....

11. Is there anything more you would have liked to know from the Police Complaints Authority? (If so, what?)

....

....

12. Is there anything more you think they could or should have done?

....

....

13. Did you contact the police, PCA or anyone else after you were told the result, in order to query anything, thank them, express dissatisfaction or try to take further action?

Yes, police ......
Yes, PCA ......
Yes, other (please say who) ......
No ......

If yes, what did you say and with what result? ....

....

....

14. Having experienced it, have you now more faith
or less faith in the whole complaints system
than you had when you first complained?

A lot more faith ......
A little more faith ......
A little less faith ......
Much less faith ......
No difference ......

15. If a similar incident to the one you complained
about occurred in the future, would you complain again?

PLEASE TICK ONE
Yes ......
No ......
Don't know ......

16. Below are a number of aims you might have had in mind when complaining.
Could you show which of these come closest to explaining what you most wanted.
Please mark a 1 by the one which was mot important to your, a 2 by the next most
important, a 3 by the next, and so on. (BUT PLEASE LEAVE BLANK ANY THAT YOU DID
NOT WANT).

MARK IN ORDER OF IMPORTANCE TO YOU 1–2–3, etc.

(BUT LEAVE BLANK ANY YOU DID NOT WANT)

Wanted an apology ......
Wanted an explanation ......
Wanted it proved that what you were saying was true ......
Wanted to express how angry or upset you felt ......
Wanted to stop it happening to somebody else ......
Wanted the officer(s) to get a ticking off ......
Wanted the officer(s) punished ......
Wanted money in compensation ......
Wanted the police to drop charges against you ......

Other (please say what) ....

17. Looking back now over the whole affair, what if anything do you think you
achieved by complaining?

....

....

18. Which of the following statements
would you most agree with:

PLEASE TICK ONE

(i)   The police should investigate complaints themselves   ......
(ii)   The police should investigate complaints themselves
        but under the supervision of an outside body   ......
(iii)   The whole investigation should be carried out by
        someone other than the police   ......

19. Is there anything else you would like to comment on? ....

....

....

....

Finally, would you be kind enough to give a few details about yourself so we can see whether complaints come equally from all sections of the population. (If you have any objections, please do not feel under any obligation to answer these questions.)

PLEASE TICK OR CIRCLE AS APPROPRIATE

Are you: Male ......   Female ......

Aged   16–19   20–29   30–39   40–49   50–59   60 or over

White ......   Black ......   Asian ......   Other ......

Employed full-time ......   Retired   ......

Employed part-time ......   Housewife ......

Unemployed   ......   Student   ......

What is your occupation – or, if not working, your last occupation?

....

(If housewife please give your partner's present or last occupation.)

THANK YOU VERY MUCH FOR YOUR PATIENCE
AND CO-OPERATION.

YOUR HELP IS MUCH APPRECIATED

223

Appendix 6

Police Discipline Code

A member of a police force commits an offence against discipline if he commits one or more of the offences set out below:

1. **Discreditable conduct:** which offence is committed where a member of a police force acts in a disorderly manner or any manner prejudicial to discipline or reasonably likely to bring discredit on the reputation of the force or the police service.

2. **Misconduct towards a member of a police force:** which offence is committed where-
   (a) the conduct of a member of a police force towards another such member is oppressive or abusive,
      or
   (b) a member of a police force assaults another such member.

3. **Disobedience to orders:** which offence is committed where a member of a police force, without good and sufficient cause, disobeys or neglects to carry out any lawful order, written or otherwise, or fails to comply with a code of practice, or contravenes any provision of the Police Regulations containing restrictions on the private lives of members of police forces or requiring him to notify the chief officer of police that he, or a relation included in his family, has a business interest, within the meaning of those Regulations.

4. **Neglect of duty:** which offence is committed where a member of a police force, without good and sufficient cause-
   (a) neglects or omits to attend to or carry out with due promptitude and diligence anything which it is his duty as a member of a police force to attend to or carry out, or
   (b) fails to work his beat in accordance with orders, or leaves the place of duty to which he had been ordered, or having left his place of duty for an authorised purpose fails to return thereto without undue delay, or
   (c) is absent without leave from, or is late for, any duty, or
   (d) fails properly to account for, or to make a prompt and true return of, any money or property received by him in the course of his duty.

5. **Falsehood or prevarication:** which offence is committed where a member of a police force:
   (a) knowingly or through neglect makes any false, misleading or inaccurate oral or written statement or entry in any record or document made, kept or required for police purposes; or
   (b) either wilfully and without proper authority or through lack of due care destroys or mutilates any record or document made, kept or required for police purposes, or
   (c) without good and sufficient cause alters or erases or adds to any entry in such a record or document, or
   (d) has knowingly or through neglect made any false, misleading or inaccurate statement in connection with his appointment to the police force.
6. **Improper disclosure of information:** which offence is committed where a member of a police force:
   (a) without proper authority communicates to any person, any information which he has in his possession as a member of a police force, or
   (b) makes any anonymous communication to any police authority, or
   (c) without proper authority makes representations to the police authority or the council of any county comprised in the police area with regard to any matter concerning the force, or
   (d) canvasses any member of that authority or of such a council with regard to any such matter.
7. **Corrupt or improper practice:** which offence is committed where a member of a police force-
   (a) in his capacity as a member of the force and without the consent of the chief officer of police or the police authority, directly or indirectly solicits or accepts any gratuity, present or subscription, or
   (b) places himself under a pecuniary obligation to any person in such a manner as might affect his properly carrying out his duties as a member of the force, or
   (c) improperly uses, or attempts so to use his position as a member of the force for his private advantage, or
   (d) in his capacity as a member of the force and without the consent of the chief officer of police, writes, signs or gives a testimonial of character or other recommendation with the object of obtaining employment for any person or of supporting an application for the grant of a licence of any kind.
8. **Abuse of authority:** which offence is committed where a member of a police force-
   (a) without good and sufficient cause makes an arrest, or

(b) uses any unnecessary violence towards any prisoner or other person with whom he may be brought into contact in the execution of his duty, or

(c) is uncivil to any member of the public.

9. **Racially discriminatory behaviour:** where an officer whilst he is on duty, on the grounds of a person's colour, race, nationality or ethnic or national origins, either behaved towards that person in a manner which, even without these grounds, amounts to the commission of the disciplinary offence of abuse of authority, or otherwise treated him improperly.

10. **Neglect of health:** which offence is committed where a member of a police force, without good and sufficient cause, neglects to carry out any instructions of a medical officer appointed by the police authority or while absent from duty on account of sickness, commits any act or adopts any conduct calculated to retard his return to duty.

11. **Improper dress or untidiness:** which offence is committed where without good and sufficient cause a member of a police force while on duty, or while off duty but wearing uniform in a public place, is improperly dressed or is untidy in his appearance.

12. **Damage to police property:** which offence is committed where a member of a police force-

(a) wilfully or through lack of due care causes any waste, loss or damage to any police property, or

(b) fails to report as soon as is reasonably practicable any loss of or damage to any such property issued to, or used by him or entrusted to his care.

13. **Drunkenness:** which offence is committed where a member of a police force renders himself unfit through drink for duties which he is or will be required to perform or which he may reasonably foresee having to perform.

14 **Drinking on duty or soliciting drink:** which offence is committed where a member of a police force while on duty-

(a) without proper authority, drinks, or receives from any other person, any intoxicating liquor, or

(b) demands, or endeavours to persuade any other person to give him, or to purchase or obtain for him, any intoxicating liquor.

15. **Entering licensed premises:** which offence is committed where a member of a police force:

(a) while on duty, or

(b) while off duty but wearing uniform, without good and sufficient cause enters any premises in respect of which a licence or permit has been granted in pursuance of the law relating to liquor licensing or betting and gaming or regulating places of entertainment.

16. **Criminal conduct:** which offence is committed where a member of a police force has been found guilty by a Court of law of a criminal offence.

17. **Being an accessory to a disciplinary offence:** which offence is committed where a member of a police force incites, connives at or is knowingly an accessory to any offence against discipline.

APPENDIX TABLES

Table A: Cases under mandatory supervision: locations of alleged assault

Location	Initial assault alleged:		Further assault alleged:	Total assaults alleged: (40 cases)
	at scene of arrest	elsewhere		
Street:	21	–	–	21
Complainant's home:	6	–	–	6
Public building:	3	–	–	3
Police vehicle:	–	7	1	8
Police station:	1	1	6	8
Court cells:	–	1	1	2
Totals	31	9	8	48

Table B: Mandatorily and discretionarily supervised cases: a comparison of complainants' characteristics

	Type of case					
	Mandatory supervision		Discretionary supervision*		Discretionary supervision—assault cases only*	
	(Total N = 40)		(Total N = 40)		(Total N = 20)	
Selected characteristics of complainants	%	(*No.*)	%	(*No.*)	%	(*No.*)
Aged under 30	68	(27)	40	(16)	55	(11)
Male	95	(38)	73	(29)	80	(16)
Non-manual	10	(4)	25	(10)	20	(4)
Previous convictions	80	(32)	63	(25)	65	(13)

*Cases referred under Section 87(1)(a)(ii), (1)(b) or (2).

Table C: Satisfaction with outcome in relation to official outcome

Satisfaction with outcome	court/tribunal		advice given	unrelated advice*	no action	All
	guilty	*NG*				
Very satisfied	1	0	0	0	1	2
Fairly satisfied	0	0	4	0	1	5
Fairly dissatisfied	2	0	1	3	13	19
Very dissatisfied	3	3	11	19	116	152
(Not answered)	(1)	(0)	(1)	(0)	(6)	(8)
Total cases	7	3	17	22	137	186

*This refers to advice given on other disciplinary matters, not directly relevant to the original complaint,which emerge during the course of inquiries.

Printed in the United Kingdom for HMSO
Dd 293640   C1   3/91